Contents

Scottish Gaelic
in Twelve Weeks

Roibeard Ó Maolalaigh

with Iain MacAonghuis
(Consultant)

BIRLINN

First published in 2008 by
Birlinn Limited
West Newington House
10 Newington Road
Edinburgh
EH9 1QS

www.birlinn.co.uk

Reprinted 2015

First published in 1996 as *Scottish Gaelic in Three Months* by Dorling
Kindersley Ltd, London

Book only
ISBN 978 1 84158 643 4

Book and CDs
ISBN 978 1 84158 644 1

British Library Cataloguing-in-Publication Data
A catalogue record for this book is available from the British Library

Chuidich Comhairle nan Leabhraichean am foillsichear
le cosgaisean an leabhair seo

Designed and typeset by Sharon McTier
Printed and bound by Bell & Bain Limited

Lesson 10

Lesson 11

Abbreviations used in this book

Mini-dictionary

adj	adjective
adv	adverb
attr	attributive
art	article
cjn	conjunction
cmp prp	composite preposition
coll	collective
def	defective
f	feminine
G, *gen*	genitive
inf	infinitive
interj	interjection
interr	interrogative
IPA	International Phonetic Alphabet
irreg	irregular
lit	literally
m	masculine
neg	negative
num	numeral
obj	object
P	prepositional
pl	plural
pron	pronoun
pos	positive
ppn	possessive pronoun
pred	predicate
prp	preposition
prt	particle
rel	relative
sing	singular
subj	subject
v	vide, see
vb	verb
vn	verbal noun
*	lenites following word

Preface

Scottish Gaelic in Twelve Weeks, which represents a revised edition of *Scottish Gaelic in Three Months*, has been written both as a self-tuition book for beginners and also for use within the classroom. You may want to learn Gaelic because of a general interest in Celtic or Scottish history and culture, or because it was the everyday language of your ancestors before they emigrated – perhaps to Nova Scotia, where, on Cape Breton Island, Gaelic speakers may still be found. The cynical observer may wonder if the exercise is worthwhile, when only less than one and a half per cent of Scotland's population speak the language. However, Gaelic is far from being dead; in some parts of the Highlands and Western Isles it is the everyday language, and it represents an important part of the United Kingdom's cultural 'mix'; there are significant numbers of Gaelic speakers in urban centres, including but not limited to Glasgow and Edinburgh. There are Gaelic-learning classes in almost every area of Scotland.

Roibeard Ó Maolalaigh, from Dublin, former lecturer at the University of Edinburgh and assistant professor at the School of Celtic Studies, Dublin Institute for Advanced Studies, now lectures in the Department of Celtic at the University of Glasgow, where he is Professor of Gaelic. His consultant Iain MacAonghuis is a native speaker of Scottish Gaelic who was born and brought up in the Isles. He lectured for many years at the School of Scottish Studies, University of Edinburgh (where he was also an Endowment Fellow), and has written and broadcast on a range of Gaelic subjects. The author is grateful to Morag MacLeod, formerly of the School of Scottish Studies, for helpful comments on the first edition of this book.

Each lesson in *Scottish Gaelic in Twelve Weeks* contains some essential points of grammar explained and illustrated, exercises, a list of new vocabulary (with a guide to pronunciation, in International Phonetics notation), and an item of conversation. Ideally, you should spend about an hour a day on the book, although this is by no means a firm rule. Do as much as you feel capable of doing at a particular time; it is much better to learn a little at a time, and to learn that thoroughly, than to force yourself beyond your daily capacity to absorb new material. Spend the first ten minutes of a daily session revising what you learned the day before.

When you have completed this book on modern, everyday Gaelic, you should have a good understanding of this wonderful language.

Gaelic: an introductory note

Scottish Gaelic has a standard orthography but otherwise tolerates quite a wide diversity. Local pronunciation and inflection are perfectly acceptable though often with the qualification that the native speaker tends to regard the speech of his or her own area as the most pleasing. Syntactical variation is minimal among the dialects of the language with phonological variation showing the greatest divergence. The present book, while adhering to a core standard, occasionally provides information on the different types of dialect variation which exist in the language.

Learners sometimes find this flexibility confusing at the start but soon realise it is essentially no different from the acceptance, say, of American, Australian or West Indian varieties of English as having equal status in pronunciation, syntax and idiom. The recently revised *Gaelic Orthographic Conventions*, published by the Scottish Qualification Authority (SQA) in 2005, has provided the basis for the standard spelling system which is utlised in this revised edition.

Gaelic had no official status in the United Kingdom until relatively recently. This situation reflects the history of the language first within Scotland and later in the United Kingdom. In particular throughout the last few centuries, when western European languages in general achieved their standard form, Gaelic has lacked the social institutions – centrally either a state-based or an independent educational system – which shape a register of the language common to all educated speakers. It is true that the Presbyterian churches and their associated schools made a signal contribution in this respect, but even that fell far short of what is normally provided by a system of secular education. Gaelic has had simply no place in the centres of political power since the high Middle Ages.

The tide has begun to change slowly in very recent years. The Gaelic Language (Scotland) Act / Achd na Gàidhlig (Alba) received Royal assent on 1 June 2005 and was commenced on 13 January 2006. As a result Bòrd na Gàidhlig ('The Gaelic Language Board') was established as a statutory Non-departmental Public Body with government funding to promote and develop the use and understanding of Gaelic. The Bòrd published in 2007 *Plana Nàiseanta na Gàidhlig 2007–12 / The National Plan for Gaelic 2007–12*, which sets out the road-map for Gaelic language development over the next 5 years. The Bòrd has the power to request public bodies in Scotland to produce Gaelic language plans.

To understand the past fortunes of Gaelic, it is necessary to see the language in an historical perspective. Gaelic was brought to Scotland by colonists from Ireland towards the end of the Roman Empire in Britain. By AD 500 these Gaels had established their Kingdom of Dàl Riada, centred on what is now Argyll in south-west Scotland; in Gaelic, Earra-Ghàidheal, 'the coastland of the Gael'. To Roman writers they were Scotti – Scotia at this time denoted Ireland – although these names cannot be traced with certainty to an origin in Gaelic itself. But from these Latin forms came the name Scotland. In Gaelic, however, the country is Alba, as in Irish Gaelic and Alban in Welsh.

By the eleventh century, Gaelic was at its highest point in Scotland and known to some degree virtually throughout the country. A Gaelic-speaking court, supported by the Columban church, gave patronage to makers of literature at the highest levels of society. With the Anglicisation of the dynasty late in that century, what has been described as a shift to an English way of life was deliberately planned and, as far as possible, implemented. The court itself became English and Norman-French in speech and the northern English dialect (Inglis) was fostered as the official language. The loss of status that these changes entailed for Gaelic had a profound and permanent effect.

In the mid-twelfth century the Lordship of the Isles, founded in part on the Norse kingdom of the Western and Southern Isles, but drawing also on the traditions of a former, wider Gaelic territory, emerged as a quasi-independent state. Until the Lordship was destroyed by the central authorities of Scotland in the late fifteenth century, Gaelic culture and learning continued to flourish. In the same twelfth century a reorganised literary order, whose main centres were in Ireland, was codifying Gaelic to produce an elegant formal register of the language, which we call Classical Gaelic. It was common to the learned classes of Ireland and Scotland and taught to the children of the aristocracy. It lasted in Scotland until the eighteenth century.

We can see this in religious prose (Bishop John Carswell's translation of the *Book of Common Order* in 1567 was the first Gaelic printed book and the first in any Celtic language), culminating in the translation of the scriptures in various phases until 1801. These literary activities involve a remarkably skilful transition from classical to vernacular Gaelic writing. On that basis, but drawing also on colloquial speech, Gaelic prose-writers developed a formal standard register whose strength is most evident in expository writings. Only in the twentieth century, however, and particularly with the founding of the periodical *Gairm* (1952–2002), and with new opportunities afforded by radio for short-story and other creative writing, was Gaelic freed from the rigidities of its older conventions. Verse too displays similar modulations from classical to vernacular Gaelic, although a tradition of oral vernacular song-poetry predominates. The renaissance of poetry in the twentieth century draws, with a variety of personal combinations, upon these resources.

Modern Gaelic offers the learner a wide spectrum of styles, ranging from formal registers, still in some degree associated with the church, to rich vivid idiomatic speech. Gaelic as a living language is now largely confined to north-western and island communities. But Gaelic speakers of local dialects are still to be found here and there throughout the Highlands. There are, besides, sizeable communities in the cities, particularly in Glasgow. A number of organisations are active in promoting the language. The oldest is An Comann Gàidhealach, founded at the end of the nineteenth century. In the last few years, the Gaelic College in Skye (at Sabhal Mòr Ostaig), Comunn na Gàidhlig (CNAG), Comann Luchd Ionnsachaidh (CLI) and Bòrd na Gàidhlig have all been established with the purpose of reviving the fortunes of the language.

While it is true that the history of the language is largely one of resistance to ethnocidal policies that sought to exclude the Gaels from the world of post-Renaissance Europe, contemporary developments in education, radio and television, and in literature generally, aim to redress the balance. And it should be noted that some of the most interesting writers now active on the literary scene are not native speakers but learners of Gaelic.

Glossary of grammatical terms

Fronting

This occurs when a word is moved from its usual position in a sentence to nearer the beginning of the sentence, for special emphasis.

Helping (Epenthetic) vowels

A vowel inserted between two consonants in certain words (usually containing **l**, **r** or **n**, e.g. **Alba** 'Scotland' is pronounced as if it were 'Alaba').

Lenition

Lenition (softening) is a process whereby certain consonants at the beginning of words are made 'softer'. This is indicated in writing by adding an 'h' to the consonant. Lenition changes **beag** ('small') to **bheag**, pronounced 'veg'.

Slenderisation/palatalisation

A process which makes consonants at the end of words sound slender (i.e. palatalised). A sound is made slender by adding a 'y' sound, as in English 'yes' to its pronunciation. A 'g' sound, for example, is slenderised by pronouncing it like the 'g' in 'argue'.

Pronunciation and Spelling

The pronunciation of Scottish Gaelic is somewhat different to English in certain respects; not all letters have an equivalent sound in English, and some consonants change their sound according to their position in the word. This being so, please bear in mind that some of the following guidelines can only be approximate. The vocabulary lists in each lesson show the pronunciation of every word in International Phonetics Alphabet (IPA); the fact that you might not have a 'standard English' accent renders the customary form of imitated pronunciation untrustworthy.

Naturally, if you wish to hear and acquire perfect pronunciation, you should use the CD recordings which we have produced as an optional 'extra' to this book. The CDs will allow you to hear the Gaelic words and phrases as you follow them in the book.

Whether you use the recordings or not, you should nevertheless read through the following notes on Scottish Gaelic pronunciation. There is no need to learn the rules by heart at this point. They should be referred to at frequent intervals, and soon you will become familiar with them. The same applies to the paragraphs dealing with lenition (a form of mutation, or change of consonant at the beginning of a word); this is a feature of the language which you cannot ignore but shouldn't get stuck on during the early stages of learning. In the meantime, you can start at **Lesson 1**.

Stress

Unlike English, the stress in Scottish Gaelic almost always falls on the first syllable of a word. Compare the word for 'police(man)' in English and Gaelic, where capital letters indicate the main stress:

English:	po**LICE**	/pə lis/
Scottish Gaelic:	**POIL**eas	/pɔləs/

There are some exceptions, however, which are stressed on the second syllable. This is generally indicated by means of a hyphen in written and printed Gaelic, e.g. **a-rithist, a-staigh, a-mach**, etc.

Spelling, Alphabet

Although Scottish Gaelic spelling may seem complicated at first sight, it is in many ways more regular than English, so that you can generally tell from the written form of a word how it is to be pronounced once you have become familiar with the spelling system.

There are eighteen letters in the Gaelic alphabet; the letters j, k, q, v, w, x, y, z are not used, except in some recent loan-words. Despite having a slightly smaller alphabet, Scottish Gaelic has far more individual sounds than English. These are represented by various combinations of the eighteen letters, as we shall see below.

Vowels

Accents

In Gaelic there are both short and long vowels. Long vowels are indicated by means of a grave accent. The traditional use of both grave and acute accents to indicate different long vowel qualities was largely, but by no means universally, abandoned with the publication of orthographic conventions for use in schools in the year 1981. The revised *Gaelic Orthographic Conventions* (2005), which continue to advocate the use only of the grave accent, are followed in this edition. Readers may, however, come across publications in which both grave and acute accents are used, the latter used only with the letters **e** and **o** (and rarely with **a**).

The difference in pronunciation between **a, o, u, i, e** and **à, ò, ù, ì, è** respectively is one of pure length. The difference on the other hand between **è, ò** and **é, ó** respectively is one of quality: no such distinction in orthography will be made in this book. The grave **è** sounds like the 'ai' in 'fair'; the 'older' acute **é** sounds like the 'ay' in 'say'. Compare the French 'è' and 'é'. See **Appendix 6** for more information.

A grave accent is occasionally also used to differentiate between 'clear' and 'unclear' vowels, e.g.

as /əs/ (unclear)   **às** /as/ (clear)

Pronunciation of Vowels

GAELIC LETTER	IPA SYMBOL	
a	/a/	like 'a' in 'hat'
à	/aː/	like 'a' in 'halve'
o	/o,ɔ,ɤ/	like 'o' in 'coat', like 'o' in 'cot' and like 'u' in 'cut'
ò	/ɔː/, /oː/	like 'au' in 'caught', like 'o' in 'owe' (with lips more rounded than for 'au' in caught'); the vowel sound in 'owe' (IPA [oː]) corresponds to the older acute **ó**
u	/u,ɯ/	like 'oo' in 'took'
ù	/uː/	like 'oo' in 'cool'
i	/i/	like 'ee' in 'deep'
ì	/iː/	like 'ea' in 'bean'
e	/e,ɛ/	like 'a' in 'gate' and 'e' in 'get'
è	/ɛː/, /eː/	like 'ai' in 'fair', like 'ay' in 'say' (IPA [eː]), the latter representing older acute **é**

When **i** is added to a vowel, there is often no change in pronunciation; however, there is much variation with the pronunciation of **oi**. The vowels appearing in the following rows are pronounced similarly:

SPELLING	ADD i	IPA	OTHER VOWELS AND THEIR ALTERNATIVE PRONUNCIATIONS
a	ai	/a/	ea (pronounced also like /ɛ/)
à	ài	/a:/	
o	oi	/ɔ,o,ɤ/	eo (usually ɔl)
ò	òi	/ɔ:/	eò, eòi
u	ui	/u,ɯ/	iu, iui
i		/i/	io (pronounced also as /u/)
ì		/i:/	ìo (pronounced also like /iə/)
e	ei	/ɛ,e/	ea (pronounced also like /ɛ/)
è	èi	/e:,ɛ:/	

Some digraphs can represent different vowel sounds, the most important of which are:

SPELLING	IPA	PRONUNCIATION	EXAMPLE
ea	/ɛ/	like 'e' in 'get'	each 'horse'
ea	/a/	like 'a' in 'hat'	each 'horse' (some dialects)
io	/i/	like 'ee' in 'deep'	fios 'knowledge'
io	/u/	like 'oo' in 'took'	rionnag 'star'
oi	/ɔ/	like 'o' in 'cot'	coire 'kettle'
oi	/ɤ/	like 'u' in 'cut'	coireach 'faulty, guilty'
ài	/a:/	like 'a' in 'halve'	càite? 'where?'
ài	/ɛ:/	like 'ai' in 'fair'	Gàidheal 'Gael'

The following vowel sounds should also be noted:

SPELLING	IPA	PRONUNCIATION	EXAMPLE
ao	/ɯ:/	has no equivalent in English. It is similar to 'oo' in 'cool' but with unrounded lips	gaol 'love'
aoi	/ɯ:/	has no equivalent in English; as ao above (we will see below that aoi can be pronounced as a diphthong in some words)	daoine 'people'

In stressed syllables the sequence (e)adh/gh is usually pronounced like 'u' in 'cut', e.g. feadh /fjəɤ/ 'during', laghach /ɫɤ-əx/ 'kind', but note the long vowel when the sequence occurs before a consonant in adhbhar /ɤ:vər/ 'reason', Raghnall /r̃ɤ̃:-əɫ/ 'Ronald'.

Diphthongs

Scottish Gaelic has a number of diphthongs, i.e. two different vowel sounds pronounced in succession within the same syllable. Diphthongs can be represented in spelling by a sequence of vowels, e.g. **ia**, **ua**, and in some words **aoi**, **eu/èa**, **ìo** (see below). Diphthongs are also representing in spelling by a combination of a vowel plus any of the following consonants, **ll, nn, m** (when not followed by a vowel) and **bh, mh, dh, gh**.

Sequence of Vowels

SPELLING	IPA	PRONUNCIATION	EXAMPLE
ia(i)	/iə/	like 'ea' in 'ear'	**biadh** 'food'
ua(i)	/uə/	like 'oo' in 'poor'	**fuar** 'cold'
eu, èa	/ia/	like 'ia' in 'Maria'	**beul** 'mouth', **dèan** 'do'
ìo	/iə/	like 'ea' in 'ear'	**sìos** 'down'
aoi	/ɤi/	has no equivalent in English; similar to 'oy' in 'boy' but with unrounded 'o'	**naoi** /n̥ɤ̃ĩ/ 'nine'

It is important to note that **eu** and **ìo** can be pronounced as diphthongs or as long vowels, depending on the word (and dialect) in question:

eu, èa	/ia/	like 'ia' in 'Maria'	**beul** 'mouth', **dèan** 'do'
eu	/eː/	like 'ay' in 'say'	**ceum** 'step, degree'
ìo	/iə/	like 'ea' in 'ear'	**sìos** 'down'
ìo	/iː/	like 'ee' in 'feet'	**pìob** 'pipe'

Vowel + ll, nn, m *or* bh, mh, dh, gh

all, ann, am	/au/	like 'ow' in 'how'	**call** 'loss'
oll, onn, om	/ou/	like 'o' in standard English 'no'	**trom** 'heavy'
aill, ainn, aim, aibh, aimh	/ai/	like 'y' in 'my'	**caill** 'lose'
einn, eim	/ei/	like 'ay' in 'say'	**seinn** 'singing'
oill, oinn, oim, aidh, aigh, oidh, oigh	/ɤi/	has no equivalent in English; it is similar to 'y' in 'my' but the first part of the diphthong is like the 'u' in 'cut'.	**taigh** 'house'
uill, uinn, uim	/ui, ɤi/	has no equivalent in English; it is similar to the previous diphthong, but the first part of the diphthong is like an unrounded form of 'oo' in 'cool'	**tuill** 'holes'

The above rules only hold when the consonants **ll, nn, m** are not followed by vowels, in which case the vowels are pronounced as normal. Compare:

ann /auṉ/   **Anna**/aṉə/
donn/d̥ouṉ/   **donna** /d̥oṉə/

Nasalised Vowels

Some vowels and diphthongs can occur nasalised, e.g. **faic** /fẽçgʲ/ 'see', **mac** /mãxg/ 'son'. However, the rules for its occurrence are far too complicated to be described in an introductory book of this nature.

Helping (Epenthetic) Vowels

A vowel is inserted between two consonants in certain words (usually containing **l, r** or **n**). This vowel is called a helping or epenthetic vowel; it is present in sound only, and is usually an exact copy of the preceding stressed vowel. (Think of someone with a good Scots accent saying 'harm' or 'film'; the 'r' and the 'l' are rolled, and a vowel is inserted after them – 'harram', 'fillim'.) Here are some examples – the square brackets in the IPA transcription show that an epenthetic syllable is pronounced differently to ordinary disyllables:

Alba   /[ala]bə/   Scotland
marbh   /m[ara]v/   dead
arm   /[ara]m/   army

The realisation of these 'helping' syllables varies a great deal in Gaelic dialects; don't worry too much about them at this stage.

Elision

Unstressed vowels are frequently elided in the vicinity of other vowels, e.g. **a òran** 'his song' is pronounced as **òran**. Similarly, **duine àrd** 'a tall man' (*lit* 'man tall') is pronounced **duin' àrd**. Such elision is often represented in spelling. However, in this book elision for the most part will not be represented in spellings so that learners can 'see' all of the elements that are present.

Consonants

In Gaelic the consonants may be divided into two groups, the 'broad' consonants and the 'slender' consonants. For most broad consonants, there is a corresponding slender consonant; so we may speak of a broad and slender **k** or **g** or **d** and so on.

A consonant is broad if it is preceded or followed by any of the broad vowels **a, o, u**; it is slender if preceded or followed by any of the slender vowels **i, e**: the **i** and **e** indicate that the tongue is raised in the mouth when the adjoining consonant is pronounced. Since a consonant cannot be both broad and slender, vowels on both sides of a consonant must agree according to 'colour' (broad or slender). This is sometimes stated as a rule:

caol ri caol is leathann ri leathann
i.e. *slender with slender and broad with broad*

Consider the following examples:

caileag, balla, gille, daoine, baga, pàipear, Seumas, **Màiri**, brògan.

As is the case with most rules, there are some exceptions, e.g. dèante, **esa**n, etc.

Broad Consonants

The pronunciation of the broad consonants is in most cases similar to their English counterparts. But some essential differences will be observed.

GAELIC LETTER	IPA	PRONUNCIATION
b	/b, p/	like 'p' in 'spot'; sounds like like 'p' in 'cap' especially after vowels
p	/p/	like 'p' in 'pad'
g	/g, k/	like 'c' in 'Scot'; sounds like 'k' in 'cook' especially after vowels
c	/k/	like 'c' in 'cat'
d	/d̪, t̪/	like 't' in 'stop'; sounds like 't' in 'cat' especially after vowels. Tongue touches upper teeth
t	/t̪/	like 't' in tap. Tongue touches upper teeth.
l, ll	/ɫ̪/	like a hollow 'l' as in 'full' with the tongue touching the upper teeth
n	/n̪̊, n/	is pronounced in a similar fashion to the hollow 'l' described above when it appears initially; otherwise broad 'n' is pronounced as in English
nn	/n̪̊/	is pronounced in a similar fashion to the hollow 'l' described above
r	/ɾ̪, r/	has no equivalent in English but is similar to a rolled 'r'; this sound appears for 'r' initially; otherwise broad 'r' is pronounced like 'r' in 'read'
rr	/ɾ̪/	has no equivalent in English but is similar to a rolled 'r'
ng	/ŋ/	like 'ng' in 'kong'

Broad **f, h, m, s** are pronounced like their English counterparts.

Slender Consonants

For the most part the pronunciation of the slender consonants involves raising the tongue towards the roof of the mouth to the position where the **i**-vowel is pronounced; linguists refer to slender consonants as palatalised consonants.

GAELIC LETTER	IPA	PRONUNCIATION
b	/b(j), p(j)/	like 'p' in 'dispute'; sounds like 'p' in 'type'
p	/p(j)/	like 'p' in 'pea' or like 'p' in 'pew'
g	/gʲ, kʲ/	like 'k' in 'skew'; sounds like 'k' in 'hike'
c	/kʲ/	like 'c' in 'cue'
d	/dʲ, tʲ/	like 't' in 'stupid' or the 'ch' in 'cheers'; sounds like 'tch' in 'match'
t	/tʲ/	like 'ch' in 'chew'

l	/ʎ, l/	like 'll' in 'million' when it appears initially; otherwise slender 'l' is pronounced like 'l' in 'silly'
ll	/ʎ/	like 'll' in 'million' or 'gli' in Italian
n	/ɲ, n/	like the first 'n' in 'onion' when it appears initially; otherwise slender 'n' is pronounced like 'n' in 'neat' and in some instances like the first 'n' in 'onion'
nn	/ɲ/	like the first 'n' in 'onion' or 'canyon'
r	/rʲ/	has no equivalent in English and varies considerably from dialect to dialect; it is in some dialects similar to 'r' in 'tree'
ng	/ŋʲ/	like 'ng' in 'king'
f	/fʲ/	like 'f' in 'few'
h	/h, ç/	like 'h' in 'happy' and 'h' in 'hue'
m	/m, m(j)/	is pronounced like 'm' in 'meal' or like 'm' in 'mule'
s	/ʃ/	is pronounced like 'sh' in 'shoe'

Recent loan-words with 't' or 'd' from English are pronounced as in English, e.g:

| tì | /tiː/ | tea |
| dola | /dɔlə/ | doll |

Preaspiration

'Preaspiration' means the placing of an h-like sound before certain consonants (**t, c, p**).

The voiceless consonants **t, c, p** following a stressed vowel are usually preaspirated in Gaelic. The preaspiration takes the form of voiceless breathing /h/ before each of the consonants. The preaspiration may be realised as a 'ch' sound especially before **c**. Preaspiration is not so noticeable in some dialects, particularly in some north-western dialects. Here are some examples:

GAELIC SPELLING		IPA
cat	cat	/kaht̪/
cait	cats	/kahtʲ/
mac	son	/māhk/, /māxk/
mic	sons	/mĩhkʲ/, /mĩçkʲ/
map	map	/mahp/

Consonant Groups

The Clusters *rt* and *rd*

Related to preaspiration is the insertion of 's' between **r** and a following **t** and **d**, e.g:

ceart	/kʲaɾs̪t̪/	right
sagart	/sagəɾ(s)t̪/	priest
àrd	/aːɾ(s)t̪/	high

All modern varieties of Scottish Gaelic insert 's' in **rt** clusters in monosyllables. However, not all dialects insert 's' in the **rd** clusters or in **rt** in unstressed (i.e. second) syllables.

The *chd* Cluster

The cluster **chd** in Scottish Gaelic is pronounced as if **chc**, e.g. **seachd** 'seven', **ochd** 'eight', **bochd** 'poor'. The word **eachdraidh** 'history' is an exception where the cluster **chd** is pronounced as **ch+d**.

The Initial *sr* Cluster

Initial **sr** is pronounced as if **str** in most dialects. However, the older pronunciation, **sr**, is retained in some southern dialects. Examples: **sràid** 'street', **sreap** 'climb(ing)', **sròn** 'nose'.

Hiatus

When two adjacent vowels within the same word belong to different syllables, we say that there is hiatus (a gap) between them. In many words **bh, mh, dh, gh** are mute when they appear between vowels. The preceding and following syllables are generally not coalesced (i.e. joined together); there is a gap or hiatus between such syllables. This hiatus is denoted by a hyphen (the symbol /-/) in the IPA transcription. Here are some examples:

laghach	/ɫɣ-əx/	kind
saoghal	/smː-əɫ̪/	world
cladhach	/kɫ̪ɣ-əx/	digging
abhainn	/ã-iɲ/	river

-th-, which is usually pronounced as /h/, is used in a small number of words to indicate hiatus, e.g.

latha	/ɫ̪a-ə/	day
fhathast	/ha-əst̪/	yet
rathad	/ɾa-əd̪/	road

More Consonants: Fricatives

In English when we write 'h' after 't', 'd', 'c', 'g', 'p', 's', 'w', we form new sounds 'th', 'dh', 'ch', 'gh', 'ph', 'sh', 'wh'. The letter **h** is used far more frequently in this way in Scottish Gaelic than in English. It is important to note that when **h** is added to a consonant in Scottish Gaelic, the resulting consonant is *never* pronounced as in English; except in the case of **fh**, which is silent, all other resulting consonants are referred to as fricatives. Once again we must distinguish between broad and slender fricative consonants. Here is a list of the consonants which may be written with **h** to form new sounds:

Broad

GAELIC LETTER	IPA	PRONUNCIATION
ph	/f/	like 'f' in 'fish'
bh	/v/	like 'v' in 'very'
ch	/x/	like 'ch' in Scottish 'loch' and German 'ch' in 'Bach'
gh	/ɣ/	the voiced version of 'ch'; like 'r' in French 'rire'
th	/h/	like 'h' in 'hat'; it is never pronounced like 'th' in 'think' or 'then'
dh	/ɣ/	like broad 'gh' (i.e. like 'r' in French 'rire')
mh	/v/	like broad 'bh' (i.e. like 'v' in 'very')
sh	/h/	like broad 'th' (i.e. like 'h' in 'hat')
fh	–	is not pronounced (except in **fhathast** 'yet', **fhuair** 'got' and **fhalbh** 'go', in which case it is pronounced as **h**).

Slender

GAELIC LETTER	IPA	PRONUNCIATION
ph	/f, f(j)/	like 'f' in 'fast' and 'f' in 'few'
bh	/v, v(j)/	like 'v' in 'very' and 'v' in 'view'
ch	/ç/	like 'h' in 'hue' or 'ch' in German 'ich'
gh	/j/	like 'y' in 'yes'
th	/h, ç/	like broad **th** or slender **ch**
dh	/j/	like slender **gh**
mh	/v, v(j)/	like slender **bh**
sh	/h, ç/	like broad **sh** or like slender **ch**
fh	–	is not pronounced except in **fhèin** 'self', in which case it is pronounced as **h**

Initial Mutations

A characteristic which is common to all Celtic languages, including Irish, Manx, Welsh, Cornish and Breton, is the change of certain consonants at the beginning of words. These changes, sometimes called mutations, appear according to grammatical context. In Scottish Gaelic, there are two initial mutations, **lenition** and **nasalisation** (sometimes referred to as eclipsis). Lenition is very important and will be dealt with presently. Nasalisation, which varies according to dialect, is perhaps not as important for learners as lenition and is discussed in **Appendix 4**.

Lenition

Lenition (softening) is a process whereby certain consonants which appear at the beginning of words are made 'softer'. This is indicated in writing by adding an **h** to the consonant. For example lenition changes **p** to an 'f' sound which is spelled **ph**. Lenition changes an initial **b** to **bh**, **g** to **gh**, **c** to **ch**, **d** to **dh**, **t** to **th**, **m** to **mh**, **s** to **sh**, **f** to **fh**. See above for the pronunciation of these lenitions. Note that **s** can be lenited in the clusters **sl**, **sn**, **sr** but never in the clusters **sg**, **sp**, **st**, **sm**. (Note: although **sr** is in most dialects pronounced as **str**, **sr** can be lenited: it becomes **shr**, pronounced **hr**.)

The -**h** form of a consonant, when it appears at the beginning of words, is referred to as the lenited form of the consonant. Those consonants which can 'add' **h** are called lenitable consonants; there are nine of them. Lenition is usually but not always caused by a preceding word. Consider the following example:

a cat   her cat

a chat   his cat

You will see that the word for 'her' and 'his' is **a**, the only difference between them being that the word for 'his' lenites a following (lenitable) consonant whereas the word for 'her' does not. We say that **a** 'his' is a leniting word and that it lenites a following word. We will distinguish between leniting and non-leniting words by placing the symbol * after those words which cause lenition. Lenition is extremely common in Scottish Gaelic and we will meet many more leniting words and particles in the lessons below. Here are some more examples of the words for 'his' and 'her':

bàta	boat	**a bàta**	her boat	**a bhàta**	his boat
piuthar	sister	**a piuthar**	her sister	**a phiuthar**	his sister
geansaidh	jumper	**a geansaidh**	her jumper	**a gheansaidh**	his jumper
cù	dog	**a cù**	her dog	**a chù**	his dog
dealbh	picture	**a dealbh**	her picture	**a dhealbh**	his picture
taigh	house	**a taigh**	her house	**a thaigh**	his house
mac	son	**a mac**	her son	**a mhac**	his son
sùil	eye	**a sùil**	her eye	**a shùil**	his eye
falt	hair	**a falt**	her hair	**a fhalt**	his hair

Note: We never write **h** after **l n r** although some dialects lenite certain varieties of **l n r** sounds, e.g. **leabaidh** /ʎɛbi/ 'bed' but **mo leabaidh** /mə lɛbi/ 'my bed'; **nigh** /ɲi/ 'wash' (imperative) but **nigh** /ni/ 'washed' (past tense); **Rob** /ɾɔb/ 'Rob' (nominative) but **a Rob** /ə ɾɔb/ or /ə rɔb/ 'Rob' (address / vocative form: see below and **Section 33**). However, the subtle differences involved are beyond the scope of this book.

Slenderisation/Palatalisation

We have seen above that for most consonants, there is a broad and a slender (palatalised) form, each one representing a separate sound in the language. For any consonant, broad and slender forms frequently alternate at the end of words, e.g. **cat** 'a cat' and **cait** 'cats'. We say that **cait** is the slenderised form of **cat**. A word is slenderised by inserting an 'i' before the last consonant or group of consonants. The **i** before a final consonant tells us that the letter is to be pronounced differently, i.e. as a slender consonant. The change of broad **t** to slender **t** is called slenderisation or palatalisation. It is important to note that slenderisation occurs only at the <u>end</u> of words. Slenderisation is used to form the plural form of some nouns. Here are some examples:

cat	cat	**cait**	cats
dùn	fort	**dùin**	forts
balach	boy	**balaich**	boys
boireannach	woman	**boireannaich**	women
òran	song	**òrain**	songs

Slenderisation of a final consonant can in some cases cause the preceding vowel to change form. A list of the common changes can be found in **Appendix 1**. Here are a few examples where the preceding vowel is affected by the process of slenderisation:

mac	son	**mic**	sons
fear	man	**fir**	men
cnoc	hill	**cnuic**	hills
bòrd	table	**bùird**	tables
fiadh	deer	**fèidh**	deer (*plural*)

Slenderisation is very important in Scottish Gaelic and we will meet many further instances of it in the lessons which follow.

Lenition and Slenderisation

Lenition and slenderisation can operate simultaneously on a word. When we address a person in Gaelic, the name is preceded by **a**, which lenites the initial consonant, e.g.

NORMAL FORM	ADDRESS FORM	
Mòrag	**a Mhòrag**	Morag
Màiri	**a Mhàiri**	Mary
Catrìona	**a Chatrìona**	Catherine

However, when we address a male, the name is also slenderised, e.g.

NORMAL FORM	ADDRESS FORM	
Seumas	**a Sheumais**	James
Dòmhnall	**a Dhòmhnaill**	Donald
Tormod	**a Thormoid**	Norman

The address form is referred to as the vocative. See **Section 33**.

Lesson 1

1 Pronouns

mi	I
thu	you
e	he/it
i	she/it
sinn	we
sibh	you (*pl*)
iad	they

In Gaelic there are two words used for 'you', **thu** and **sibh**. **Sibh** is used to refer to (a) 'you' plural and (b) 'you' in formal or polite contexts, usually when addressing one's elders or superiors. **Thu** is used otherwise, generally in familiar contexts.

2 The verb '*tha*' ('to be')

In sentences like 'John is young', 'Ann is small', 'James is tired' we use the verb **tha**. In Gaelic the order of words in such sentences is the same as English except that the verb comes first in the sentence. Consider the following examples:

Tha Iain òg.	John is young.
Tha Anna beag.	Ann is small.
Tha Seumas sgìth.	James is tired.
Tha Màiri toilichte.	Mary is happy.
Tha Dòmhnall an seo.	Donald is here.
Tha Uilleam an sin.	William is there.
Tha Raghnall an siud.	Ronald is yonder.
Tha Iain math.	John is good.
Tha Anna gu math.	Ann is well.
Tha mi sgìth.	I am tired.
Tha thu làidir.	You are strong.
Tha e fuar.	He/it is cold.
Tha sinn blàth.	We are warm.
Tha sibh fliuch.	You are wet.
Tha iad an seo.	They are here.

1

3 Indefinite nouns

There is no indefinite article in Gaelic. **Cat** (*sing*) may be translated as 'cat' or 'a cat'. Likewise **cait** (*pl*) means 'cats' or 'some cats'.

cù	/kuː/	(a) dog
càr	/kaːr/	(a) car
deoch	/dʲɔx/	(a) drink
balach	/baʈ̪əx/	(a) boy
caileag	/kalag/	(a) girl
rùm	/ɼuːm/	(a) room
taigh	/t̪ɤj/	(a) house
airgead	/[arʲa]gʲəd̪/, /[ɛrʲɛ]gʲəd̪/	money

3a 'There is/are'

A noun not preceded by the definite article is referred to as an indefinite noun. When the subject of **tha** is an indefinite noun, we can translate 'there is' or 'there are':

Tha cat an seo.	There is a cat here.
	(*lit* 'a cat is here')
Tha craobh an sin.	There is a tree there.
	(*lit* 'a tree is there')
Tha caistealan an Glaschu.	There are castles in Glasgow.
	(*lit* 'castles are in Glasgow')

4 'To have'

Gaelic has no verb 'to have'. Instead a periphrastic (or 'long') construction involving the verb **tha** and the preposition **aig** 'at' is used. 'John has a cat' becomes:

Tha cat aig Iain.	(*lit* 'a cat is at John')

Similarly:

Tha cù aig Màiri.	Mary has a dog.
Tha leabhar aig Anna.	Ann has a book.
Tha taigh aig Seumas.	James has a house.
Tha airgead aig Iain.	John has money.

4a Prepositional pronouns

Prepositions normally combine with pronouns to give prepositional pronouns, e.g.

aig + mi = agam	at me
aig + thu = agad	at you
aig + e = aige	at him/it
aig + i = aice	at her/it
aig + sinn = againn	at us
aig + sibh = agaibh	at you
aig + iad = aca	at them
Tha càr agam. (NOT aig mi)	I have a car.
Tha leabhar agad.	You have a book.
Tha taigh aige.	He has a house.
Tha airgead aca.	They have money.

For more prepositional pronouns, see **Appendix 2**.

Exercise 1.1

Translate

1   Mary is happy.
2   John is strong.
3   I am warm.
4   They are cold.
5   We are here.
6   Ann has a book.
7   James has a car.
8   I have a drink.
9   We have a house.
10   She has a boy.

4b 'To know'

A periphrastic construction involving the verb **tha**, the noun **fios** 'knowledge' and the preposition **aig** 'at' is used to translate 'know' in Gaelic as follows:

tha f(h)ios aig Iain	John knows
tha f(h)ios agam	I know

This is generally used for 'know' in the sense of knowing facts as opposed to knowing a person. We will learn a different idiom for 'knowing people' in **Lesson 4**. In this idiom there is variation between **fios** and **fhios** which literally means **a fhios** 'its knowledge, knowledge of it'.

5 Negative and interrogative forms of '*tha*'

To negate **tha**, simply replace **tha** with **chan eil**:

Chan eil Iain mòr.	John is not big.
Chan eil Anna toilichte.	Ann is not happy.
Chan eil mi sgìth.	I am not tired.
Chan eil iad an seo.	They are not here.
Chan eil cat aig Màiri.	Mary doesn't have a cat / has no cat.
Chan eil deoch aig Dòmhnall.	Donald doesn't have a drink / has no drink.
Chan eil airgead agam.	I don't have (any) money / I have no money.

To form the interrogative (positive), replace **tha** with **a bheil** (sometimes written as **am bheil**):

A bheil Seumas sgìth?	Is James tired?
A bheil Màiri fuar?	Is Mary cold?
A bheil Iain an seo?	Is John here?
A bheil cat aig Anna?	Does Ann have a cat?
A bheil airgead agad?	Do you have (any) money?

To form the interrogative (negative), replace **tha** with **nach eil**:

Nach eil Anna toilichte?	Isn't Ann happy?
Nach eil iad math?	Aren't they good?
Nach eil cù aig Dòmhnall?	Doesn't Donald have a dog?
Nach eil taigh aice?	Doesn't she have a house?

6 Answering questions

There is no single word for 'yes' or 'no' in Scottish Gaelic. A question is always answered by repeating or echoing the main verb of the question. There is no need to repeat the subject of the sentence. Consider the following examples:

A bheil thu gu math?	Are you well?
Tha.	Yes.
Chan eil.	No.

Nach eil i an sin?	Is she not there?
Tha.	Yes.
Chan eil.	No.

Where are you from?

Study the following phrases:

Cò às a tha thu?	Where are you from?
tha à Glaschu	from Glasgow
tha à Dùn Èideann	from Edinburgh
tha à Alba	from Scotland
tha à Èirinn	from Ireland
tha à Sasainn	from England
Tha Iain à Glaschu.	John is from Glasgow.
Tha Anna à Sasainn.	Ann is from England.

7 'I have only'

Consider the following examples:

Chan eil not agam.	I haven't got a pound.
Chan eil agam ach not.	I have only a pound.
Chan eil sgillinn aig Seumas.	James hasn't got a penny.
Chan eil aig Seumas ach sgillinn.	James has only a penny.

Ach normally means 'but'. **Chan eil aig Seumas ach sgillinn** translates literally as 'James hasn't but a penny'.

Exercise 1.2

Translate

1 Ann is not tired.
2 James is not there.
3 Mary doesn't have a dog.
4 We have no money.
5 Is John cold?
6 Does Donald have a drink?
7 Do they have any money?
8 I have only a penny.
9 Isn't Donald happy?
10 Doesn't he have a car?

8 Adverbs

Adverbs are frequently formed by placing **gu** before adjectives:

math	good	(*adj*)	**gu math**	well	(*adv*)
dona	bad	(*adj*)	**gu dona**	badly	(*adv*)
snog	nice	(*adj*)	**gu snog**	nicely	(*adv*)

1

Other adverbs with **gu** are:

gu dòigheil	fine
gu luath	quickly

Watch out for more examples which follow.

8a 'How are you?'

Study the following phrases:

Ciamar a tha thu?	How are you?
tha gu math	well
tha gu dòigheil	fine
chan eil gu dona	not bad
chan eil mi gu math idir	I am not well at all
chan eil ach meadhanach	only middling, so-so
tha thu fhèin gu math?	are you well yourself?
	(*lit* 'you are well yourself?')

Vocabulary

ach (*cjn*)	/ax/	but
agus (*cjn*)	/agəs/, /ɣgəs/	and
A bheil fios agad?	/ə vel fis agəd̪/	Do you know?
an-diugh (*adv*)	/əɲ d̪ʲu/	today
a-nis (*adv*)	/ə niʃ/	now
brèagha (*adj*)	/brʲia-ə/	lovely
cuideachd (*adv*)	/kud̪ʲəxk/	also
fios (*m*)	/fis/	knowledge
gu dearbh (*adv*)	/gə d̪ʲ[ɛrɛ]v/	indeed
idir (*adv*)	/id̪ʲərʲ/	at all
no (*cjn*)	/nɔ/	or
rùm (*m*)	/ɾuːm/	room
slàinte (*f*) **mhath**	/sɫaːɲd̪ʲə vã/	good health
uile (*adj*)	/ulə/	all

CÒMHRADH (CONVERSATION)

1

Iain agus Anna

Iain	A bheil taigh aig Seumas an seo?
Anna	Tha, tha taigh aig Seumas an siud. Tha taigh aig Dòmhnall cuideachd agus tha e brèagha.
Iain	A bheil cù agus cat aca, a bheil fios agad?
Anna	Chan eil, chan eil cù no cat aca.
Iain	Gu dearbh! A-nis, a bheil càr agad?
Anna	Tha, tha càr agam ach chan eil e mòr idir.
Iain	Agus a bheil taigh agad?
Anna	Chan eil, chan eil taigh agam. Chan eil airgead agam. Agus chan eil taigh aig Uilleam no aig Màiri. Tha caileag agus balach aca.
Iain	A bheil Raghnall an seo?
Anna	Tha, tha Raghnall an seo. Tha rùm aige. Tha e toilichte an seo. Tha leabhar aige agus tha e math.
Iain	A bheil sibh uile toilichte an seo?
Anna	Chan eil, chan eil sinn uile toilichte idir. Tha e fuar agus fliuch an-diugh agus tha sinn sgìth.
Iain	A bheil deoch agad?
Anna	Tha, tha deoch agam an seo – blàth agus làidir. Slàinte mhath!

TRANSLATION

John and Ann

John	Does James have a house here?
Ann	Yes, James has a house over there. Donald has a house also and it's lovely.
John	Do they have a dog and a cat, do you know?
Ann	No, they don't have a dog or a cat.
John	Indeed! Now, do you have a car?
Ann	I have a car but it's not big at all.
John	And do you have a house?
Ann	I have no house. I have no money. And neither William nor Mary have a house. They have a girl and a boy.
John	Is Ronald here?
Ann	Ronald is here. He has a room. He is happy here. He has a book and it's good.
John	Are you all happy here?
Ann	We aren't all happy at all. It's cold and wet today and we are tired.
John	Do you have a drink?
Ann	I have a drink here – warm and strong. Good health!

Lesson 2

9 Emphatic pronouns

mise	I
t(h)usa	you
esan	he
ise	she
sinne	we
sibhse	you
iadsan	them

Gaelic normally uses emphatic suffixes (rather than tone or stress) for emphatic and contrastive purposes.

Tha Iain beag ach tha <u>mise</u> mòr.	John is small but *I'm* big.
Tha Anna sgìth ach chan eil <u>mise</u>.	Ann is tired but *I'm* not.
Ciamar a tha thu?	How are you?
Ciamar a tha <u>thusa</u>?	How are *you*?

9a 'Who are you?'

To ask who someone is, we use **cò** 'who?' with either the emphatic or unemphatic form of the pronouns as follows:

Cò thusa? OR Cò thu?	Who are you?
Cò ise? Cò i?	Who is she?
Cò esan? Cò e?	Who is he?
Cò sibhse? Cò sibh?	Who are you? (*formal, polite* and *plural*)
Cò iadsan? Cò iad?	Who are they?

10 The verb '*is*' ('to be')

There are two verbs 'to be' in Gaelic, **tha** and **is**. We met **tha** in **Lesson 1**. In sentences like 'I am John', 'you are Ann', 'he is James', we use the verb **is**. This verb is traditionally referred to as the copula since it 'couples' or joins two entities together.

As with **tha,** the copula **is** comes first in the sentence. You will note from the following examples that the emphatic forms of the pronouns are usually used with **is**:

Is mise Iain.	I am John.
Is tusa Anna.	You are Ann.

Is esan Seumas.	He is James.
Is ise Peigi.	She is Peggy.
Is sinne an clas Gàidhlig.	We are the Gaelic class.
Is sibhse an tidsear.	You are the teacher.
Is iadsan Màiri agus Calum.	They are Mary and Calum.

Note: **tusa** (pronounced **dusa**) rather than **thusa** is used with **is**.

10a A note on the difference between '*tha*' and '*is*'

In sentences like 'John is young' and 'she is Ann' we refer to 'young' and 'Ann' as being predicates (i.e. that which is being said about the subject of the sentence) of the verb 'to be'. A useful rule on the use of **tha** and **is** is as follows:

> when the predicate is a noun, use **is**

> when the predicate is anything else (e.g. adjective, adverb, etc), use **tha**

Note: this is one of the most basic rules of Gaelic grammar and one of the most important to remember.

Another minor difference between the verbs **tha** and **is** is that **is** is unstressed and is usually pronounced as **s**.

10b Negative and interrogative forms of '*is*'

To negate **is** replace **is** with **cha** or **chan** as follows:

Cha mhise Iain.	I am not John.
Cha tusa Anna.	You aren't Ann.
Chan esan Seumas.	He isn't James.
Chan ise Peigi.	She isn't Peggy.
Cha sinne an clas Gàidhlig.	We aren't the Gaelic class.
Cha sibhse an tidsear.	You aren't the teacher.
Chan iadsan Màiri agus Calum.	They aren't Mary and Calum.

You will note that **cha** becomes **chan** before a following vowel (i.e. before **esan, ise, iadsan**) and that **cha** lenites **mise**.

To form the interrogative (positive) replace **is** with **an** (**am** before **mise**):

Am mise Iain?	Am I John?
An tusa Anna?	Are you Ann?
An esan Seumas?	Is he James?
An ise Peigi?	Is she Peggy?
An sinne an clas Gàidhlig?	Are we the Gaelic class?
An sibhse an tidsear?	Are you the teacher?
An iadsan Màiri agus Calum?	Are they Mary and Calum?

To form the interrogative (negative) replace **is** with **nach**:

Nach mise Iain?	Am I not John?
Nach tusa Anna?	Aren't you Ann?
Nach esan Seumas?	Isn't he James?

To answer any of the above **is** questions, the answer must always include either the positive or the negative form of **is** and also the appropriate unemphatic pronoun:

POSITIVE	NEGATIVE
is mi	**cha mhi**
is tu	**cha tu**
is e (usually spelled **'s e**)	**chan e**
is i (usually spelled **'s i**)	**chan i**
is sinn	**cha sinn**
is sibh	**cha sibh**
is iad (usually spelled **'s iad**)	**chan iad**

Note: **tu** is pronounced **du**.

Some examples:

An tusa Iain? Is mi.	Are you John? Yes.
An ise Anna? Is i.	Is she Ann? Yes.
An sibhse Màiri agus Peigi?	Are you Mary and Peggy?
Cha sinn.	No.
An iadsan an clas Gàidhlig?	Are they the Gaelic class?
Chan iad.	No.

Exercise 2.1

Translate

1. I am Ann.
2. He is Calum.
3. She is Peggy.
4. You aren't James.
5. They aren't the Gaelic class.
6. She isn't Mary.
7. Aren't you Donald? No.
8. Are you John? Yes.
9. They are Peggy and Mary.
10. You are the teacher.

11 Gender

Scottish Gaelic has two genders – feminine and masculine. Nouns are either feminine or masculine. The gender of a noun must be learnt by heart as there is no easy way of telling a word's gender. A good example of this is the word **boireannach** 'woman' which is grammatically a masculine noun. The main difference between masculine and feminine nouns is that (a) feminine nouns are generally lenited after the definite article (nominative) and (b) adjectives following feminine nouns are generally lenited, e.g.

MASCULINE		FEMININE	
an gille beag	the little boy	**a' chaileag bheag**	the little girl

Here are some useful phrases which illustrate the difference between masculine and feminine nouns:

madainn (*f*) **mhath**	good morning
feasgar (*m*) **math**	good evening
oidhche (*f*) **mhath**†	good night
slàinte (*f*) **mhath**	good health

For exceptions such as **sgian** (*f*) **dubh**, see **Appendix 7**.
† Oidhche mhath is also used to wish someone 'goodnight'.

12 The pronouns *'fear'* and *'tè'*

The words **fear** (*m*) and **tè** (*f*), which normally mean 'man' and 'woman', respectively, can act as pronouns meaning 'one'. **Fear** meaning 'one' is used when referring to masculine nouns; **tè** is used when referring to feminine nouns:

leabhar (*m*)	book	**fear mòr**	a big one
deoch (*f*)	drink	**tè bheag**	a small one

13 Case in Gaelic

There are three cases in Gaelic: nominative, prepositional and genitive. The nominative is the dictionary form of a word (article, noun, adjective) and corresponds to the traditional cases of nominative (subjects) and accusative (objects). The prepositional corresponds partly to the traditional dative case and is used only after prepositions. The prepositional and genitive will be discussed in **Lessons 6** and **7** respectively.

14 Definite article ('the')

The definite article always precedes the noun it qualifies and agrees in gender, number and case with it. We can distinguish between four main forms of the article in Gaelic: **an, an*, na, nan** (recall that * indicates that lenition follows).

As we shall see, each of these four forms represents a distinct set of variants (usually 2 or 3) of the article. We will deal only with the first two forms here, **an** and **an***.

NOMINATIVE FORMS

The article has two nominative forms: **an**, which is used before masculine nouns, and **an***, which is used before feminine nouns. The spelling of each form of the article changes slightly according to the initial sound of the following word. These changes are helpful as they reflect the pronunciation in each case.

(i) Masculine article an

The masculine article **an** is spelt:

am	before all labial sounds, i.e. **b f m p**
an t-	before all vowels
an	otherwise

am fear	the man	**an t-uisge**	the water	**an tidsear**	the teacher
am balach	the boy	**an t-airgead**	the money	**an sagart**	the priest
am ministear	the minister	**an t-ìm**	the butter	**an taigh**	the house
am peann	the pen	**an t-eilean**	the island	**an loch**	the lake

It will be seen that the change in spelling of **an** to **am** reflects the pronunciation of **an** before the labials **b f m p**. Compare your pronunciation of **n** in the English word **input**; you will more than likely pronounce this **n** as an **m**. A **t-** is prefixed before all masculine nouns beginning in a vowel after the masculine (nominative) article **an**.

(ii) Feminine article an*

The feminine article **an*** is spelt:

a' + lenition	before all lenitable consonants (except **d t s f**), i.e. **b c g m p**
an t-	before **s sl sr sn**, but NOT before **sg sp st sm**
an + lenition	before **f** (which becomes **fh**)
an	otherwise, i.e. before all vowels, **d n t l r** and **sg sp st sm**

a' chlach	the stone	**an fhuil**	the blood	**an deoch**	the drink
a' bhò	the cow	**an fheòil**	the meat	**an teanga**	the tongue
a' Bheurla	(the) English	**an t-sùil**	the eye	**an obair**	the work
a' Ghàidhlig	(the) Gaelic	**an t-sràid**	the street	**an sgoil**	the school

The feminine definite article generally lenites a following consonant, in which case the **n** of the article is not pronounced (except before **fh-**) and therefore dropped in spelling, hence **a'**. The **n** is pronounced and therefore retained before **fh-**. The dentals (i.e. sounds made at the teeth) **d t** are NOT lenited by the feminine article; the lenition is 'blocked' in such instances: see **Appendix 7**.

This means that it is difficult to distinguish between masculine and feminine nouns beginning with **d t** when they are preceded by the article, e.g.

an duine (*m*)	the man
an deoch (*f*)	the drink
an taigh (*m*)	the house
an tì (*f*)	the tea

The feminine article prefixes **t-** to feminine nouns beginning with **s** (**sl sr sn**), in which case the **s** is not pronounced. It follows that the groups **t-s, t-sl, t-sr, t-sn** are pronounced, respectively, as **t, tl, tr, tn** (also **tr**). The reason that **t** is not prefixed to feminine words beginning with **sg, sp, st, sm** is that the initial clusters **tg, tp, tt, tm** are not possible in Gaelic.

14a Use of article

When a noun is used to designate an entire class, the singular article is often used, e.g.

am bradan	salmon
an t-each	horses (in general)
am feur	grass

The article is always used before abstract nouns, e.g.

an aois	age
an sgìths	tiredness
am blàths	warmth

Exercise 2.2

Put the proper form of the nominative article before the following nouns:

1	**leabhar** (*m*)	/ʎɔ-ər/	book
2	**ceòl** (*m*)	/kʲɔːɫ/	music
3	**craobh** (*f*)	/krɯːv/	tree
4	**pìob** (*f*)	/piːb/	pipe
5	**bean** (*f*)	/bɛn/	wife
6	**feannag** (*f*)	/fjaṉag/	crow
7	**sràid** (*f*)	/sʈraːdʲ/	street
8	**sporan** (*m*)	/spɔran/	purse
9	**pàipear** (*m*)	/pɛːhpɛrʲ/	paper
10	**tè** (*f*)	/tʲeː/	woman

15 Possessive constructions

There are two possessive constructions in Scottish Gaelic, each involving the use of personal pronouns. The first construction involves the use of possessive pronouns which precede the noun they qualify. The second construction involves the use of the definite article and the prepositional pronouns formed from the preposition **aig** 'at'.

(i) Possessive pronouns

Before consonants		Before vowels and **fh** + vowel			
Before consonants		Before vowels		Before **f** + vowel	
mo*[†]		**m'**		**m' fh-**	my
do*		**d'** or **t'**		**d' fh-** or **t' fh-**	your
a*		**a**		**a fh-**	his
a		**a h-**		**a f-**	her
ar		**ar n-**		**ar f-**	our
ur		**ur n-**		**ur f-**	your
an / am		**an / am**		**am f-**	their
mo mhàthair	my mother	**m' athair**	my father	**m' fhalt**	my hair
do bhràthair	your brother	**d' aodann**	your face	**d' fhalt**	your hair
a phiuthar	his sister	**a athair**	his father	**a fhalt**	his hair
a cas	her foot	**a h-athair**	her father	**a falt**	her hair
ar mac	our son	**ar n-athair**	our father	**ar falt**	her hair
ur nighean	your daughter	**ur n-athair**	your father	**ur falt**	your hair
an làmhan	their hands	**an athair**	their father	**am falt**	their hair

Note: **an** 'their' becomes **am** before labials, e.g. **am bràthair** 'their brother'. Possessive pronouns are normally used with the so-called inalienables, i.e. parts of the body and blood relations, e.g. **làmh** 'arm', **cas** 'leg', **sùil** 'eye', **màthair** 'mother', **athair** 'father', **mac** 'son', **nighean** 'daughter' (also means 'girl').

[†] Recall that an asterisk is used in this book to show that a word lenites.

(ii) Alternative possessive construction involving prepositional pronouns

This construction involves the definite article, which precedes the noun, and the appropriate prepositional pronoun formed from the preposition **aig** 'at' which follows the noun. 'My cat' becomes **an cat agam** in Gaelic, *lit* 'the cat at-me'. Here are some further examples:

an cù agad	your dog
an leabhar aige	his book
an t-airgead aice	her money
a' bhò againn	our cow

an obair agaibh	your work
an deoch aca	their drink

This possessive construction is generally used with the so-called 'alienables', i.e. nouns which are not parts of the body or blood relations. Note that the alternative construction is always used with the pronouns **fear** and **tè** introduced in **Section 12**, e.g. **an tè agam** 'my one' .

Exercise 2.3

Translate

1. my sister
2. your mother
3. her father
4. their son
5. his foot
6. our dog
7. their money
8. your cow
9. her work
10. her eye

16 Position and status of adjectives

Adjectives normally follow the noun they qualify. There is a small number of exceptions which precede the noun, and these will be discussed below. An adjective following a feminine noun is lenited (nominative form); an adjective following a masculine noun is not lenited (nominative form).

MASCULINE		FEMININE	
cù mòr	a big dog	**caileag bheag**	a small girl
rùm dorcha	a dark room	**slàinte mhath**	good health
còta dearg	a red coat	**lèine gheal**	a white shirt
taigh beag	a small house	**uinneag shalach**	a dirty window
òran math	a good song	**oidhche mhath**	a good night

A noun can be followed by more than one adjective. There is a certain order in which these adjectives may occur. Adjectives denoting size (e.g. **mòr** 'big', **beag** 'small') tend always to appear first in a string of adjectives, e.g.

cù mòr dubh	a big black dog
lèine bheag gheal	a small white shirt

You will note that a feminine noun lenites all (attributive) adjectives which follow it.

Note: it is only attributive and not predicative adjectives which are affected by lenition. Consider the following two examples which contain attributive adjectives:

bròg bheag	a small shoe
clach throm	a heavy stone

The following two examples, on the other hand, contain predicative adjectives (which are not lenited by the preceding feminine nouns):

Tha a' bhròg beag.	The shoe is small.
Tha a' chlach trom.	The stone is heavy.

The following example contains both attributive and predicative adjectives:

> **Tha [a' chlach <u>bheag</u> (*attr*)] <u>trom</u> (*pred*).** The small stone is heavy.

Attributive adjectives belong to the same noun phrase as the noun they qualify, i.e. they can be included within the same bracket as the noun as in the above example. Predicative adjectives on the other hand do not belong to the same noun phrase as the noun they qualify; in English predicative adjectives follow the verb as in the above examples.

(i) Adjectives which precede a noun

We have already mentioned that there are some adjectives which precede the noun they qualify, the most important of which are:

seann*	old
deagh*	good
droch*	bad

These adjectives lenite the initial consonant of a following noun (except **d t s** in the case of **seann**: see **Appendix 7**) irrespective of the gender of the noun in question.

seann chroitear	an old crofter
seann duine	an old man
deagh sheinneadair	a good singer
droch bhiadh	bad food

The nominative article, when it appears, always precedes the adjectives **seann, deagh, droch**. It always appears as **an** before **deagh** and **droch**. **An** is used before **seann** when **seann** precedes a masculine noun; **an t-** is used when **seann** precedes a feminine noun. Study the following examples:

an deagh sheinneadair (*m*)	the good singer
an droch shìde (*f*)	the bad weather
an t-seann bhròg (*f*)	the old shoe
an seann chòta (*m*)	the old coat

2

(ii) 'The same'

The adjectives **aon*** and **dearbh*** also precede the noun they qualify and are usually preceded by the article **an** 'the', e.g.

an aon bheachd	the same opinion
an aon chàr	the same car
an dearbh bhalach	the very boy
an dearbh rud	the very thing

Some write **an t-aon** in the above examples. **Aon** does not lenite nouns beginning with **d** or **t**: see **Appendix 7**.

(iii) 'Very' and 'too'

The words **glè*** 'very' and **ro*** 'too' lenite a following adjective. Study the following:

glè mhath	very well
glè bheag	very small
glè mhòr	very big
ro mhath	too good
ro bheag	too small
ro mhòr	too big

Vocabulary

balach (*m*)	/baḻəx/	boy
bàta (*m*)	/baːht̪ə/	boat
bò (*f*)	/boː/	cow
bòrd (*m*)	/bɔːrṣt̪/	table
bròg (*f*)	/brɔːg/	shoe
caileag (*f*)	/kalag/	girl
deagh (*adj*)	/dʲoː/	good
dearg (*adj*)	/dʲ[ɛra]g/, /dʲ[ara]g/	red
dorcha (*adj*)	/d̪[ɔrɔ]xə/	dark
gorm (*adj*)	/g[ɔrɔ]m/	blue
oidhche (*f*)	/r̃ĩçə/	night
salach (*adj*)	/saḻəx/	dirty
sìde (*f*)	/ʃiːdʲə/	weather

Exercise 2.4

Remove the brackets, make the necessary adjustments and translate:

1 **bòrd (beag)**
2 **bò (mòr)**
3 **balach (math)**
4 **oidhche (dorcha)**
5 **bròg (salach)**
6 **bàta (dearg)**
7 **seann (bàta)**
8 **deagh (caileag)**
9 **droch (sìde)**
10 **seann (càr) (gorm)**

Vocabulary

an seo (*adv*)	/əɲ ʃɔ/	here
an sin (*adv*)	/əɲ ʃin/	there
basaidh (*m*)	/basi/	basin (note **mias** is also used for 'basin')
beagan (*adv*)	/began/	a little
blàth (*adj*)	/bɫaː/	warm
ceàrr (*adj*)	/kʲaːr/	wrong (note **ceàrr** can also mean 'left')
clì (*adj*)	/kliː/	left
comhfhurtail (*adj*)	/kõ-ərsʈal/	comfortable
cruaidh (*adj*)	/kruəj/	hard
cuideachd (*adv*)	/kudʲəxk/	also
deas (*adj*)	/dʲes/	right(-hand)
glan (*adj*)	/gɫan/	fine, nice (*lit* 'clean')
goirt (*adj*)	/gɔrsʈʲ/	sore
madainn (*f*) **mhath**	/mãḏiɲ vã/	good morning
ma-thà (*interj*)	/mã haː/	then! so!
nurs (*m*)	/nɤrs/	nurse
ospadal (*m*)	/ɔspəḏəɫ/	hospital
suidh (*vb*)	/suɪj/	sit down
tapadh (*m*) **leibh**	/ʈahpə lʲɤiv/	thank you
teann (*adj*)	/tʲaun̪/	tight
ùr (*adj*)	/uːr/	new

CÒMHRADH (CONVERSATION)

Balach òg, Iain, aig an ospadal

Nurs	Madainn mhath. Is mise an nurs. Cò thusa?
Iain	Is mise Iain.
Nurs	Ciamar a tha thu?
Iain	Chan eil mi gu math idir.
Nurs	Dè a tha ceàrr?
Iain	Tha mo chas goirt.
Nurs	A' chas dheas no a' chas chlì?
Iain	An tè dheas ach tha an tè chlì beagan goirt cuideachd.
Nurs	A bheil a' bhròg agad ro theann?
Iain	Chan eil ach tha mo bhrògan ro chruaidh. Tha iad ùr, tha fios agaibh.
Nurs	Suidh an sin, ma-thà. Tha basaidh agam an seo.
Iain	O, tha sin glan. Tha an t-uisge blàth.
Nurs	A bheil sin comhfhurtail?
Iain	Tha gu dearbh. Tapadh leibh.

TRANSLATION

A young boy, John, at the hospital

Nurse	Good morning. I'm the nurse. Who are you?
John	I'm John.
Nurse	How are you?
John	I am not well at all.
Nurse	What's the matter?
John	My foot is sore.
Nurse	The right foot or the left foot?
John	The right foot but the left one is a little sore, too.
Nurse	Is your shoe too tight?
John	No, but my shoes are too hard. They are new, you know.
Nurse	Sit down here then. I've got a basin here.
John	Oh, that's nice. The water is warm.
Nurse	Is that comfortable?
John	It certainly is. Thank you.

Lesson 3

17 Verbal nouns

With every verb (except the verb **tha**), there is an associated verbal noun which corresponds to participles in other languages. In most cases the verbal noun is formed by adding a suffix to the verb, although this is not always the case. Here are some examples with variants given in brackets:

VERB		VERBAL NOUN	
(a) VERB + **adh**			
leugh	→	**leughadh**	reading
sgrìobh	→	**sgrìobhadh**	writing
geàrr	→	**gearradh**	cutting
mol	→	**moladh**	praising
pòs	→	**pòsadh**	marrying
buail	→	**bualadh**	striking

Note the long **à** in **geàrr** but short **a** in **gearradh**.

(b) VERB + **(a)inn, sinn, tinn**			
faic	→	**faicinn (faiceail)**	seeing
faigh	→	**faighinn (faotainn)**	getting
feuch	→	**feuchainn**	trying
tuig	→	**tuigsinn**	understanding
creid	→	**creidsinn**	believing
cluinn	→	**cluinntinn (cluinnteail)**	hearing
can	→	**cantainn (cantail)**	saying

(c) VERB + **ail, tail**			
gabh	→	**gabhail**	taking
fàg	→	**fàgail**	leaving
cùm	→	**cumail**	keeping
tog	→	**togail**	lifting, building
lean	→	**leantail (leantainn)**	following

Note the long **ù** in **cùm** but short in **cumail**.

(d) VERB + **achadh**			
lag(aich)	→	**lagachadh**	weakening

(e) VERB + e

ith	→	ithe	eating
laigh	→	laighe	lying
suidh	→	suidhe	sitting
nigh	→	nighe	washing

(f) VERB = verbal noun

seinn	→	seinn	singing
òl	→	òl	drinking
falbh	→	falbh	going away
fàs	→	fàs	growing
ruith	→	ruith	running
obair	→	obair	working

(g) other forms

cuir	→	cur	putting
iarr	→	iarraidh	wanting
fuirich	→	fuireach	living
ceannaich	→	ceannach	buying
fairich	→	faireachdainn	feeling
ionnsaich	→	ionnsachadh	learning
smaoinich	→	smaoineachadh (smaointinn)	thinking
èist	→	èisteachd	listening
èigh	→	èigheachd	shouting
dèan	→	dèanamh (dèanadh)	doing, making
seas	→	seasamh	standing
tuit	→	tuiteam	falling
innis	→	innse	telling, relating

Some irregular verbs form their verbal nouns from different roots:

rach	→	dol	going
thig	→	tighinn (tighean)	coming
abair	→	ràdh(a) (gràdh(a))	saying

18 The present tense

The present tense in Gaelic is formed by using the verbal noun with the (auxiliary) verb **tha** as follows:

THA	SUBJECT	VERBAL NOUN PARTICLE	VERBAL NOUN
tha	mi	ag	**èisteachd**
is	I	at	listening

I am listening, I listen

This literally means 'I am at listening'. In the present tense this periphrastic ('long') construction covers both the continuous and simple present. In other words, **tha mi ag èisteachd** can be translated as 'I am listening' or 'I listen'.

The verbal noun is preceded by **ag** when used with **tha** to form the present tense. The final **g** of **ag** is not pronounced before a following consonant and is dropped in writing: **ag** → **a'**, e.g.

tha mi a' sgrìobhadh	I am writing, I write
tha Anna a' leughadh	Ann is reading, Ann reads

Here are some further examples:

Tha Iain a' leughadh leabhar.
John is reading a book, John reads a book.

A bheil Anna a' sgrìobhadh litir?
Is Ann writing a letter? Does Ann write a letter?

Chan eil mi a' faicinn sìon.
I don't see anything.

Tha mi a' cluinntinn ceòl brèagha.
I hear lovely music.

Chan eil iad a' dol a-mach.
They are not going out, they do not go out.

A bheil Màiri a' fuireach (ann) an Glaschu?
Does Mary live in Glasgow?

A bheil thu a' tuigsinn Gàidhlig?
Do you understand Gaelic?

Tha mi ag iarraidh ìm agus càise.
I want butter and cheese.

The final **g** of **ag** is preserved before the the verbal noun **ràdh** 'saying', **ag ràdh**. In many dialects a new verbal noun **gràdh** has been formed as a result.

As the term implies, verbal nouns may function as either nouns or verbs. As nouns they may be preceded by the definite article, e.g.

an leughadh (*m*)	the reading
an sgrìobhadh (*m*)	the writing
an t-òl (*m*)	the drinking
an fhaireachdainn (*f*)	the feeling

19 'What do you want?', etc.

To ask a question 'what ... ?', put **dè a** ('what is it that') in front of the verb as follows:

Dè a tha thu ag iarraidh?	What do you want?
Dè a tha thu a' dèanamh?	What are you doing?
	What do you do?
Dè a tha thu ag òl?	What are you drinking?
	What do you drink?
Dè a tha thu a' faicinn?	What are you seeing?
	What do you see?
Dè a tha a' dol?	What is going (on)?

Vocabulary

a-mach	/ə max/	out (movement)
bàrdachd (f)	/baːʀ(s)d̪axh/	poetry
ceart gu leòr	/kʲaʀsṭ ga ʎɔːr/	all right, O.K.
cupa cofaidh (m)	/kuhpə kɔfi/	a cup of coffee
Dùn Èideann	/d̪un eːdʲəŋ̊/	Edinburgh
Fraingis (f)	/fraŋʲgʲəʃ/	French
obair (f)	/obərʲ/	work, working
rannsachadh (m)	/ʀãũn̥səxəɣ/	research

Exercise 3.1

Translate

1 What are you thinking?
2 Ann lives in Edinburgh.
3 Do you understand French?
4 John is writing poetry.
5 Mary is doing research.
6 Are you coming out?
7 They want a cup of coffee.
8 James works in Glasgow.
9 Do you feel all right?
10 I don't understand.

20 Definite nouns: definition

We say that a noun is definite if it is (a) a proper noun, e.g. **Iain** 'John', **Glaschu** 'Glasgow', (b) preceded by the article, e.g. **an tidsear** 'the teacher', (c) preceded by a possessive pronoun, e.g. **mo mhàthair** 'my mother'.

21 More on the verb '*is*' ('to be')

We have already dealt with **is** sentences of the following type:

IS	SUBJECT	PREDICATE	
Is	mise	Iain.	I am John.
Is	tusa	an tidsear.	You are the teacher.
Is	esan	am ministear againn.	He is our minister.
Is	ise	mo mhàthair.	She is my mother.

Our sentences so far have included those where the subject is a pronoun (**mise, tusa,** etc.) and the predicate is a definite noun. If the subject, however, is a definite noun instead of a pronoun and the predicate remains a definite noun, we use **is e** (where **e** is sometimes referred to as an augment) rather than **is** and the same order of elements as before, as follows:

IS	SUBJECT	PREDICATE	
Is e	Iain	an tidsear.	John is the teacher.
Is e	m' athair	am ministear.	My father is the minister.
Is e	Màiri	mo phiuthar.	Mary is my sister.
Is e	Seumas	an sagart againn.	James is our priest.

3

Note: **Is e** is pronounced and usually written **'s e**. However, **is e** is retained for the sake of transparency in this beginners' book.

Note: Agreement between the augment and a following feminine subject sometimes occurs, e.g. **is i Màiri mo phiuthar** 'Mary is my sister'. However, more often than not the augment is **e** irrespective of the gender of the subject.

To negate **is e** sentences, replace **is e** with **chan e**:

Chan e do bhràthair an sagart.	Your brother is not the priest.
Chan e Iain an tidsear.	John is not the teacher.
Chan e Seumas mo bhràthair.	James is not my brother.

To form the interrogative (positive), replace **is e** with **an e**:

An e Dòmhnall an tidsear?	Is Donald the teacher?
An e Anna do mhàthair?	Is Ann your mother?
An e am post d' athair?	Is the postman your father?

To form the interrogative (negative), replace **is e** with **nach e**:

Nach e Iain am ministear?	Isn't John the minister?
Nach e Uilleam do bhràthair?	Isn't William your brother?
Nach e an sagart do charaid?	Isn't the priest your friend?

To answer any of the above questions beginning with **an e** or **nach e**, the answer forms are always as follows:

POSITIVE		NEGATIVE	
Is e (or **'s e**)	yes	**Chan e**	no

In **Lesson 2** we learnt several simple **is** sentences:

Is mise Iain.	I am John.
Is tusa Anna.	You are Ann.
Is esan Seumas.	He is James.
Is ise Peigi.	She is Peggy.
Is sinne an clas Gàidhlig.	We are the Gaelic class.
Is sibhse an tidsear.	You are the teacher.
Is iadsan Màiri agus Calum.	They are Mary and Calum.

We may note at this stage that **is e** can replace **is** before the personal pronouns in certain contexts as follows:

Is e mise Iain.	I am John.
Is e thusa Anna.	You are Ann.

Is e esan Seumas.	He is James.
Is e ise Peigi.	She is Peggy.
Is e sinne an clas Gàidhlig.	We are the Gaelic class.
Is e sibhse an tidsear.	You are the teacher.
Is e iadsan Màiri agus Calum.	They are Mary and Calum.

Note: **thusa** follows **is e**, not **tusa**.

Similarly, **cha, an, nach** may be replaced by **chan e, an e, nach e** in which case **thu** (not **tu**) is used. Note also that **mise** is not lenited when it is preceded by **chan e**; **cha mhise** becomes **chan e mise**.

Here are some further examples:

Chan e mise Dòmhnall.	I am not Donald.
Chan e thusa Anna.	You are not Ann.
An e esan Iain?	Is he John?
An e ise Peigi?	Is she Peggy?
Nach e sibhse am ministear?	Aren't you the minister?
Nach e iadsan an clas Gàidhlig?	Aren't they the Gaelic class?

Vocabulary

Catrìona (*f*)	/ka triːnə/, /ka trianə/, /ka triənə/	Catherine
Dòmhnall (*m*)	/d̪ɔ̃ːəɫ/	Donald
mac (*m*)	/mãhk/, /mãxk/	son
Màiri (*f*)	/mãːrʲi/	Mary
ministear (*m*)	/miniʃtʲerʲ/	minister
Seòras (*m*)	/ʃɔːras/	George
Uilleam (*m*)	/uʎam/	William

Exercise 3.2

Translate

1   I am John.
2   She is Ann.
3   Is he the teacher? Yes.
4   James is not my teacher.
5   Mary is the nurse.
6   Donald is her father.
7   Isn't William your son? No.
8   Catherine is the big sister.
9   You are small George.
10   Mary is their new minister.

22 Demonstratives

Gaelic, like Lowland Scots (a language closely related to English), distinguishes between 'this', 'that' and 'yon'; and also between 'here', 'there' and 'yonder'. The main difference between 'that' and 'yon' and between 'there' and 'yonder' in Gaelic is that the former ('that', 'there') are generally more specific in their reference, whereas the latter ('yon', 'yonder') are usually more 'remote' in either spatial, temporal or emotional terms.

(a) Demonstrative adjectives

These adjectives, like most other adjectives, follow the noun they qualify. However, they are not affected by the initial mutation of lenition. Nouns followed by demonstrative adjectives are usually preceded by the definite article. The forms are as follows:

an dealbh seo	this picture
an taigh sin	that house
a' bheinn ud	yon mountain

The plural form of the article is **na**:

na taighean seo	these houses
na dealbhannan sin	those pictures
na caileagan ud	yon girls

In a string of adjectives, the demonstrative adjectives usually appear in final position:

a' bheinn mhòr àrd sin	that big high mountain
an dealbh bheag bhrèagha seo	this small fine picture

(b) Demonstrative pronouns

seo	this
sin	that
siud	that (yon)

There is a distinction between singular and plural forms. These are formed by placing the third person plural pronoun **iad** before the above demonstrative forms:

iad seo	these
iad sin	those
iad siud	those (yon)

It is also possible to distinguish between masculine and feminine singular forms although the basic demonstrative forms normally suffice. The forms are as follows:

e seo	this (*masculine*)
i seo	this (*feminine*)
e sin	that (*masculine*)
i sin	that (*feminine*)
e siud	that/yon (*masculine*)
i siud	that/yon (*feminine*)

The demonstrative pronouns act like other pronouns and nouns and therefore can be the subject (or object) of a verb, e.g.

Tha seo math.	This is good.
Tha sin blasta.	That is tasty.
Tha siud dìreach àlainn.	That is just beautiful.

Note: the demonstrative pronouns **seo**, **sin** and **siud** may also be used as the subject of an **is** sentence, in which case the **is e** construction introduced earlier in this lesson is used, e.g.

Is e seo Màiri.	This is Mary.
Is e sin Iain.	That is John.
Is e siud Anna.	That (yon) is Ann.

Is e may be omitted before the demonstrative pronouns and so the following sentences often replace the above: (note that we can translate 'this is' or 'here is', etc.)

Seo Màiri.	This is Mary; here is Mary.
Sin an tidsear.	That is the teacher; there is the teacher.
Siud Iain.	That (yon) is John; there (yonder) is John.

Sentences beginning with **seo, sin, siud** or **is e seo, is e sin, is e siud** are negated by **chan e** as follows:

Chan e seo Màiri.	This is not Mary.
Chan e sin Iain.	That is not John.
Chan e siud an tidsear.	That is not the teacher.

When the predicate is feminine, the feminine pronoun may be used, e.g.

Is i seo Màiri.	This is Mary.
Chan i seo Anna.	This is not Ann.

(c) Demonstrative adverbs

an seo	here
an sin	there
an siud	yonder

22a 'Càite a bheil...?' ('Where is ...?')

Study the following phrases:

Càite a bheil a' bhùth?	Where is the shop?
Càite a bheil am banca?	Where is the bank?
Càite a bheil oifis a' phuist?	Where is the post office?
Càite a bheil an stèisean?	Where is the station?
Càite a bheil an taigh-beag?	Where is the toilet?

Note: The form **Càite bheil . . .?** is also used.

Note the difference between:

Tha an cat an sin	The cat is there.
Sin an cat	That is the cat; there is the cat.

Vocabulary

a' bhasgaid (*f*)	/ə vaskɛdʲ/	the basket
a' bheinn (*f*)	/ə vẽĩɲ/	the mountain
a' bhròg (*f*)	/ə vrɔːg/	the shoe
a' bhùth (*f*)	/ə vuː/	the shop
a' chaileag (*f*)	/ə xalag/	the girl
a' chas (*f*)	/ə xas/	the foot, leg
am baga (*m*)	/əm bagə/	the bag
am baile (*m*)	/əm balə/	the town
am balach (*m*)	/əm baɫəx/	the boy
am boireannach (*m*)	/əm bɔrʲəɳəx/	the woman
am manaidsear (*m*)	/əm manədʲʃɛrʲ/	the manager
an duine (*m*)	/əɳ ḏuɲə/	the man
an làmh (*f*)	/əɳ ɫãːv/	the hand
an sgian (*f*)	/əɳ skʲiən/	the knife
an t-airgead (*m*)	/əɳ ṯ[arʲa]gʲəḏ/, /əɳ ṯ[ɛrʲɛ]gʲəḏ/	the money
an t-aran (*m*)	/əɳ ṯaran/	the bread
an t-sùil (*f*)	/əɳ ṯuːl/	the eye
a-rithist (*adv*)	/ə rʲi-əʃtʲ/	again
piuthar (*f*)	/pʲu-ər/	sister

Exercise 3.3

Translate

1 this girl
2 that shop
3 yon town
4 that woman there
5 This is my sister.
6 There is the knife.
7 The bread is yonder.
8 There is that mountain again.
9 This is cold.
10 That is very good.

23 Numerals 0–19

The basic numerals from zero to ten are as follows:

0	**neoni**
1	**aon**
2	**dà**
3	**trì**
4	**ceithir**
5	**còig**
6	**sia**
7	**seachd**
8	**ochd**
9	**naoi**
10	**deich**

If counting, and when there is no following noun, the numbers between one and nineteen prefix **a**, which lenites **dà** and prefixes **h-** to **aon** and **ochd**; however, the prefix is often dropped in speech:

1	**a h-aon** or **aonan**
2	**a dhà**
3	**a trì**
4	**a ceithir**
5	**a còig**
6	**a sia**
7	**a seachd**
8	**a h-ochd**
9	**a naoi**
10	**a deich**

The numbers from eleven to nineteen are formed by adding **deug** which corresponds to 'teen' in English as follows:

11	**a h-aon-deug**	eleven
12	**a dhà-dheug**	twelve
13	**a trì-deug**	thirteen
14	**a ceithir-deug**	fourteen
15	**a còig-deug**	fifteen
16	**a sia-deug**	sixteen
17	**a seachd-deug**	seventeen
18	**a h-ochd-deug**	eighteen
19	**a naoi-deug**	nineteen

Note: **deug** is lenited following **d(h)à**.

Exercise 3.4

Complete the following sums, writing the answers in words:

(a) $1 + 8 =$

(b) $2 + 3 =$

(c) $8 - 2 =$

(d) $6 \times 3 =$

(e) $14 \div 2 =$

(f) $12 + 7 =$

(g) $10 \div 10 =$

(h) $7 + 8 =$

24 Adverbs of direction

Adverbs which denote position in relation to the speaker generally distinguish between forms which imply *location* and forms which imply *motion*. In some cases, motion *to* and *away* from the speaker is also differentiated.

(a) 'Up' and 'down'

In words for 'up' and 'down', Gaelic makes a distinction between (i) position of being up or down, (ii) going 'up' and 'down', i.e. motion away from/towards the speaker, and (iii) coming 'up' and 'down', i.e. motion towards the speaker.

(i)	**shuas**	up (location)
(ii)	**suas**	up, upwards (away from the speaker)
(iii)	**a-nuas**	down, downwards (towards the speaker, *lit* from above)
(i)	**shìos**	down (location)
(ii)	**sìos**	down, downwards (away from the speaker)
(iii)	**a-nuas**	up, upwards (towards the speaker, *lit* from below)

Note: **a-nuas** is used for both 'up' and 'down' (towards the speaker) which can be confusing at first. It is also useful to note that it is incorrect to say **a' dol a-nuas** or **a' tighinn sìos**, although younger speakers sometimes use them. Note also that some dialects do distinguish between 'up' and 'down' (towards the speaker); these dialects use **a-nìos** 'up', 'from below' (towards the speaker).

Note: **suas** has the variant **an-àird**; similarly, **sìos** has the variant **a-bhàn**.

Examples:

Tha Iain shuas an staidhre.	John is upstairs.
Tha Anna a' dol suas an staidhre.	Ann is going up the stairs.
Tha Màiri a' tighinn a-nuas.	Mary is coming up/Mary is coming down.

(b) 'Over here' and 'over there'

Gaelic makes a distinction in words for 'over here' and 'over there' both in terms of location and motion:

a-bhos	over here (location at speaker)
a-nall	(coming) over here (motion towards speaker, *lit* from over there)
thall	over there (location not at speaker)
a-null	(going) over there (motion away from speaker)

Examples:
Tha Anna a-bhos ann an Dùn Èideann.
Ann is over here in Edinburgh.

Tha Màiri a' tighinn a-nall à Glaschu.
Mary is coming over here from Glasgow.

The Màiri thall ann an Glaschu.
Mary is over there in Glasgow.

Tha Anna a' dol a-null a Ghlaschu.
Ann is going over there to Glasgow.

Note: for **a*** < **do*** 'to', see **Section 44**.

These adverbs of motion are frequently used with the demonstrative adverbs **an seo, an sin** and **an siud** which we met earlier in this lesson, e.g.

Tha Màiri a-bhos an seo.	Mary is over here.
Tha Iain thall an sin.	John is over there.

There is a difference between **a-bhos** and **an seo** on the one hand and between **thall** and **an sin** (**an siud**) on the other. The demonstrative adverbs are definite and specific in their reference; the directional adverbs **thall** and **a-bhos** are non-specific in their reference. **Thall** means 'not in the vicinity of the speaker'; **a-bhos** means 'in the vicinity of the speaker' without specifying the exact location.

'Here and there' is translated in Gaelic as **thall is a-bhos**.

(c) 'In' and 'out'

Gaelic makes a distinction in words for 'in' and 'out' between location and motion:

a-staigh	in, inside (location)
a-steach	in, inwards (motion)
a-muigh	out, outside (location)
a-mach	out, outwards (motion)

Not all varieties of Gaelic use **a-steach**. Indeed there is a tendency to use **a-staigh** to convey both location and motion.

Tha mi a-staigh an-dràsta.	I am in now.
Tha Anna a' tighinn a-steach.	Ann is coming in.
Tha Iain a-muigh a' cluich ball-coise.	John is out playing football.
Tha Màiri a' dol a-mach.	Mary is going out.

25 Days, months and seasons

DAYS

Diluain	Monday	**Oidhche Luain**	Monday night
Dimàirt	Tuesday	**Oidhche Mhàirt**	Tuesday night
Diciadain	Wednesday	**Oidhche Chiadain**	Wednesday night
Diardaoin	Thursday	**Oidhche Ardaoin**	Thursday night
Dihaoine	Friday	**Oidhche Haoine**	Friday night
Disathairne	Saturday	**Oidhche Shathairne**	Saturday night
Didòmhnaich/ Latha na Sàbaid	Sunday	**Oidhche Dhòmhnaich/ Oidhche na Sàbaid**	Sunday night

Note that all of the days of the week beginning with **Di-** are stressed on the second syllable.

The use of **Didòmhnaich** and **Latha na Sàbaid** depends to a certain extent on denominational factors although there are no absolutely clear lines of demarcation between the use of both. Generally speaking **Didòmhnaich** tends to be used by Catholics and by Episcopalians, and **Latha na Sàbaid** by Presbyterians.

MONTHS

am Faoilleach/Faoilteach	January
an Gearran	February
am Màrt	March
an Giblean	April
an Cèitean	May
an t-Ògmhios	June
an t-Iuchar	July
an Lùnastal	August
an t-Sultain	September
an Dàmhair	October
an t-Samhain	November
an Dùbhlachd	December

Note that the names of the months all appear with the article, which can be spelled **An**, etc.

SEASONS

an t-Earrach	Spring
an Samhradh	Summer
am Foghar	Autumn
an Geamhradh	Winter

The seasons are all masculine. Study the following:

as t-earrach	in Spring
as t-samhradh	in Summer
as t-fhoghar	in Autumn

BUT

anns a' Gheamhradh	in Winter

3

26 Emphatic suffixes

We saw in **Lesson 2** how Scottish Gaelic uses emphatic suffixes to give emphatic or contrastive power to the pronouns, e.g.

Tha Iain beag ach tha mise mòr.   John is small but *I* am big.

The emphatic pronouns consist of the pronoun followed by an emphatic suffix as follows:

PRONOUN	EMPHATIC SUFFIX		EMPHATIC PRONOUN	
mi	+ se	→	**mise**	*I*
thu	+ sa	→	**thusa**	*you*
e	+ san	→	**esan**	*he*
i	+ se	→	**ise**	*she*
sinn	+ ne	→	**sinne**	*we*
sibh	+ se	→	**sibhse**	*you*
iad	+ san	→	**iadsan**	*they*

Emphatic suffixes are also used with other parts of speech to give them emphatic or contrastive power. They are principally used with (a) prepositional pronouns and (b) following nouns preceded by possessive pronouns. In each case they emphasise the pronominal element. The emphatic suffixes are the same as those used with the pronouns listed above except that **-sa** rather than **-se** is used with the first person singular. Note that the hyphen used with emphatic suffixes does not indicate a change in stress. The italics in the English translations indicate emphatic or contrastive use:

an cù agamsa	**mo chù-sa**	*my* dog
an cat agadsa	**do chat-sa**	*your* cat
an taigh aigesan	**a thaigh-san**	*his* house
an càr aicese	**a càr-se**	*her* car
an t-aodach againne	**ar n-aodach-ne**	*our* clothes
an leabhar agaibhse	**ur leabhar-se**	*your* book
an sgoil acasan	**an sgoil-san**	*their* school

Note that a hyphen is not usually used when these suffixes are added to prepositional pronouns.

Vocabulary

an toiseach (*adv*)	/ən t̪ɔʃəx/	first
a-nis (*adv*)	/ə niʃ/	now
a-nochd (*adv*)	/ə n̪ɔ̃xk/	tonight
bainne (*m*)	/baɲə/	milk
banca (*m*)	/baŋkə/	bank
beannachd (*f*) **leibh**	/bʲan̪əxk lʲiv/	good-bye
biadh (*m*)	/biəɣ/	food
brot (*m*)	/brɔht̪/	soup
cò mheud? (*pl*) (*interr adv*)	/koː vĩãd̪/	how many (+ singular form of the noun)
dad (*m*)	/d̪ad̪/	anything
doras (*m*)	/d̪ɔrəs/	door
duine (*m*), **daoine**	/d̪uɲə/, /d̪uːɲə/	man/person, men/people
eile (*adj*)	/elə/	other, else
gu (*prp*)	/gu/, /gə/, /gɔ/	to
mar sin leibh	/maɾ ʃin lʲiv/	good-bye to you
mas e ur toil e	/ma ʃe ər t̪ɔl ɛ/	please (polite, formal)
oifis (*f*) **a' phuist**	/ɔfiʃ ə fuʃtʲ/	post office
orainsear (*m*), **orainsearan** (*pl*)	/ɔrəɲʃerʲ/, /ɔrəɲʃerʲən/	oranges
salann (*m*)	/sal̪ən̪/	salt
sgeilp (*f*)	/skʲɛlp/	shelf
siùcar (*m*)	/ʃuːhkərʲ/, /ʃuːxkərʲ/	sugar
thig (*vb*)	/higʲ/	come
ugh (*f*), **uighean** (*pl*)	/u/, /ujən/	egg, eggs
uinnean (*m*), **uinneanan** (*pl*)	/ũɲan/, /ũɲanən/	onions

CÒMHRADH (CONVERSATION)

Anna ann am bùth

Fear na bùtha	Thig a-staigh. Tha e fuar an-diugh.
Anna	Tha, tha e fuar agus fliuch.
Fear na bùtha	Dè a tha sibh ag iarraidh?
Anna	An toiseach, ma-thà, tha mi ag iarraidh siùcar. Càite a bheil e, mas e ur toil e?
Fear na bùtha	Tha thall an sin aig an doras. Dè eile a tha sibh ag iarraidh?
Anna	Bainne agus uighean agus orainsearan.
Fear na bùtha	Cò mheud ugh?
Anna	A sia, tha mi a' smaoineachadh.
Fear na bùtha	Glè mhath. Cò mheud orainsear?

Anna	A seachd. Tha mi ag iarraidh uinneanan cuideachd. Tha mi a' dèanamh brot. Tha daoine a' tighinn a-nochd gu biadh.
Fear na bùtha	A-nis seo bainne, uighean, orainsearan agus uinneanan. A bheil sibh ag iarraidh dad eile?
Anna	Tha. Tha mi ag iarraidh salann. Càite a bheil e?
Fear na bùtha	Tha e shuas air an sgeilp sin. A bheil sibh ag iarraidh dad eile?
Anna	Chan eil, tapadh leibh. Tha gu leòr agam. O, a bheil fios agaibh càite a bheil am banca agus oifis a' phuist?
Fear na bùtha	Tha, shìos an rathad. Beannachd leibh.
Anna	Mar sin leibh.

TRANSLATION

Ann in a shop

Shopkeeper	Come in. It's cold today.
Ann	Yes, it's cold and wet.
Shopkeeper	What do you want?
Ann	Well, first I want sugar. Where is it please?
Shopkeeper	It's over there at the door. What else do you want?
Ann	Milk and eggs and oranges.
Shopkeeper	How many eggs?
Ann	Six, I think.
Shopkeeper	Very good. How many oranges?
Ann	Seven. I want onions too. I'm making soup. People are coming to dinner tonight.
Shopkeeper	Now here are milk, eggs, oranges and onions. Do you want anything else?
Ann	Yes. I want salt. Where is it?
Shopkeeper	It's up there on that shelf. Do you want anything else?
Ann	No, thank you. I have enough. Oh, do you know where the bank and the post-office are?
Shopkeeper	Yes, down the road. Goodbye.
Ann	Goodbye.

Lesson 4

27 Past tense of 'tha'

We have already met the present tense of the verb **tha** 'to be'. The past tense forms are listed below with the present tense forms for comparison:

	PAST	PRESENT
Positive	**bha**	**tha**
Negative	cha **robh**	chan **eil**
Interrogative (positive)	an **robh**?	a **bheil**?
Interrogative (negative)	nach **robh**?	nach **eil**?

27a Independent and dependent verbal forms

It will be clear that there is a correspondence between **tha** and **bha** on the one hand, and between **(bh)eil** and **robh** on the other. **Tha** and **bha** appear 'independently' and usually appear at the beginning of an utterance. **Tha** and **bha** are therefore called *independent* verbal forms. **(Bh)eil** and **robh** on the other hand only appear after certain particles (e.g. **cha, an, nach**) and their occurrence 'depends' on the occurrence of these particles. **(Bh)eil** and **robh** are called *dependent* verbal forms. The distinction between independent and dependent forms is of fundamental importance in the verbal system of Gaelic. Here are some examples of the past tense of **tha:**

Bha Iain sgìth.	John was tired.
Cha robh e blàth.	It was not warm.
An robh Seumas an seo?	Was James here?
Nach robh an t-airgead agad?	Did you not have the money?

27b Past tense of 'tha' with the verbal noun

In **Lesson 3** we saw that the periphrastic construction (in the present tense) involving the verb **tha** and the verbal noun covered both the continuous tense and the simple present tense. When the past tense of **tha** is used in the periphrastic construction, however, the meaning for most verbs is continuous past, not simple past. In other words, **bha mi ag òl** means 'I was drinking' and not 'I drank'. Here are some further examples:

Bha Iain a' sgrìobhadh litir.	John was writing a letter.
Cha robh Anna a' dèanamh sìon.	Ann wasn't doing anything.
An robh sibh a' seinn a-raoir?	Were you singing last night?
Bha mi ag ithe mo bhracaist.	I was eating my breakfast.

However, the following verbal nouns when used in the periphrastic construction in the past, present and future correspond to the simple past, present and future tenses respectively in English: **iarraidh** 'wanting', **fuireach** 'living', **tuigsinn** 'understanding', **smaoineachadh** 'thinking'. Consider the following examples in the past tense:

Bha mi ag iarraidh aran.	I wanted bread.
Bha Anna a' fuireach (ann) an Glaschu.	Ann lived in Glasgow.
Bha mi a' tuigsinn.	I understood.
Bha Iain a' smaoineachadh.	John thought.

Note: For the preposition **an / ann an** 'in', see **Section 44**.

28 Irregular verbs: simple past tense

The simple past tense is not formed by using a periphrastic construction; the simple past consists of one-word (short) verbal forms. There are 12 irregular verbs in Scottish Gaelic. We have already met the verbs 'to be' **is** and **tha**. One of the distinguishing features of irregular verbs, as we will see, is that their independent and dependent forms are frequently formed from different roots. It is possible to group the past tense formation of irregular verbs into the following four groups:

(i) Verbs whose independent and dependent forms differ substantially:

INDEPENDENT	DEPENDENT	
bha	robh	was
chunnaic	faca	saw
chaidh	deach/deachaidh	went

(ii) Verbs whose independent and dependent forms begin with **th-** and **t-** respectively:

INDEPENDENT	DEPENDENT	
thàinig	tàinig	came
thug	tug	gave, brought
thuirt	tuirt	said

Note: the dependent forms **tàinig, tug, tuirt** are pronounced with initial **d-**, and some writers prefer to spell the dependent forms with an initial **d-** or even **d'th**.

(iii) Verbs whose dependent form is formed by prefixing **do** (or **d'**) to the independent form:

INDEPENDENT	DEPENDENT	
ràinig	**do ràinig**	reached
rug	**do rug**	caught
rinn	**do rinn**	did, made
fhuair	**d' fhuair**	got

4

(iv)

INDEPENDENT	DEPENDENT	
chuala	**cuala**	heard

Subjects including subject pronouns follow the above verbal forms as follows:

chuala mi	I heard
chuala t(h)u	you heard
chuala e/i	he, she heard
chuala sinn	we heard
chuala sibh	you heard
chuala iad	they heard

Bha Seumas an seo.	James was here.
Cha robh Anna sgìth.	Ann was not tired.
Chunnaic sinn Màiri.	We saw Mary.
Am faca iad an cù?	Did they see the dog?
Chaidh Iain a-mach.	John went out.
Cha deach Uilleam a-mach.	William did not go out.
Ràinig i Dùn Èideann.	She reached Edinburgh.
An do ràinig sibh Glaschu?	Did you reach Glasgow?
Thàinig iad dhachaigh.	They came home.
Cha tàinig iad riamh.	They never came.
Thug Anna pòg do Raghnall.	Ann gave a kiss to Ronald.
An tug a mhàthair airgead dha?	Did his mother give money to him?
Thuirt Iain sin.	John said that.
Cha tuirt mise sin.	*I* did not say that.
Rug mi air Catrìona.	I caught Catherine.
An do rug thu air Uilleam?	Did you catch William?
Rinn mi m' obair.	I did my work.
An do rinn thusa an obair agadsa?	Did *you* do *your* work?
Fhuair mi an t-airgead.	I got the money.
An d' fhuair e sìon?	Did he get anything?

Chuala mi an t-òran brèagha.	I heard the beautiful song.
An cuala sibh Màiri a-raoir?	Did you hear Mary last night?

Note: **nach** lenites **f** in **faca**, e.g.

Nach fhaca Iain am bus?   Did John not see the bus?

Note: **cha*** becomes **chan*** before **faca**, e.g.
  Chan fhaca mi Seumas.   I didn't see James.

Note: of the verbs given here **cha*** lenites only the dependent form **cuala**, e.g.
  Cha chuala mi thu.   I didn't hear you.

Note: both **tu/thu** may be used with the following verbal forms: **chunnaic, faca; thàinig, tàinig; ràinig, do ràinig; chuala, cuala**.

Note that the simple past tense can sometimes be translated as a perfect, e.g.
  An tàinig Iain fhathast?   Has John come yet?
  An cuala t(h)u an naidheachd?   Have you heard the news?

The following text contains instances of all of the irregular verbs (in **bold**) in the past tense (positive). Study it carefully. Learning it by heart may be a useful way of learning the irregular verbs:

POSITIVE:

Am Meàirleach ('the Robber')

Bha mi aig an taigh Diluain. **Chuala** mi fuaim shuas an staidhre. **Chaidh** mi suas. **Chunnaic** mi meàirleach. **Rinn** e bùrach. **Thuirt** mi: 'Cò thusa?'. **Thàinig** am Poileas agus **rug** iad air a' mheàirleach. **Fhuair** am meàirleach buille. **Thug** e an t-airgead air ais. **Ràinig** iad an stèisean. **Bha** e duilich.

I was at home on Monday. I heard a noise upstairs. I went up. I saw a robber. He made a mess. I said: 'Who are you?'. The police came and they caught the robber. The robber got a thump. He gave the money back. They reached the station. He was sorry.

NEGATIVE:

Cha robh mi aig an taigh Diluain. **Cha chuala** mi fuaim shuas an staidhre. **Cha deach** mi suas. **Chan fhaca** mi meàirleach. **Cha do rinn** e bùrach. **Cha tuirt** mi: 'Cò thusa?'. **Cha tàinig** am Poileas agus **cha do rug** iad air a' mheàirleach. **Cha d' fhuair** am meàirleach buille. **Cha tug** e an t-airgead air ais. **Cha do ràinig** iad an stèisean. **Cha robh** e duilich.

I wasn't at home on Monday. I didn't hear a noise upstairs. I didn't go up. I didn't see a robber. He didn't make a mess. I didn't say: 'Who are you?'. The police didn't come and they didn't catch the robber. The robber didn't get a thump. He didn't give the money back. They didn't reach the station. He wasn't sorry.

Exercise 4.1

Rewrite the above passage in the interrogative (positive and negative):

Vocabulary

an-dè (*adv*)	/ən dʲeː/	yesterday
a-raoir (*adv*)	/ən ɾⱳir/	last night
chuir mi seachad bliadhna	/xurʲ mi ʃɛxəd̪ bliəŋə/	I spent a year
fhathast (*adv*)	/ha-əst̪/	yet

Exercise 4.2

Translate

1 I was happy.
2 I saw Ann yesterday.
3 John went out.
4 They came in.
5 We spent a year there.
6 You didn't do your work.
7 Did you get the money?
8 Did you not reach Edinburgh yet?
9 She didn't say anything.
10 I heard Mary last night.

29 Answering questions (past tense)

In **Lesson 1** we saw that when answering a question in Gaelic, we repeat the main verb of the question, usually without the subject. To answer 'yes', we repeat the independent form of the verb. To answer 'no', we repeat the dependent form of the verb preceded *always* by the negative particle **cha**. Consider the following examples:

An robh thu aig a' chèilidh?	Were you at the ceilidh?
Bha.	Yes.
Cha robh.	No.
Am faca t(h)u Seumas?	Did you see James?
Chunnaic.	Yes.
Chan fhaca.	No.
An do rinn thu an obair?	Did you do the work?
Rinn.	Yes.
Cha do rinn.	No.

30 Imperative

The imperative form of the verb is the form which is used for giving orders. It is also the most basic form of the verb. It is the imperative form which appears as the head word in dictionaries. We will see later that all tenses (other than periphrastic constructions) of regular verbs are derived from the imperative form. For this reason the imperative is sometimes referred to as the verbal root.

The two imperative forms which are most frequently used in Gaelic are the 2nd person singular and plural forms, corresponding to the use of the pronouns **thu** and **sibh**. The plural (also the polite or formal) form is formed by adding **-(a)ibh** (pronounced '-iv' or '-u') to the singular form as follows:

SINGULAR	PLURAL	
òl	òlaibh	drink
glan	glanaibh	clean
seas	seasaibh	stand
suidh	suidhibh	sit
ith	ithibh	eat
dùin	dùinibh	close

Note the following useful phrases:

Gabh do bhiadh.	Eat your food.
Gabh mo lethsgeul.	Excuse me (*lit* 'accept my excuse').

The singular imperative form is made emphatic by using the pronoun **thusa** as follows:

Òl thusa do thì.	*you* drink your tea.
Suidh thusa an sin.	*you* sit there.

30a Negative imperative

To negate the imperative forms, place **na** before the above forms e.g.

Na òl sin.	Don't drink that.
Na suidh an sin.	Don't sit there.
Na dùin an doras fhathast.	Don't close the door yet.
Na gabh thusa dragh.	Don't *you* be worried.

The most commonly used imperative forms of the irregular verbs are as follows:

SINGULAR	PLURAL	
bi	bithibh	be
rach	rachaibh	go
dèan	dèanaibh	do, make
faigh	faighibh	get
thig	thigibh	come
thoir	thoiribh	give, bring (to)

The last two verbs, **thig** and **thoir** become **tig** and **toir** (both pronounced with initial **d**-) after the negative **na**:

Na tig an seo.	Don't come here.
Na tigibh an seo.	Don't (*pl*) come here.
Na toir airgead dha.	Don't give him money.
Na toiribh airgead do Pheigi.	Don't (*pl*) give money to Peggy.

30b Other imperative forms

There are also first person plural and third person imperatives. The first person plural imperative is formed by adding **(e)amaid** to the verbal root (= imperative second singular form):

seasamaid	let us stand
suidheamaid	let us sit

The third person imperative is formed by adding **(e)adh** to the verbal root. This imperative form must always be followed either by one of the pronouns **e (esan), i (ise), iad (iadsan)** or by a noun, e.g.

seinneadh e	let him sing
suidheadh ise	let *her* sit
seasadh iad	let them stand
thigeadh Anna	let Ann come

Examples of the imperative

cuir	put (*sing*)
cuireadh e	let him put
cuireamaid	let us put
cuiribh	put (*pl*)
cuireadh iad	let them put

Vocabulary

a-màireach (*adv*)	/ə maːrʲəx/	tomorrow
an-dè (*adv*)	/ən dʲeː/	yesterday
an-diugh (*adv*)	/ən dʲu/	today
dìnnear/dinnear (*f*)	/dʲiːɲɛrʲ/	dinner
mas e do thoil e	/ma ʃe ḍə hɔl e/	please (*lit* 'if it is your wish') (*informal*)
mas e ur toil e	/ma ʃe ər ṭɔl e/	please (*lit* 'if it is your wish') (*pl/informal*)
sàmhach (*adj*)	/sãːvəx/	quiet
sìon (*m*); **càil** (*m*)†	/ʃĩən/, /ʃĩ̃ən/; /kaːl/	anything
sìos (*adv*)	/ʃiəs/	down
suas (*adv*)	/suəs/	up
tì (*f*)	/tiː/	tea

† The dialectal variants **sìon** and **càil** are used only with negative and interrogative verbs.

Exercise 4.3

Translate

1	Drink your tea.		6	Come in.
2	Eat your dinner.		7	Give that to James.
3	Stand up.		8	Don't do anything.
4	Sit down.		9	Find it today.
5	Be quiet.		10	Close the door please.

31 Past tense of '*is*'

The Gaelic verb **is** is a defective verb since it occurs only in the present, past and conditional. It has no future tense forms. The past and conditional forms are identical. The past tense of **is** is **bu*** (**b'** before vowels and **f** + vowel). **Bu** does not usually lenite a following **d, t, s**. Here are some examples:

Bu mhise an tidsear.	I was the teacher.
Bu tusa am ministear.	You were the minister.
B' esan an saor.	He was the joiner.
B' ise an dotair.	She was the doctor.
Bu sinne an clas Gàidhlig.	We were the Gaelic class.
Bu sibhse an clas Beurla.	You were the English class.
B' iadsan an clas Gearmailtis.	They were the German class.

31a Idioms with '*is*'

There are very many idioms in Gaelic involving the use of nouns, adjectives and prepositions with the verb **is**. Here is one example which we will study in more detail in the next lesson:

is	**toil**	**le**	**Iain**	**cofaidh**
is	pleasing	with	John	coffee

John likes coffee

This could be translated literally as 'it (i.e. coffee) is pleasing to John'

If we substitute **bu** for **is** in the above idiom, we get past or 'conditional' meaning:

bu toil le Iain cofaidh   John would like coffee

OR John liked coffee

Watch out for other examples of **bu** below in our discussion of idioms involving the preposition **do** 'to'. We will translate **bu** as 'conditional' in what follows. For the prepositional pronouns associated with **le** 'with', see **Section 42b**.

32 Prepositional pronouns: '*do**' ('to, for')

dhomh	to me	**dhuinn**	to us
dhut	to you	**dhuibh**	to you (*pl*)
dha	to him	**dhaibh**	to them
dhi	to her		

Note: In the second person singular the variant **dhuit** occurs in place of **dhut** in some dialects.

32a Idioms involving '*do*'

The preposition **do** lenites a following noun, e.g. **do Sheumas** 'to James' and prefixes **dh'** to vowels, e.g. **do dh'Anna** 'to Ann'.

(a) can

The basic pattern is:

IS	+	URRAINN	+	DO*	+	SUBJ
is		**urrainn**		**do**		**Chalum**
is		capability		to		Calum

Calum can

Study the following phrases:

Is urrainn do Sheumas.	James can.
Is urrainn dhomh.	I can.

B' urrainn do Mhàiri.	Mary could.
B' urrainn dha.	He could.

NEGATIVE FORMS:

Chan urrainn do Dhòmhnall.	Donald cannot.
Cha b' urrainn dhi.	She couldn't.

INTERROGATIVE (POSITIVE) FORMS:

An urrainn dhut?	Can you?
Am b' urrainn do Shìle?	Could Sheila?

INTERROGATIVE (NEGATIVE) FORMS:

Nach urrainn do Dhòmhnall?	Can't Donald?
Nach b' urrainn dhaibh?	Couldn't they?

ANSWERS:

An urrainn ...? / Nach urrainn ...?	**Is urrainn.**	Yes.
	Chan urrainn.	No.
Am b' urrainn ...? / Nach b' urrainn ...?	**B' urrainn**	Yes.
	Cha b' urrainn.	No.

(b) to know (a person)

The basic pattern is:

IS	+	AITHNE	+	DO*	+	SUBJ	+	OBJ
is		**aithne**		**do**		**Sheumas**		**Màiri**
is		knowledge		to		James		Mary

James knows Mary

Study the following phrases:

Is aithne do Mhàiri Seumas.	Mary knows James.
Is aithne dhomh e.	I know him.

NEGATIVE FORMS:

Chan aithne do Dhòmhnall an duine sin.
Donald doesn't know that man.

Chan aithne dha Seumas.
He doesn't know James.

INTERROGATIVE (POSITIVE) FORMS:

An aithne dhut Peigi?	Do you know Peggy?
An aithne dhuibh a chèile?	Do you know one another?

INTERROGATIVE (NEGATIVE) FORMS:

Nach aithne dhut am ministear?	Do you not know the minister?
Nach aithne dhi e?	Does she not know him?

ANSWERS:

An/Nach aithne do ...?	**Is aithne.**	Yes.
	Chan aithne.	No.

In the past tense **is aithne** becomes **b' aithne**:

B' aithne dhomh Anna.	I knew Ann.
Am b' aithne dhut Seumas?	Did you know James?
Nach b' aithne do dh'Anna Seumas?	Didn't Ann know James?

ANSWERS:

B' aithne.	Yes.
Cha b' aithne.	No.

(c) should

The basic pattern is:

BU	+	CHÒIR	+	DO*	+	SUBJ	
bu		**chòir**		**do**		**Mhàiri**	
is		proper		for		Mary	...

Mary should . . .

Study the following phrases:

Bu chòir dha.	He should.
Bu chòir do Pheigi.	Peggy should.

NEGATIVE FORMS:

Cha bu chòir do Dhòmhnall.	Donald shouldn't.
Cha bu chòir dhut.	You shouldn't.

INTERROGATIVE (POSITIVE) FORMS:

Am bu chòir dhomh?	Should I?
Am bu chòir do Mhàrtainn?	Should Martin?

INTERROGATIVE (NEGATIVE) FORMS:

Nach bu chòir dhuinn?	Shouldn't we?
Nach bu chòir dhomh?	Shouldn't I?

ANSWERS:

Am bu chòir ...? / Nach bu chòir ...?	**Bu chòir.**	Yes.
	Cha bu chòir.	No.

33 Vocative (or address form)

When addressing a person or calling them by their name, Gaelic uses a special form of the noun, called the vocative (or address form). All vocative forms are preceded by the unstressed vocative particle **a*** which lenites. The vocative particle **a***, like other unstressed particles, is usually elided (i.e. not pronounced) in the vicinity of other vowels in speech and frequently in writing, but is retained here for reasons of clarity.

(a) Feminine personal nouns

Feminine personal nouns are lenited in the vocative.

VOCATIVE

a **Mhòrag**	Morag
a **Chatrìona**	Catherine
a **Mhàiri**	Mary
a **Sheonag**	Joan
a **Sheònaid**	Janet
a **Anna** (pronounced **Anna**)	Ann

(b) Masculine proper nouns

Masculine proper nouns are lenited and the final consonant slenderised:

VOCATIVE

a **Sheumais**	James
a **Dhòmhnaill**	Donald
a **Raghnaill**	Ronald
a **Chaluim**	Calum
a **Iain** (pronounced **Iain**)	John
a **Mhata**	Matthew

Exercise 4.4

Put the following names into the vocative:

1 **Donnchadh** (*m*)   Duncan
2 **Mairead** (*f*)   Margaret
3 **Mìcheal** (*m*)   Michael
4 **Murchadh** (*m*)   Murdo
5 **Sìne** (*f*)   Sheena

Note: For other vocative forms, see **Section 70a**.

34 The reflexive pronoun '*fhèin*' ('self')

The reflexive pronoun **fhèin** is used with personal, possessive and prepositional pronouns as follows. Note that **fhìn** (or **fhèin**, pronounced [ɛ:], in some dialects) is used with the first person singular and plural; otherwise **fhèin** is pronounced [e:].

mi fhìn	myself
thu fhèin	yourself
e fhèin	himself
i fhèin	herself
sinn fhìn	ourselves
sibh fhèin	yourselves
iad fhèin	themselves

Note that **fhìn** and **fhèin** are both pronounced with initial **h-**. However, **sibh** + **fhèin** is generally pronounced as **si** + **pèin**.

The reflexive pronoun **fhèin** is used with both possessive constructions as follows:

an cù agam fhìn	OR	**mo chù fhìn**	my own dog
an cat agad fhèin		**do chat fhèin**	your own cat
an taigh aige fhèin		**a thaigh fhèin**	his own house
an càr aice fhèin		**a càr fhèin**	her own car
an t-aodach againn fhìn		**ar n-aodach fhìn**	our own clothes
an leabhar agaibh fhèin		**ur leabhar fhèin**	your own book
an sgoil aca fhèin		**an sgoil fhèin**	their own school

Note that **agaibh** + **fhèin**, etc. is generally pronounced as **aga** + **pèin**.

34a Adverbial use of '*fhèin*'

Fhèin is also used adverbially with emphatic meaning. Study the following:

gu dearbh	certainly
gu dearbh fhèin	certainly (more emphatic)
Tha am biadh fhèin daor.	The food itself is expensive/even the food is expensive.
Tha an deoch daor fhèin.	The drink is terribly expensive.

Vocabulary

a dh'aithghearr (*adv*)	/ə ɣaçaɼ/	soon
a-staigh (*adv*)	/ə st̪ɣj/	inside, in
bruidhinn (*vb, vn*)	/bri-iɲ/	speak(ing)
coinneachadh (*vn*)	/kɣɲəxəɣ/	meeting
dearg (*adj*)	/dʲ[ɛra]g/, /dʲ[ara]g/	red
deigh (*f*)	/dʲɣj/	ice
dràibheadh (*vn*)	/d̪raivəɣ/	driving
falamh (*adj*)	/fal̪əv/	empty
fhathast (*adv*)	/ha-əst̪/	yet
fion (*m*)	/fĩãn/, /fĩə̃n/	wine
firinn (*f*)	/fiːrʲiɲ/	truth
geal (*adj*)	/gʲal̪/	white
ged-thà (*adv*)	/gə t̪aː/	though, however
gloine (*f*)	/gl̪aɲə/	glass
guth (*m*)	/gu/	voice
inntinneach (*adj*)	/iː ɲdʲiɲəx/	interesting
leth-phinnt (*f*)	/ʎe fiːɲdʲ/	a half pint
mar-thà (*adv*)	/mər haː/	already
mas urrainn dhut	/mas uɼiɲ ɣuht̪/	if you can
math fhèin (*interj*)	/ma heːn̂/	splendid, that's excellent
naidheachd (*f*)	/n̂ɛ̃-əxk/	news
oileanach (*m*), **oileanaich** (*pl*)	/ɣlanəx/, /ɣlaniç/	student, students
siuga (*m*)	/ʃɣgə/	jug
suas ri chèile (*adv*)	/suəs rʲi çeːlə/	going out together, courting
taigh-òsta (*m*)	/t̪ɣj ɔːst̪ə/	hotel, pub
uisge-beatha (*m*)	/uʃkʲə bɛhə/	whisky

CÒMHRADH (CONVERSATION)

Oileanaich a' coinneachadh ann an taigh-òsta

Anna	An tàinig Beathag fhathast? Chuala mi an guth aice, bha mi a' smaoineachadh.
Màiri	Tha i a-muigh an sin a' bruidhinn ach cha tàinig i a-staigh fhathast. Tha i a' tighinn a dh'aithghearr.
Anna	Math fhèin! An cuala tu an naidheachd? Tha Beathag agus Iain suas ri chèile.
Màiri	O, chan eil mi a' creidsinn sin.
Anna	An fhìrinn, ged-thà.
Màiri	Nach eil sin inntinneach?
Anna	A-nis càite a bheil Dòmhnall?
Màiri	Thàinig esan mar-thà. Tha e thall an sin a' ceannach uisge-beatha.
Anna	A Dhòmhnaill, an d' fhuair thu gloine dhòmhsa?
Dòmhnall	Fhuair. Fhuair mi fìon dearg dhut, a Anna. Agus seo fìon geal dhutsa a Mhàiri. Thoir dhomh siuga uisge, a Sheumais, agus faigh dhomh gloine fhalamh agus deigh mas urrainn dhut.
Anna	Dè a tha thu fhèin ag òl an sin a Dhòmhnaill?
Dòmhnall	Chan eil agam ach leth-phinnt agus gloine orains. Tha mi a' dràibheadh a-nochd.

TRANSLATION

Students meeting in a pub

Ann	Has Rebecca come yet? I heard her voice, I thought.
Mary	She's out there talking but she hasn't come in yet. She's coming soon.
Ann	Have you heard the news? Rebecca and John are courting.
Mary	Oh, I don't believe that.
Ann	The truth, though.
Mary	Isn't that interesting?
Ann	Now where's Donald?
Mary	He has come already. He's over there buying whisky.
Ann	Donald, did you get a glass for me?
Donald	Yes. I got red wine for you, Ann. And here's white wine for you, Mary. Give me a jug of water, James, and fetch me an empty glass and some ice if you can.
Ann	What are you drinking there yourself, Donald?
Donald	I've only got a half pint and a glass of orange. I'm driving tonight.

Lesson 5

35 Preposition '*ann an*' ('in')

So far we have met the prepositional pronouns associated with the preposition **aig** 'at' and **do** 'to'. The prepositional pronouns associated with the preposition **ann an** 'in' (**ann am** before labials) are as follows:

annam	in me	**annainn**	in us
annad	in you	**annaibh**	in you (*pl*)
ann	in him/it	**annta**	in them
innte	in her/it		

Note: **ann** 'in it' can be used as an adverb meaning 'there' and in statements concerning 'existence', e.g. **bha Iain ann a-raoir** 'John was there last night'. **Tha thu ann** 'you are there/in existence' is often used as an initial statement in a conversation or as a form of address.

The preposition **ann an** combines with the possessive pronouns **mo*, do*, a*, a, ar, ur, an/am** as follows (see **Section 46b**):

nam*	in my	**nar**	in our
nad*	in your	**nur**	in your (*pl*)
na*	in his	**nan/m**	in their
na	in her		

Note: **na** 'in her' prefixes **h-** to vowels, and both **nar** and **nur** prefix **n-** to vowels.

35a Idiomatic use of '*ann an*' ('in')

The forms **nam, nad**, etc. are used in a small number of idioms involving the verb **tha** and certain verbal nouns. The idioms involved normally denote a state or a condition such as: sleep, being awake, lying, running, standing, stretching out, sitting:

Tha mi nam chadal.	I am asleep.
Tha thu nad dhùisg.	You are awake.
Tha e na laighe.	He is lying down.
Tha i na ruith.	She is running.
Tha sinn nar seasamh.	We are standing (up).
Tha sibh nur sìneadh.	You are stretched out.
Tha iad nan suidhe.	They are sitting (down).

Exercise 5.1

Translate

1   John is asleep.
2   Are you awake?
3   Mary is lying down.
4   He was standing there.
5   We are sitting down.

36 More on the use of '*is*'

We have already dealt with the following types of **is** sentence:

IS	SUBJECT	PREDICATE	
Is/Is e	**mise**	**Iain**	I am John
Is e	**Seumas**	**an tidsear**	James is the teacher
Is e	**Anna**	**mo phiuthar**	Ann is my sister

So far we have dealt only with cases where the predicate is a definite noun. We will now deal with sentences where the predicate is an indefinite noun, i.e. a noun which is (a) not a proper noun, (b) not preceded by the article and (c) not preceded by a possessive pronoun. We will be dealing with sentences like 'John is a teacher' and 'she is a doctor'.

So far our **is** sentences have involved the order: **is** + **subject** + **predicate**. When the predicate is indefinite, however, the order is reversed and becomes: **is** + **predicate** + **subject**. In such sentences the verb **tha** and the preposition **ann an** are used as follows:

IS E	PREDICATE	RELATIVE	THA	ANN AN	SUBJECT
Is e	**tidsear**	**a**	**tha**	**ann an**	**Iain**
it is	a teacher	that	is	in	John

John is a teacher

The **a** which appears before **tha** is a relative pronoun meaning 'that' and is explained further in **Lesson 9**. Here are some more examples:

Is e croitear a tha ann an Seumas.	James is a crofter.
Is e nurs a tha ann an Anna.	Ann is a nurse.
Is e ministear a tha ann an Uilleam.	William is a minister.
Is e oileanach a tha ann am Màiri.	Mary is a student.
Is e seinneadair a tha ann an Ailean.	Alan is a singer.
Is e actair a tha ann an Seonag.	Joan is an actor.

If the subject is a personal pronoun, we use the prepositional pronouns associated with the preposition **ann an**. 'I am a teacher' in Gaelic is literally 'it is a teacher that is in-me': **is e tidsear a tha annam**. Here are some further examples:

Is e oileanach a tha annam.	I am a student.
Is e seinneadair a tha annad.	You are a singer.
Is e actair a tha ann.	He is an actor.
Is e dotair a tha innte.	She is a doctor.

Note: there is a certain amount of ambiguity in cases like **Is e nurs a tha ann**, since **ann** can refer to 'him' or 'it'. **Is e nurs a tha ann** could therefore be translated as 'he is a nurse' or 'it is a nurse'. It depends on what **ann** refers to. In all of the above examples **tha** is often written as **th'**.

Vocabulary

borbair (*m*)	/b[ɔrɔ]bɛrʲ/	barber, hairdresser
croitear (*m*)	/krɔhtʲɛrʲ/	crofter
dotair (*m*)	/dɔht̪ɛrʲ/	doctor
seinneadair (*m*)	/ʃeɲədɛrʲ/	singer

Exercise 5.2

Translate

1 John is a minister.
2 Ann is a singer.
3 Joan is a teacher.
4 William is a crofter.
5 Donald is a student.
6 I am a student also.
7 She is a doctor.
8 You (*pl*) are a hairdresser.
9 Are you a teacher?
10 Is he a minister?

36a Negative and question forms (interrogative) of '*is e*'

To negate **is e**, replace **is e** with **chan e**. To form the positive interrogative, replace **is e** with **an e**. To form the negative interrogative, replace **is e** with **nach e**.

Study the following forms:

An e tidsear a tha annad?	Are you a teacher?
Chan e saor a tha annam.	I am not a carpenter.
Nach e ministear a tha ann an Iain?	Isn't John a minister?

Answering questions An e ...? / Nach e ...?

We have already noted that there is no single word for 'yes' or 'no' in Gaelic. To answer a question beginning **An e ...?** or **Nach e ...?**, the answer for 'yes' and 'no' is **is e** and **chan e**, respectively. Study the following examples:

An e tidsear a tha annad?	Are you a teacher?
Is e.	Yes.
Chan e.	No.

An e saor a tha ann an Iain?	Is John a carpenter?
Is e.	Yes.
Chan e.	No.

Nach e seinneadair a tha ann an Anna?	Isn't Ann a singer?
Is e.	Yes.
Chan e.	No.

36b Alternative construction: using '*tha*' instead of '*is*'

There is an alternative way of dealing with the above type of 'is' sentence by using the verb **tha** instead of the verb **is**.

THA + SUBJECT + {ANN AN + POSS PRON (agreeing with subject)} + PREDICATE

Tha	**Iain**	**na**	**mhinistear**

lit John is in his minister
John is a minister.

Very often this construction is used to describe temporary states, including one's profession, whereas the **is** / **is e** construction tends to describe more permanent states. Here are some further examples:

Tha Anna na seinneadair.	Ann is a singer.
Tha Seonag na tidsear.	Joan is a teacher.
Tha Uilleam na chroitear.	William is a crofter.
Tha Dòmhnall na oileanach.	Donald is a student.
Tha mi nam oileanach cuideachd.	I am a student also.
Tha i na seinneadair.	She is a singer.
Tha sibh nur tidsear.	You (*formal*) are a teacher.
A bheil e na mhinistear?	Is he a minister?

36c 'It is ...'

To translate any sentence 'it is ...', we use the formula **is e ... a tha ann**, irrespective of the nature of the predicate (i.e. whether it is definite or indefinite):

Is e cù a tha ann.	It's a dog.
Is e Seumas a tha ann.	It's James.
Is e an tidsear ùr a tha ann.	It's the new teacher.

To negate or ask questions, we replace **is e** with **chan e, an e, nach e** as usual:

Chan e ministear a tha ann.	It's not a minister.
An e càr a tha ann?	Is it a car?
Nach e call a tha ann?	Isn't it a loss/pity?

(Note: **tha ann** is often written as **th' ann**.)

37 Past tense

The past tense of sentences like **is e tidsear a tha ann an Iain** 'John is a teacher' or **is e Iain a tha ann** 'it is John' is normally formed by putting **tha** in the past tense, e.g.

Is e tidsear a <u>bha</u> ann an Iain.	John was a teacher.
Is e oileanach a <u>bha</u> annam.	I was a student.
Is e Anna a <u>bha</u> ann.	It was Ann.
Chan e Màiri a <u>bha</u> ann.	It wasn't Mary.
An e Uilleam a <u>bha</u> ann?	Was it William?

(Note: **bha ann** is often written as **bh' ann**.)

38 'This is', 'that is'

We have already learnt (see **Lesson 3**) how to translate 'this is ...' and 'that is ...' sentences when the predicate is a definite noun, e.g.

(Is) seo Iain	OR	**Is e seo Iain**	this is John
(Is) sin an tidsear	OR	**Is e sin an tidsear**	that is the teacher

When the predicate is an indefinite noun, we use the construction, introduced earlier on in this lesson, i.e. **is e X a tha (ann an) seo/sin/siud,** the only difference being that the preposition **ann an** is often omitted:

IS E	+	PREDICATE	+	A THA	+	SEO/SIN/SIUD
Is e		**cù**		**a tha**		**seo**

This is a dog.

Note: In some dialects the **ann an** does occur before **seo**, and **ann an seo** can be heard as **ann a sheo**, e.g.

Is e cù a tha ann a sheo.
This is a dog.

Here are some further examples (without the **ann an**, which is what is recommended in this book):

Is e ionad-spòrs a tha sin.	That's a sports centre.
Is e sionnach a bha siud.	That was a fox.

5

39 Asking 'What is …?'

Dè a tha ann?	What is it?
Dè a tha seo?	What is here/what is this?
Dè a tha sin?	What is there/what is that?
Dè a tha siud?	What is there (yonder)/what is that (yon)?

40 Word order: fronting

Fronting occurs when a word is moved from its usual position nearer to the front of the sentence. When this occurs emphasis is usually implied. The normal order of elements in a Gaelic sentence is as follows:

VERB	+	SUBJECT	+	OBJECT	+	INDIRECT OBJECT	+	ADVERB
chunnaic		**mi**		**Seumas**		**air a' bhus**		**an-dè**
saw		I		James		on the bus		yesterday

I saw James on the bus yesterday

It is, however, possible to place any of these elements at the beginning of the sentence for special emphasis. Such fronted sentences are very common indeed in Gaelic and are therefore important to learn. Fronted elements are preceded either by **Is e** or **Is ann** and are 'joined' to the remainder of the sentence by a relative pronoun **a** 'that', for which see **Lesson 9**. The use of **Is e** and **Is ann** is straightforward and is as follows:

(a) **Is e** is used to front pronouns and nouns

(b) **Is ann** is used to front everything else, e.g. adjectives, adverbs, prepositional phrases, verbal phrases, etc.

Note: **Is ann** is often written as **'S ann**.

Here is how we would front each of the elements in the above sentence:

Chunnaic mi Seumas air a' bhus an-dè:

mi

Is e mise a chunnaic Seumas air a' bhus an-dè. OR
Is mise a chunnaic Seumas air a' bhus an-dè.
It is *I* who saw James on the bus yesterday.

Note that the emphatic forms of the pronoun are used with **is e** as before.

Seumas

Is e Seumas a chunnaic mi air a' bhus an-dè.
It is James that I saw on the bus yesterday.

air a' bhus

Is ann air a' bhus a chunnaic mi Seumas an-dè.
It is on the bus that I saw James yesterday.

an-dè

Is ann an-dè a chunnaic mi Seumas air a' bhus.
It is yesterday that I saw James on the bus.

chunnaic

Is ann a chunnaic mi Seumas air a' bhus an-dè.
I saw James on the bus yesterday.

Note: The latter sentence is more emphatic than the sentence **Chunnaic mi Seumas air a' bhus an-dè**.

Here are some further examples of fronted sentences:

Is e Seumas a thàinig a-staigh.	It is James that came in.
Is e cù a chunnaic mi.	It is a dog that I saw.
Is e ise a chuala mi.	It is she that I heard.
Is ann sgìth a tha Seumas.	It is tired that James is.
Is ann an-dè a chunnaic mi Anna.	It is yesterday that I saw Ann.
Is ann (ann) an Glaschu a tha Màiri.	It is in Glasgow that Mary is.
Is ann agamsa a tha an leabhar.	It is at me that the book is/ *I* have the book.
Is ann a thàinig Iain anmoch.	It is that John came late/ John (really) did come late.

Note that all 'it is' sentences involve the relative **a** 'that'.
Study the following negative and interrogative forms:

Chan ann sgìth a tha mi.	It is not tired that I am.
An ann an-dè a chunnaic thu Seumas?	Was it yesterday that you saw James?
Nach ann agadsa a bha an iuchair?	Wasn't it you who had the key? (*lit* 'Was it not at you that the key was?'

> *****IMPORTANT*****
>
> Compare:
>
> | | |
> |---|---|
> | **Is e Seumas a tha ann.** | It is James. |
> | **Is e Seumas a chunnaic mi.** | It is James that I saw. |
>
> In 'it is ...' sentences when the predicate is followed by a relative clause, **a tha ann** is not used.

Exercise 5.3

Front each of the elements **sinn, Anna, a' seinn, aig a' chèilidh, a-raoir, chuala** *in the following sentence:*

Chuala sinn Anna a' seinn aig a' chèilidh a-raoir.
We heard Ann singing at the ceilidh last night.

41 Answering questions

To answer a question beginning with **An e?** ('Is it?'), **Nach e?** ('Is it not?') or **An ann?** ('Is it?'), **Nach ann?** ('Is it not?'), the answers are:

QUESTION	ANSWER YES	NO
An e? Nach e?	Is e.	Chan e.
An ann? Nach ann?	Is ann.	Chan ann.

42 Ownership

We have already learnt how to translate 'have' sentences; we use the verb **tha** and the preposition **aig** 'at'. However, if we want to say that something 'belongs to' someone as opposed to someone 'having' something, we use **is ann** and the preposition **le** 'with'. To say 'James owns the book' or 'the book belongs to James', in Scottish Gaelic we use a fronted sentence: 'it is with James that the book is':

Is ann le Seumas a tha an leabhar.	The book belongs to James.

Study the following phrases:

Is ann le Màiri a tha an càr.	The car belongs to Mary.
Is ann le mo bhràthair a tha a' bhùth.	The shop belongs to my brother.

42a 'Who owns?'

To ask the question 'who owns …?', we say:

Cò leis a tha an leabhar? Who owns the book? (*lit* 'With whom is the book?')
Cò leis a tha seo? Who owns this?

42b Prepositional pronouns '*le*' ('with')

leam	with me	**leinn**	with us
leat	with you	**leibh**	with you
leis	with him/it	**leotha**	with them
leatha	with her/it		

Study the following phrases:

Is ann leamsa a tha an cat sin. That cat is mine/belongs to me.
Is ann leatsa a tha an cù sin. That dog is yours/belongs to you.
Is ann leinne a tha an t-airgead. The money is ours/belongs to us.

Note that the prepositional pronouns are usually used with the emphatic suffixes in this construction.

42c Idioms involving '*le*' ('with')

(i) Thank you

Study the following phrases:

tapadh leat thank you (sing *informal*)
tapadh leibh thank you (*pl* or *sing formal*)

'Thank you' is also expressed as follows in some south-western dialects, which resembles very closely the Irish Gaelic form:

gu robh math agad thank you (sing *informal*)
gu robh math agaibh thank you (*pl* or *sing formal*)

The latter phrase literally means 'may you have good'; see **Section 110**.

(ii) I like, I would like

Study the following phrases:

Is toil le Ailean ceòl-mòr. Alan likes 'pibroch' (*lit* 'big music').
Is toil leinn dealbh-chluich. We like drama.
Bu toil le Catrìona deoch orains. Catherine would like a drink of orange.
Bu toil leotha geama ball-coise. They would like a game of football.

Some dialects use **is caomh** and **bu chaomh** instead of **is toil** and **bu toil** respectively in the above phrases.

Note that **dràma** 'drama' is also used.

NEGATIVE FORMS:

Cha toil (cha chaomh) leam uisge-beatha.	I don't like whisky
Cha bu toil leam rola.	I wouldn't like a bread roll.

INTERROGATIVE (POSITIVE) FORMS:

An toil (an caomh) leat an fhidheall?	Do you like the fiddle?
Am bu toil leat pinnt?	Would you like a pint?

INTERROGATIVE (NEGATIVE) FORMS:

Nach toil le Alasdair lionn?	Doesn't Alasdair like beer?
Nach bu toil leat aran?	Wouldn't you like (some) bread?

ANSWERS:

An toil ...?/Nach toil ...?	**Is toil.**	Yes.
	Cha toil.	No.
Am bu toil ...?/Nach bu toil ...?	**Bu toil.**	Yes.
	Cha bu toil.	No.

(iii) I prefer, I would prefer

Study the following phrases:

Is fheàrr le Iain aran donn.	John prefers brown bread.
Is fheàrr leatha tì na cofaidh.	She prefers tea to coffee.
B' fheàrr le Anna feòil na iasg.	Ann would prefer meat to fish.
B' fheàrr leam sgadan.	I would prefer herring.

Note: **na** in Gaelic corresponds to 'to'; **seach**, which means 'rather than, in contrast to', is also used, e.g.

Is fheàrr le Anna tì seach cofaidh.	Ann prefers tea rather than coffee.

NEGATIVE FORMS:

Chan fheàrr le Sìle golf.	Sheila doesn't prefer golf.
Cha b' fheàrr leis drama.	He wouldn't prefer a dram (drink).

INTERROGATIVE (POSITIVE) FORMS:

An fheàrr leat buntàta?	Do you prefer potatoes?
Am b' fheàrr leat fion?	Would you prefer wine?

INTERROGATIVE (NEGATIVE) FORMS:

Nach fheàrr le Anna dannsa?	Doesn't Ann prefer dancing/to dance?
Nach b' fheàrr le Uilleam buntàta?	Wouldn't William prefer potatoes?

ANSWERS:

An fheàrr ...?/ Nach fheàrr ...?	**Is fheàrr.**	Yes.
	Chan fheàrr.	No.
Am b' fheàrr ...?/Nach b' fheàrr ...?	**B' fheàrr.**	Yes.
	Cha b' fheàrr.	No.

5

(iv) I don't mind, it doesn't matter to me

Study the following phrases:

Is coingeis le Calum.	Calum doesn't mind, it doesn't matter to Calum.
Is coingeis leam.	I don't mind.

Tha mi coingeis and **tha mi coma** are also used for the latter.

Vocabulary

ceòl-mòr (*m*)	/kʲɔɫ moːr/	pibroch
dannsa (*m*)	/d̪aun̪sə/, /d̪ãũsə/	dancing
donn (*adj*)	/d̪õũn̪/	brown
feòil (*f*)	/fjɔːp/	meat
lionn (*m*)	/ʎũːn̪/	beer

Exercise 5.4

Translate the following:

1 **Is toil leam a' Ghàidhlig.**
2 **Is fheàrr leatha Iain.**
3 **Am b' fheàrr leat lionn?**
4 **Am bu toil leat cupa tì?**
5 **Chan fheàrr leotha aran donn.**
6 **Nach toil le Anna dannsa?**
7 **Cha toil leamsa feòil.**
8 **B' fheàrr leam lionn na uisge-beatha.**
9 **An toil leat Run Rig?** †
10 **Nach b' fheàrr leat ceòl-mòr?**

† Run Rig is the name of a popular band.

43 The weather

The weather **sìde** (*f*) or **aimsir** (*f*) is an important part of daily conversation in Gaelic. Most conversations begin with comments on the weather. Here are some useful examples:

Is e latha brèagha a tha ann.	It is a lovely day.
Is e latha fuar a tha ann.	It is a cold day.
Is e latha fliuch a tha ann.	It is a wet day.
Is e latha blàth a tha ann.	It is a warm day.

Alternatively, we can simply use the verb **tha** as follows:

Tha e brèagha an-diugh.	It is fine today.
Tha e fuar an-diugh.	It is cold today.
Tha e fliuch an-diugh.	It is wet today.
Tha e blàth an-diugh.	It is warm today.

The feminine pronoun **i** rather than **e** is used in some dialects to refer to the weather in the above phrases; the feminine reference refers to, or originally referred to, **oidhche** 'night' which is a feminine noun.

44 Prepositions

Prepositions may be classified into two groups according to whether they lenite a following noun or not:

DO NOT LENITE A FOLLOWING NOUN		LENITE A FOLLOWING NOUN	
aig	at	**bho***	from
air	on	**fo***	under
à	out of, from	**do***	to, into, for
ann an	in	**de***	of
le	with, by	**mu***	about
ri	against†	**ro***	before
gu	to (the point of)	**tro***	through

† The meaning of **ri** changes according to idiom, e.g. **bruidhinn ri** 'speak to', **tachair ri** 'meet with' (also **tachair air**), etc.

Some examples

aig balla	at a wall	**bho Sheumas**	from James
air sèithear	on a chair	**fo bhaga**	under a bag
à Glaschu	from Glasgow	**do Mhàiri**	to Mary
ann an cabhag	in a hurry	**ro chàr**	before a car
le Seumas	with James	**tro dhoras**	through a doorway

Note: **do** and **de** prefix **dh'** to a following vowel or **fh-** e.g. **do dh'Anna** 'to Ann', **de dh'fhalt** 'of hair', **do dh'Iain** 'to John'. **Do*** is frequently reduced to **a*** especially before place-names, e.g.

a Ghlaschu	to Glasgow
a Dhùn Èideann	to Edinburgh

Note: The preposition **ann an** is frequently reduced to **an** (**am** before labials) before placenames, e.g.

an Glaschu	in Glasgow
an Dùn Èideann	in Edinburgh
an Alba	in Scotland
an Èirinn	in Ireland
an Sasainn	in England

5

Vocabulary

àm (*m*)	/aum/	time
baile (*m*)	/balə/	town
bòrd (*m*)	/bɔːɼs̪t̪/	table
càr (*m*)	/kaːr/	car
duine (*m*)	/d̪ujɲə/, /d̪ujɲə/	man
geata (*m*)	/gʲeht̪ə/	gate
Inbhir Nis (*m*)	/iɲər ɲiʃ/	Inverness
taigh (*m*)	/t̪ɤj/	house

Exercise 5.5

Translate

1 in a house
2 on a table
3 with a man
4 through a town
5 before James
6 from time to time
7 to Inverness
8 from Edinburgh
9 at a gate
10 under a car

45 More prepositional pronouns: '*air*' ('on')

orm	on me	**oirnn**	on us
ort	on you	**oirbh**	on you (*pl*)
air	on him/it	**orra**	on them
oirre	on her/it		

(i) The preposition **air** is frequently used in the following expressions expressing hunger, thirst, etc. or physical conditions which are generally to one's disadvantage.

Tha an t-acras orm.	I am hungry. (*lit* 'The hunger is on-me')
Tha am pathadh ort.	You are thirsty.
Tha an cnatan air.	He has a cold.
Tha an t-eagal oirre.	She is afraid.
Tha cabhag oirnn.	We are in a hurry.

(ii) **Air** is also used to express 'wearing clothes, etc.':

Tha còta snog oirre.	She is wearing a nice coat.
Tha peitean air Iain.	John is wearing a jumper.
Tha brògan àrda orra.	They are wearing boots (*lit* high shoes).
Tha ad air.	He is wearing a hat.

(iii) **Air** is also used to ask someone's name:

Dè an t-ainm a tha ort?	What is your name?
OR	(*lit* 'What name is on-you?')
C' ainm a tha ort?	
Is e Iain (an t-ainm) a tha orm.	John is my name.
OR	
Tha, Iain.	John.

(iv) **Dislikes, loathes**

IS	+	BEAG	+	AIR	+	SUBJ	+	OBJ
Is		**beag**		**air**		**Màiri**		**feòil**

Mary dislikes meat

Here are some further examples:

Is beag air Seumas còcaireachd.	James dislikes/loathes cooking.
Is beag orm an leabhar sin.	I dislike that book.

The comparative/superlative **lugha** (see **Section 90**) is also used in place of **beag** in this idiom:

Is lugha air Anna ball-coise.   Ann dislikes football.

(v) **Hurry up**

| **Greas ort!** | Hurry up! (*informal*) |
| **Greasaibh oirbh!** | Hurry up! (*pl or formal*) |

Vocabulary

aimsir (*f*)	/[ɛmɛ]ʃərʲ/	weather
a-null thairis (*adv*)	/ə n̪uːt̪ harʲiʃ/	abroad (motion to)
baga (*m*), **bagaichean** (*pl*)	/baɡə/, /baɡiçən/	bag, bags
beannachd (*f*) **leat**	/bʲan̪əxk laht̪/	good-bye, farewell
cadal (*vn*)	/kaḏət̪/	sleep
cairt-shiubhail (*f*)	/kaɾst̪ʲ çu-əl/	passport
ceart gu leòr (*adv*)	/kʲaɾst̪ ɡə ʎɔːr/	fine, right enough
co-dhiù (*adv*)	/ko juː/	anyway, however
Dùn (*m*) **Èideann**	/d̪un eːdʲən̪/	Edinburgh
faisg air (*cd prp*)	/faʃkʲ ɛrʲ/	near
fear-lagha (*m*)	/fɛr t̪ɣɣə/	lawyer
Glaschu (*m*)	/ɡɫasəxə/	Glasgow
is beag orm	/s beɡ [ɔrɔ]m/	I dislike, I don't care for
is coingeis leam	/əs kainʲɡʲəʃ ləːm/	I don't care, it's all the same
mar sin leat fhèin	/mər ʃin laht̪ heːn/	the same to you (in farewells)
mas e do thoil e	/ma ʃe d̪ə hɔl ɛ/	please (informal)
na gabh (*vb*) **dragh** (*m*)	/n̪a ɡav d̪rɣɣ/	don't worry
obair (*f*)	/obərʲ/	work
Paras (*m*)	/parəs/	Paris
plèan (*m*), **plèanaichean** (*pl*)	/pleːn/, /pleːniçən/	plane, planes
port-adhair (*m*)	/pɔɾst̪ a-ərʲ/	airport
sam bith (*adv*)	/səm bi/	any, at all
seall (*vb*) **dhomh**	/ʃaut̪ d̪ɔ̃/, /ʃaut̪ ɣɔ̃/	show (to) me
suidheachan (*m*)	/suɪjəxan/	seat
tidsear (*m*)	/tidʲʃɛrʲ/	teacher
turas (*m*)	/t̪urəs/	trip, journey
uinneag (*f*)	/ũɲaɡ/	window

CÒMHRADH (CONVERSATION)

Aig port-adhair

Oifigear†	Càite a bheil thu a' dol?
Iain	Tha mi a' dol a-null thairis a Pharas.
Oifigear	Seall dhomh an tiocaid agad agus do chairt-shiubhail, mas e do thoil e.
Iain	Seo agad i.
Oifigear	Ceart gu leòr. Is ann à Glaschu a tha thu, an ann?
Iain	Is ann. Ach tha mi a' fuireach ann an Dùn Èideann.
Oifigear	Agus dè an obair a tha agad an sin?
Iain	Is e tidsear a bha annam ach tha mi nam fhear-lagha a-nis.
Oifigear	An ann leatsa a tha na bagaichean sin uile?
Iain	Is ann ach am fear seo.
Oifigear	Am bu toil leat suidheachan faisg air uinneag?
Iain	B' fheàrr leam suidheachan eile ach is coingeis leam. Tha an cadal orm agus is beag orm plèanaichean co-dhiù.
Oifigear	Na gabh thusa dragh sam bith. Tha an aimsir math.
	Turas math dhut agus beannachd leat.
Iain	Mar sin leat fhèin.

† *Oifigear* tends to be used more commonly than *oifigeach* nowadays.

TRANSLATION

At an airport

Officer	Where are you going?
John	I'm going abroad to Paris.
Officer	Show me your ticket and your passport, please.
John	Here it is.
Officer	Fine. You're from Glasgow?
John	Yes. But I live in Edinburgh.
Officer	And what's your job there?
John	I was a teacher, but I'm now a lawyer.
Officer	Are all those bags yours?
John	Yes, except this one.
Officer	Would you like a seat near a window?
John	I'd prefer another seat but it's all the same. I'm sleepy and I don't like planes anyway.
Officer	Don't you worry at all. The weather's good. Good journey to you and good-bye.
John	The same to you.

Lesson 6

46 The prepositional (P) case

Gaelic has a prepositional case, traditionally referred to as the dative case, which is used after most prepositions. The only parts of speech which regularly change form after prepositions are the singular article and to a lesser extent singular feminine nouns. Masculine nouns do not change form in the prepositional case. The use of the prepositional case of feminine nouns is disappearing in Gaelic and in many dialects is confined to a handful of singular feminine nouns and then usually only when the definite article precedes.

The prepositional form of the article may affect the initial consonant of a following noun. We have actually met the prepositional form of the article already; it is the leniting article **an*** (irrespective of the gender of the following noun), which as you will recall is the form of the feminine nominative singular article. The forms are:

a' + lenition	before all lenitable consonants (except **d t s f**), i.e. **b c g m p**
an t-	before **s** (**s sl sr sn**, NOT **sg sp st sm**)
an + lenition	before **f** (which becomes **fh**)
an	otherwise, i.e. before **d n t l r** and all vowels

Some examples

NOMINATIVE		PREPOSITIONAL	
am bòrd	the table	**air a' bhòrd**	on the table
an cèilidh	the ceilidh	**aig a' chèilidh**	at the ceilidh
an sagart	the priest	**air an t-sagart**	on the priest
an t-sràid	the street	**air an t-sràid**	on the street

Note that the above applies to all prepositions whether they themselves lenite an immediately following noun or not, e.g.

air càr	on a car	**air a' chàr**	on the car
fo chàr	under a car	**fon a' chàr**	under the car

Most prepositions change form before the article with the exception of **air** and **aig**. These may be classified into two groups as follows:

(a)   Prepositions which add **-s** before the definite article:

PREPOSITION		PREPOSITION BEFORE THE ARTICLE
à	→	**às**
ann an	→	**anns**
le	→	**leis**
ri	→	**ris**
gu	→	**gus**

(b)   Prepositions which add **-n** before the definite article:

PREPOSITION		PREPOSITION BEFORE THE ARTICLE
bho	→	bhon
fo	→	fon
mu	→	mun
ro	→	ron
tro	→	tron

Note that the prepositions **do** and **de** can change form slightly before the article:

do	→	don/dhan
de	→	den/dhen

Before we proceed to look at more examples, it will be well to explain what we mean by some singular feminine nouns changing form in the prepositional case, especially when preceded by the article. Feminine nouns which end in a consonant are slenderised following prepositions (see **Introduction**: sounds). Note that this slenderisation may alter the preceding vowel (see **Appendix 1**). Some examples:

NOMINATIVE SINGULAR FEMININE		PREPOSITIONAL FORM: SINGULAR	
làmh	→	làimh	hand
cluas	→	cluais	ear
bròg	→	bròig	shoe
cas	→	cois	foot
bas	→	bois	palm
clann	→	cloinn	children
caileag	→	caileig	girl
cailleach	→	caillich	old woman

> ### LITERARY GAELIC
> In practice the slenderisation of nouns following prepositions is confined to a handful of nouns, including the above examples.
>
> The slenderisation is far more common in literary Gaelic.

Watch out for more examples in the samples below (marked with P). Some examples of prepositions + article:

às a' bhaile	out of the town
anns a' Ghàidhlig[†]	in (the) Gaelic
leis a' mhinistear	with the minister
ris an t-sagart	against/with[††] the priest

[†] Gaelic uses both **ann an Gàidhlig** 'in Gaelic' and **anns a' Ghàidhlig** 'in the Gaelic' for English 'in Gaelic'.
[††] Recall the translation of **ri** depends on the idiom in which it is used.

fon a' bhòrd	under the table
dhan a' chaileig (P)	to the girl
ron an fhear	before the man
mun an taigh	about the house
tron an latha	through the day
anns an òran	in the song
aig an uinneig (P)	at the window

Note: **bhon an, fon an, dhan an** etc. have the variants **bhon, fon, dhan** respectively, e.g.

fon bhòrd	under the table
dhan chaileig (P) *or* **don chaileig (P)**	to the girl

46a Irregular nouns

Nominative		Prepositional	Examples	
bean (*f*)	wife	**mnaoi**	**le mo mhnaoi**	with my wife
bò (*f*)	cow	**boin**	**aig a' bhoin**	at the cow
sgian (*f*)	knife	**sgithinn**	**leis an sgithinn**	with the knife

Vocabulary

airgead (*m*)	/[ɛrʲɛ]gʲəd̪/	money
Beurla (*f*)	/bjɤːɾɫə/	English
craobh (*f*)	/krɯːv/	tree
seòmar (*m*)	/ʃɔːmər/	chamber, room

Exercise 6.1

Translate

1. at the door
2. in the room
3. with the boy
4. to the girl
5. before the ceilidh
6. with the money
7. in the car
8. in (the) English
9. under a tree
10. through the town

46b Prepositions and possessive pronouns

When the prepositions which end in a consonant (i.e. **aig** 'at' and **air** 'on') are followed immediately by possessive pronouns the spelling is straighforward. They are spelled as two separate words, e.g.

aig mo mhàthair	at my mother
air do chù	on your dog

However, the remaining prepositions, all of which which end in a vowel, combine with the possessive pronouns as follows:

	mo* 'my'	**do*** 'your'	**a*** 'his'/**a** (**h-**) 'her'	**ar** (**n-**) 'our'	**ur** (**n-**) 'your'	**an/am** 'their'
do	**dom***/**dham*** 'to my'	**dod***/**dhad*** 'to your'	**da/dha** 'to his/her'	**dor/dar/dhar** 'to our'	**dur/dhur** 'to your'	**don/dan/dhan** or **dom/dam/dham** 'to their'
de	**dem***/**dhem*** 'of my'	**ded***/**dhed*** 'of your'	**de** (**a**)/**dhe** (**a**) 'of his/her'	**der/dher** 'of our'	**dur/dhur** 'of your'	**den/dhen** or **dem/dhem** 'of their'
le	**lem*** 'with my'	**led*** 'with your'	**le** (**a**) 'with his/her'	**ler** 'with our'	**lur** 'with your'	**len/lem** 'with their'
bho	**bhom*** 'from my'	**bhod*** 'from your'	**bho** (**a**) 'from his/her'	**bhor** 'from our'	**bhur** 'from your'	**bhon/bhom** 'from their'
fo	**fom*** 'under my'	**fod*** 'under your'	**fo** (**a**) 'under his/her'	**for** 'under our'	**fur** 'under your'	**fon/fom** 'under their'
ro	**rom*** 'before my'	**rod*** 'before your'	**ro** (**a**) 'before his/her'	**ror** 'before our'	**rur** 'before your'	**ron/rom** 'before their'
tro	**trom*** 'through my'	**trod*** 'through your'	**tro** (**a**) 'through his/her'	**tror** 'through our'	**trur** 'through your'	**tron/trom** 'through their'
gu	**gum*** 'to my'	**gud*** 'to your'	**gu** (**a**) 'to his'	**gar** 'to our'	**gur** 'to your'	**gun/gum** 'to their'
mu	**mum*** 'about my'	**mud*** 'about your'	**mu** (**a**) 'about his/her'	**mar** 'about our'	**mur** 'about your'	**mun/mum** 'about their'
ri	**rim*** 'to my'	**rid*** 'to your'	**ri** (**a**) 'to his/her'	**rir** 'to our'	**rur** 'with your'	**rin/rim** 'to their'
ann an/am	**nam*** 'in my'	**nad*** 'in your'	**na** 'in his/her'	**nar** 'in our'	**nur** 'in your'	**nan/nam** 'in their'

Note: all first and second plural forms prefix **n-** to vowels; all third singular feminine forms prefix **h-** to vowels.

It is also acceptable to write the full forms without coalescence, e.g:

bho mo mhàthair	from my mother
le ar n-athair	with our father
tro ur taigh	through your house

Note that the third person singular forms lenite when the possessive is masculine, e.g.

da thaigh	to his house
da taigh	to her house
le (a) bhràthair	with his brother
le (a) bràthair	with her brother

The preposition **à** 'out of, from' becomes **às** before all possessive pronouns and thus resembles the pattern exhibited by **aig** and **air**, e.g.

às mo thaigh	out of my house
às a beul	from her mouth

6

47 Prepositions followed by the nominative: *'gun'* ('without'); *'mar'* ('like'); *'gu ruige'* ('to')

Most, but not all, prepositions are followed by the prepositional form. Some prepositions are followed by the genitive as we will see later (see **Section 62a**). Others are followed by the nominative, e.g. **gun(*)** 'without', **mar*** 'like' and **gu ruige** 'to' (in sense 'as far as' or 'up to'). **Gun** may or may not lenite according to dialect. **Mar*** lenites a following noun. (Some northern dialects use **man** for **mar**, which does not lenite.) Here are some examples:

gun f(h)acal	without a word
gun sgillinn	without a penny
gun an t-airgead	without the money
mar dhuine	like a man
mar chat	like a cat
mar am fiadh	like the deer
gu ruige an t-Òban	to Oban
gu ruige a' Ghearmailt	to Germany

The difference between the use of the prepositional and the nominative form after certain prepositions is seen in the following examples:

leis a' chaillich (P)	with the old woman
mar a' chailleach	like the old woman
anns an Òban (P)	in (the) Oban
gu ruige an t-Òban	to Oban

Note the following idioms involving **gun**:

gun teagamh	without doubt, certainly
gun fhiosta do	unknown to
Thàinig Iain gun fhiosta dhomh.	John came unknown to me.

Note: On the lack of lenition in **gun teagamh**, see **Appendix 7**.

48 The past tense of regular verbs: independent forms

In **Lesson 4** we met the continuous past (a periphrastic construction) and also the simple past tense of irregular verbs. The simple past tense of regular verbs is derived from the root of the verb, which in Gaelic is the imperative 2nd singular form. We will see later that the simple future and conditional/past habitual tenses are also derived from the verbal root.

To form the independent form of the past tense of a regular verb, we lenite (see **Introduction**: sounds) the initial consonant of the root, e.g.

IMPERATIVE	PAST	
brist	**Bhrist Seumas an uinneag.**	James broke the window.
dùin	**Dhùin Anna an doras.**	Ann closed the door.
ceannaich	**Cheannaich Iain am pàipear.**	John bought the paper.
gabh	**Ghabh am balach òran.**	The boy sang a song.
coisich	**Choisich an nighean a-mach.**	The girl walked out.
bruidhinn	**Bhruidhinn Màiri.**	Mary spoke.

Note: some dialects have **bris** rather than **brist** for the verb 'break'.
If the verb begins with an unlenitable consonant or consonant cluster, e.g. **sg**, the initial remains unchanged in writing, e.g.

sgrìobh	**Sgrìobh Anna litir.**	Ann wrote a letter.

Similarly, verbs beginning with **l n r** show no difference in writing (although there are subtle phonetic differences in the pronunciation of **l n r** in certain lenition contexts: see the section on lenition in the Pronunciation and Spelling chapter at the beginning of the book):

Verbal root and imperative	Pronunciation	Past Tense	Pronunciation of past tense forms	Translation
leugh	like *ll* in 'million' or Italian 'gli" IPA /ʎ/	**Leugh Dòmhnall an leabhar.**	like English *l*; IPA alveolar /l/	Donald read the book.
nigh	like *ny* in 'canyon'; IPA /ɲ/	**Nigh Màiri a làmhan.**	like English *n*; IPA alveolar /n/	Mary washed her hands.
ruith	like a rolled 'r'; IPA /r̪/	**Ruith Calum a-mach.**	like English tapped *r*; IPA /ɾ/ or /ɾ/	Calum ran out.

If the verb begins with a **vowel** or **f** followed by a vowel, then the verb is preceded by **dh'** as follows:

innis	**Dh'innis Mòrag dhomh.**	Morag told (to) me.
ith	**Dh'ith Seòras a bhiadh.**	George ate his food.
òl	**Dh'òl Uilleam pinnt.**	William drank a pint.
fòn	**Dh'fhòn Iain.**	John phoned.

Note: the past is a simple past tense. It implies a completed action in the past and does **not** have continuous or progressive meaning. **Bhrist Seumas** means 'James broke', **not** 'James was breaking'.

The pronouns are used just as with the verb **tha**. Note that the subject always follows the verb in Scottish Gaelic.

Dhùin mi an doras.	I closed the door.
Ghabh thu òran.	You sang a song.
Dh'ith e am biadh aige.	He ate his food.
Ruith i a-mach.	She ran out.
Cheannaich sinn aran.	We bought (some) bread.
Choisich sibh air a' chabhsair.	You walked on the pavement.
Dh'ionnsaich iad a' Ghàidhlig.	They learnt (the) Gaelic.

Exercise 6.2

Translate

1 James closed the window.
2 Ann walked home.
3 Mary bought the paper.
4 Catherine drank her tea.
5 John sang a song.
6 Calum read the paper.
7 He told me.
8 I learnt Gaelic.
9 She ate bread.
10 William ran and closed the door.

49 Some more prepositional pronouns

ri 'to'

rium	to me	**ruinn/rinn**	to us
riut	to you	**ruibh/ribh**	to you
ris	to him/it	**riutha**	to them
rithe	to her/it		

Note: The **r** in **ruinn/rinn** and **ruibh/ribh** is pronounced with broad single **r**. It is difficult to translate the preposition **ri** exactly as its sense varies according to idiom. See below for examples.

do* 'to, for'			
dhomh[†]	to me	**dhuinn**	to us
dhut	to you	**dhuibh**	to you
dha	to him	**dhaibh**	to them
dhi	to her		

† **dhomh** but emphatic **dhòmhsa**.

50 Verbs and prepositions

There are very many verbs in Gaelic which are complemented by prepositions. **Ri** is frequently used with the verbs **can** 'say' and **bruidhinn** 'speak', e.g. **can rium** 'say to me', **bhruidhinn Seumas ris** 'James spoke to him'. **Do** is frequently used with the irregular verb **thoir** 'give, bring', e.g. **thoir dhomh** 'give (to) me'. Note that when using the following verbs and prepositions that the subject follows the verb directly and not the preposition, e.g. **bhruidhinn Seumas** (subject) **ri Anna** 'James spoke to Ann'. Here are some more examples consisting mostly of regular verbs which are complemented by prepositions. In each case the verbal root, i.e. the imperative 2nd singular form is given.

can ri	say to
bruidhinn ri	speak to
tachair ri	meet (with)
innis do	tell (to)
thoir do	give to
iarr air	ask
faighnich de / faighneachd de	ask (information) of, enquire of
còrd ri	enjoy (accord with)

Such prepositions combine in the usual way with nouns and pronouns. Here are some sample sentences in the past tense:

Thuirt Iain ri Dòmhnall...	John said to Donald...
Thug Anna pòg do Chalum.	Ann gave a kiss to Calum.
Bhruidhinn mi ri Seumas a-raoir.	I spoke to James last night.
Thachair Anna ri Màiri an-dè.	Ann met (with) Mary yesterday.
Dh'innis mi an naidheachd do Sheumas.	I told the story to James.
Dh'iarr mi air an tidsear.	I asked the teacher.
Chòrd an cèilidh rium.	I enjoyed the ceilidh. (*lit* the ceilidh accorded with-me)

51 More on the regular past tense: dependent forms

You will recall from **Lesson 4** the distinction between independent and dependent verbal forms. The forms given above for the past tense are the independent forms which are used independently and in other instances to be discussed shortly. The dependent past forms are formed by prefixing **do** to the independent past form:

Cha do dh'òl mi an tì.	I did not drink the tea.
An do bhrist Anna an uinneag?	Did Ann break the window?
Nach do cheannaich thu am pàipear?	Did you not buy the paper?
Cha do bhruidhinn Iain rithe.	John did not speak to her.
An do thachair thu ris an tidsear fhathast?	Did you meet the teacher yet?
Nach do dh'innis mi dhut mar-thà?	Did I not tell you already?
Cha do chòrd an oidhche riutha.	They did not enjoy the night.

6

51a 'Never', 'ever'

The Gaelic word for 'never', **riamh** is used with verbs in the past tense, e.g.

Cha do dh'òl mi lionn riamh.	I never drank beer.
Cha do shreap mi Beinn Nibheis riamh.	I never climbed Ben Nevis.
An do dh'ith thu bradan riamh?	Did you ever eat salmon?
Nach do thachair thu ri Iain riamh?	Did you never meet John?

Riamh can mean 'ever, always', e.g.

Bha sinn a' fuireach an Glaschu riamh.	We have always lived in Glasgow.

Riamh can in some dialects have future reference, e.g.

Cha tachair sin riamh.	That will never happen.

See also **Section 67b.**

51b 'Only'

The word for 'only' in Gaelic is **ach** which means literally 'but'. **Ach** is usually placed immediately before the subject or the object of the sentence. Consider the following examples:

Cha tàinig ach Anna. (subj)	Only Ann came.
Cha do dh'òl mi ach gloine fìon. (obj)	I drank only a glass of wine.
Chan eil mi ag iarraidh ach pìos beag. (obj)	I want only a small piece.

52 Independent and dependent verbal particles

We have defined independent verbal forms as being forms which occur 'independently', i.e. at the beginning of sentences or phrases/clauses. Similarly, we have defined dependent verbal forms as forms whose occurrence is 'dependent' upon the presence of particles like **cha** 'not', **an** 'is?', **nach** 'is ... not?' We refer to these particles as dependent particles. We will learn some other dependent verbal particles shortly. Independent verbal forms can also occur after certain verbal particles e.g. **ciamar a** 'how' and **cuin a** 'when'; such particles are referred to as independent particles. Consider the following examples:

INDEPENDENT VERBAL FORMS:

<u>Bha</u> Iain ann.	John was there.
<u>Ciamar a</u> bha an cèilidh?	How was the ceilidh?
<u>Cuin a</u> bha an cèilidh ann?	When was the ceilidh?
<u>Bhrist</u> thu an iuchair.	You broke the key.
<u>Ciamar a</u> bhrist thu an iuchair?	How did you break the key?
<u>Cuin a</u> bhrist thu an iuchair?	When did you break the key?

INDEPENDENT PARTICLES		DEPENDENT PARTICLES	
a	that, who, which	**cha**	not
	(*rel pron*)	**an**	*interr particle positive*
dè a?	what?	**nach**	*interr particle negative, negative form of rel pron, cjn etc.*
cò a?	who?		
ciamar a?	how?	**càite an?**†	where?
cuin a?††	when?	**far an**	where (the place that)
ged a	although	**gun**	that (*cjn*)
nuair a	when (the time that)	**gus an**	until
mar a	as, how	**nan**	if
ma	if	**mura**	if not mur (also **mur/mur an**)
na	what, that which	**mus**	before

† **Càite an** has the variant **cà an**, which occurs as **cà** before irregular **bheil** and **robh**.
†† **Cuin** in some dialects has the variant **cuine**.

Examples:

INDEPENDENT:

An duine a <u>chunnaic</u> mi a-raoir.	The man that I saw last night.
Cò a <u>bhrist</u> an uinneag?	Who broke the window?
Ciamar a <u>chòrd</u> an cèilidh riut?	How did you enjoy the ceilidh?
Cuin a <u>thill</u> thu dhachaigh?	When did you return home?
Chan aithne dhomh e ged a <u>thachair</u> mi ris.	I don't know him although I met him.
Dè a <u>thuirt</u> Anna?	What did Ann say?
Ma <u>cheannaich</u> thu am pàipear.	If you bought the paper.
Seo na <u>tha</u> agam.	Here's what I have.

DEPENDENT:

An duine <u>nach fhaca</u> mi a-raoir.	The man that I didn't see last night.
Càite an <u>do dh'fhalbh</u> iad?	Where did they go?
Cha <u>do choisich</u> sinn an oidhche ud.	We did not walk that night.
An <u>do thachair</u> thu ri Tormod riamh?	Did you ever meet Norman?
Nach <u>do leugh</u> thu an leabhar aig Iain?	Did you not read John's book?
Càite an <u>do cheannaich</u> thu na suiteis?	Where did you buy the sweets?
Tha an còta agad far an <u>do dh'fhàg</u> thu e.	Your coat is where you left it.

6

52a How to recognise an independent verbal particle

All independent particles (with the exception of **ma** 'if' and **na** 'that which') end in the particle **a**, which as we will see in a later lesson is in fact the relative pronoun **a** 'that' (see **Section 77**). However, the **a** is frequently dropped in writing following particles ending in a vowel such as **cò** 'who' and **dè** 'what' in order to reflect pronunciation, but is retained here for reasons of clarity.

> USEFUL RULE
>
> Verbal particles which end in **a** are independent particles and are therefore followed by independent verbal forms. All other verbal particles (except **ma** and **na**) are dependent and are followed by dependent verbal forms.

53 Understanding the difference between:

cò a?	who?	~	**a**	who
cuin a?	when?	~	**nuair a**	when
càite an?	where?	~	**far an**	where
dè a?	what?	~	**na**	what
ciamar a?	how?	~	**mar a**	how, as

The question mark following the words in the first column indicates that these forms are question (also called interrogative) forms. Note that many of them begin with **c-** (compare English **wh-**). The forms without question marks are not question forms. **A** 'who' is a relative pronoun for which sometimes 'that' is used. **Nuair a** means 'when' in the sense 'the time that'. **Far an** means 'where' in the sense 'the place that'. **Na** means 'what' in the sense 'that which' or 'all that'. **Mar a** means 'how' in the sense 'the way' or 'the manner'.

The question forms of 'who, when, where, what' are usually used with idioms such as **tha fios aig** 'know', **innis do** 'tell to', etc. e.g.

Chan eil fios agam cò a chuir an litir.
I don't know who sent the letter.

A bheil fios agaibh cuin a thàinig an trèan?
Do you know when the train came?

A bheil fios agad càite a bheil an stèisean?
Do you know where the station is?

Chan eil fios aig Anna dè a thachair.
Ann doesn't know what happened.

Innis dhomh cò a bha ann.
Tell me who was there.

Note: some dialects use **far an** 'where' and **na** 'what' in indirect questions like the above.

The difference between **ma** 'if' and **an** 'if, whether' is discussed in **Lesson 10**, **Section 88**.

Vocabulary

cèilidh (*m*)	/kʲeːli/	ceilidh
cuir (*vb*)	/kurʲ/	put
doras (*m*)	/d̪ɔrəs/	door
dùin (*vb*)	/d̪uːɲ/	close
iuchair (*f*)	/juxərʲ/	key
leabhar (*m*)	/ʎɔ-ər/	book
òg (*adj*)	/ɔːg/	young
seinn (*vb*)	/ʃeiɲ/	sing
sgìth (*adj*)	/skʲiː/	tired

Exercise 6.3

Translate

1   Who closed the door?
2   When did they go out?
3   Where did you put the key?
4   I didn't tell him.
5   Did you enjoy the ceilidh?
6   I read that book when I was young.
7   Leave it where you got (found) it.
8   There's the man that sang at the ceilidh.
9   I didn't see James if he was there.
10 He came although he was tired.

6

54 Time

Dè an uair a tha e?	What time is it?
Tha e ...	It is ...

In telling the time, the word which corresponds to 'o'clock' in English is **uair**, which means 'hour' or 'time'. The singular form **uair** is used with **dà** 'two', but the plural **uairean** is used with the numerals from three to ten. Note that **aon** 'one' is not used to translate 'one (o'clock)' in Scottish Gaelic (**aon uair** can, however, be used in Cape Breton Gaelic) but is used in the translation of 'eleven (o'clock)'. The time in simple hours is therefore as follows:

uair	one o'clock
dà uair	two o'clock
trì uairean	three o'clock
ceithir uairean	four o'clock
còig uairean	five o'clock
sia uairean	six o'clock
seachd uairean	seven o'clock
ochd uairean	eight o'clock
naoi uairean	nine o'clock
deich uairean	ten o'clock
aon uair deug	eleven o'clock
dà uair dheug	twelve o'clock

Note the lenition of **deug** in **dà uair dheug**; it is often pronounced as if it were **dà reug. Meadhan latha** is used for 'midday' and **meadhan oidhche** is used for 'midnight'. If we want to indicate time a.m., we usually add **anns a' mhadainn**, literally 'in the morning'. If we want to indicate p.m., we usually add **feasgar** which literally means 'evening'. However, there is some overlap between **feasgar** and **as t-oidhche / a dh'oidhche** which literally means 'at night'. **Feasgar** is generally used up to about 6 o'clock and in some cases possibly up until 9 o'clock. **As t-oidhche / a dh'oidhche** are generally used from about 9 o'clock onwards although when using **feasgar** there is some overlap, with 9 o'clock as a rough boundary.

54a   Other times of the year

Study the following:

a' Bhliadhna Ùr	(the) New Year
Oidhche Challainn	Hogmanay, New Year's Eve
an Nollaig	Christmas
a' Chàisg	Easter
Latha Bealltainn	May Day
Oidhche Shamhna	Halloween
am-bliadhna	this year
an-uiridh	last year
a' bhòn-uiridh	the year before last
an-dè	yesterday
a' bhòn-dè	the day before yesterday
a-raoir	last night
a' bhòn-raoir	the night before last
a-màireach	tomorrow
an-earar	the day after tomorrow

54b 'Last', 'next'

Study the following phrases:

a' bhliadhna (seo/sa) a chaidh	last year
an t-seachdain (seo/sa) a chaidh	last week
a' mhìos (seo/sa) a chaidh	last month

A' bhliadhna seo/sa a chaidh literally means 'this year that has passed'. The **a** before **chaidh** is usually elided in speech. **Seo/sa** can also be omitted. The adverb **seachad** 'past' can also be used with this idiom:

a' bhliadhna a chaidh seachad	last year (*lit* the year that went past)
an ath-bhliadhna	next year
an ath-sheachdain	next week
an ath-oidhch(e)	tomorrow night

Ath* 'next' is a leniting word and is usually preceded by the article **an**. Note that the common adverbial expressions 'next year', 'next week' and 'tomorrow night' are spelled with a hyphen; note the distinction between **an ath-sheachdain** 'next week' and **an ath sheachdain** 'the following week' and

an ath-bhliadhna 'next year' and **an ath bhliadhna** 'the following year'. Otherwise no hyphen is needed (when **ath** means 'next, following'). Here are some other useful phrases involving **ath***:

an ath dhuine	the next person
an ath fhear (*m*)/**t(h)è** (*f*)	the next one (*m*, *f*)
an ath dhoras	(the) next door
an ath mhìos	the next month
an ath latha	(the) next day

'Next' can also be translated as follows:

a' bhliadhna seo/sa a' tighinn	next year
an t-seachdain seo/sa a' tighinn	next week
a' mhìos seo/sa a' tighinn	next month

A' bhliadhna seo a' tighinn literally means 'this year coming'. The **a'** before **tighinn** is usually elided in speech.

55 'Some'

The word for 'some' in Gaelic is **eigin** which is affixed to a small number of nouns, e.g.

cuideigin	some person, someone
rudeigin	something
uaireigin	sometime
àiteigin	somewhere
tèigin	someone (*f*)
feareigin	someone (*m*)

The phrase **air choreigin** 'some … or other' can also be used with this group and is regularly used with other nouns, e.g.

taigh air choreigin	some house or other
leabhar air choreigin	some book or other
rud air choreigin	some thing or other

55a *'Feadhainn'*

The indefinite pronoun **feadhainn** (*f*) can mean 'some people' or 'some things', e.g.

Dh'fhalbh feadhainn a Ghlaschu agus thill feadhainn eile à Peairt.
Some people went away to Glasgow and others returned from Perth.

Tha dealbhannan aig Màiri agus tha feadhainn aig Anna cuideachd.
Mary has photographs and Ann also has some.

On the use of plural adjectives with the collective noun **feadhainn**, see **Section 92**.

56 'Every'

The word for 'every' in Gaelic is **a h-uile** which prefixes **h-** to vowels; **gach** is also used, e.g.

a h-uile rud	every thing	**gach rud**
a h-uile duine	every man, everyone	**gach duine**
a h-uile h-àite	every place	**gach àite**
a h-uile h-uair	every time	**gach uair**

Vocabulary

a h-uile duine	/ə hulə d̪u ɲə/	everyone
a' bhòn-dè (*adv*)	/ə vɔːɲ d̠ʲeː/	the day before yesterday
aithnich (*vb*)	/aɲiç/	recognise, know
an Fhraing (*f*)	/əŋ ɾaiŋʲgʲ/	France
an t-Òban (*m*)	/əŋ t̪ɔːban/	Oban
an-diugh (*adv*)	/əɲ d̠ʲu/	today
bho chionn ghoirid (*adv*)	/ɔ çuːɲ ɣɤɾʲəd̠ʲ/	recently
bruidhinn (*vb*)	/bruɪ-iɲ/	speak
ceann-suidhe (*m*)	/kʲauŋ suɪjə/	president
cothrom (*m*)	/kɔɾəm/	chance
cuideigin (*f*)	/kud̠ʲigʲin/	somebody
cùirt (*f*)	/kuːɾstʲ/	court
dad às ùr?	/d̠ad̠ as uːr/	anything new?
dùthaich (*f*)	/d̠uː-iç/	country, district
goid (*vb*)	/gɤd̠ʲ/	steal, rob
gu ruige (*cmp prp*)	/gə ɾugʲə/	to
gu sealladh sealbh ort	/gə ʃal̪ə ʃ[al̪ə]v ɔɾst̪/	asseveration of surprise or disbelief: good lord!
leugh (*vb*)	/ʎeː(v)/	read
manaidsear (*m*)	/manad̠ʲʃɛɾʲ/	manager
meàirleach (*m*),	/mʲaːɾʎex/,	thief, robber
meàirlich (*pl*)	/mʲaːɾʎiç/	
mìltean (*pl*)	/miːl̪t̠ʲən/	thousands
mòran (*adv*)	/moːran/	much
muilleanan (*pl*)	/muʎɛnən/	millions
pàipear-naidheachd (*m*)	/pɛːhpɛɾʲ n̪ɛ̃-əxk/	newspaper
poileas (*m*)	/pɔləs/	police
prìosanach (*m*),	/prʲiːsanəx/, /prʲiːsaniç/	prisoner, prisoners
prìosanaich (*pl*)		
sgeul (*m*)	/skʲiaɫ/	sign, news
tagh (*vb*)	/t̪ɤɣ/	elect, select
taghadh-pàrlamaid (*m*)	/t̪ɤ-əɣ paːɾl̪əmɛd̠ʲ/	parliamentary election
teich (*vb*)	/tʲeç/	escape, flee
Telebhisean (*m*) **na Gàidhlig**	/tɛləviʃən nə gaːligʲ/	Gaelic Television

CÒMHRADH (CONVERSATION)

A bheil dad às ùr?

Anna	An do leugh thu am pàipear-naidheachd an-diugh?
Sìm	Cha do leugh. Cha d' fhuair mi cothrom fhathast. A bheil dad às ùr ann?
Anna	Tha. Fhuair Telebhisean na Gàidhlig airgead mòr: muilleanan.
Sìm	Gu sealladh sealbh ort!
Anna	Agus theich prìosanaich a bha a' dol gu ruige cùirt. Thachair sin an t-seachdain seo a chaidh.
Sìm	Agus nach robh taghadh-pàrlamaid anns an Fhraing?
Anna	Bha agus thagh iad ceann-suidhe ùr air a' phàrlamaid aca. Ach cha do chòrd sin ris a h-uile duine.
Sìm	Dè a thachair anns an dùthaich seo bho chionn ghoirid?
Anna	Cha do thachair mòran. Bhrist meàirlich a-staigh dhan a' bhanca anns an Òban. Agus ghoid iad mìltean.
Sìm	Dh'innis cuideigin sin dhomh a' bhòn-dè ceart gu leòr. Cha do rug am poileas orra fhathast, chuala mi.
Anna	Cha do rug. Bhruidhinn am poileas ris a' mhanaidsear ach ged a dh'aithnich esan na meàirlich, chan eil sgeul aca orra.

6

TRANSLATION

Anything new?

Ann	Have[†] you read the newspaper today?
Simon	No. I haven't had a chance yet. Is there anything new in it?
Ann	There is. Gaelic Television got a lot of money: millions.
Simon	Good lord!
Ann	And prisoners who were going to court escaped. That happened last week.
Simon	And wasn't there a parliamentary election in France?
Ann	Yes, and they elected a new president for their parliament. But that didn't please everyone.
Simon	What happened in this country recently?
Ann	Not much happened. Robbers broke into a bank in Oban. And they stole thousands.
Simon	Somebody told me that the day before yesterday right enough. The police didn't catch them yet, I heard.
Ann	No. The police spoke to the manager but although he recognised the thieves, they don't have a sign of them.

† Note that Scottish Gaelic uses the simple past tense here where English uses the perfect.

Lesson 7

57 The genitive case

Gaelic, as well as having a nominative and a prepositional case also has a genitive case, denoted here by G or *gen*. The genitive has various functions. It can be used (a) to express possession and (b) to give adjectival or attributive force to a noun.

(a) **taigh Dhòmhnaill** (G)	Donald's house
(b) **sgian-arain** (G)	bread-knife

(a) Possession

There are two ways of expressing that something belongs to someone, only one of which involves the genitive case:

(i)	POSSESSEE	+	POSSESSOR (GEN)
	taigh		**Dhòmhnaill**

Donald's house

Here are some other examples:

leabhar Sheumais (G)	James' book
cat Mòraig (G)	Morag's cat
mac ministeir (G)	a son of a minister
ad caileig(e) (G)	a girl's hat

It will be clear from the above that the genitive of masculine proper names is formed by leniting the initial consonant of the noun and by slenderising the final consonant. The genitive of feminine proper names is formed by slenderising the final consonant of the noun. These rules apply only when there are initial consonants to lenite and/or when there are non-slender final consonants to slenderise. Consider the following examples whose genitive and nominative forms are identical:

leabhar Iain	John's book
cat Alasdair	Alasdair's cat
cù Anna	Ann's dog
càr Catrìona	Catherine's car

The alternative possessive construction is formed as follows:

(ii)	ART	+	POSSESSEE	+	AIG	+	POSSESSOR
	an		**taigh**		**aig**		**Dòmhnall**

Donald's house

This construction should be familiar to you. It is essentially the 'alternative possessive construction' which we learnt in **Lesson 2, Section 15**. Here are some further examples:

an leabhar aig Seumas	James' book
an cat aig Mòrag	Morag's cat
an leabhar aig Iain	John's book
an cat aig Aonghas	Angus' cat
an cù aig Anna	Ann's dog
an càr aig Catrìona	Catherine's car

(b) Adjectival force

The genitive is also used to give adjectival or attributive force to a noun. In other words, if a noun is used adjectivally, it appears in the genitive case. Let us compare the following two noun phrases:

sgian <u>bheag</u>	a small knife
sgian-<u>arain</u> (G)	a bread-knife

It is clear that **beag** and **arain** both function as attributive adjectives: they both tell us more about **sgian** 'knife' and as adjectives they both follow the noun they qualify. However, **beag** is an adjective proper and **ara(i)n** is a noun. When **aran** 'bread' is used adjectivally or attributively it appears in the genitive case. The genitive of **aran** is **arain**. Hyphens are used in such noun phrases when they are deemed to be compounds. (Compound noun formation is beyond the scope of this book.) Here are some further examples with the genitive noun underlined:

leabhar-<u>sgoile</u>	a school book
solas-<u>sràide</u>	a street light
seòmar-<u>leughaidh</u>	a reading-room

Even when the genitive indicates possession, the genitive noun also acts as an adjective. Consider the following examples, the genitive noun being underlined in each case:

mac <u>ministeir</u>	a minister's son
còta <u>balaich</u>	a boy's coat
ad <u>caileig(e)</u>	a girl's hat

57a Forming the genitive case

Leaving aside irregular nouns, there are five types of genitive formation, the most important and productive of which are types 1 and 2 below. All regular genitive forms are based on the nominative singular form. In the table below, '+ slenderisation' means that the genitive is formed by slenderising the nominative singular form. Similarly, '+a' means that the genitive is formed by adding **a** to the nominative singular form.

Type	Formation	
1	+ **slenderisation**	applies to masculine nouns only
2	+ **slenderisation + e**	applies to feminine nouns only
3	+ **a**	applies to masculine and feminine nouns
4	+ **ach**	applies to feminine nouns (usually ending in -**ir**)
5	**no change**	applies to masculine and feminine nouns

The process of slenderisation may affect the preceding vowel (as was pointed out in the introduction; see also **Appendix 1**) e.g. **cas** > **coise**; **bòrd** > **bùird**; **mac** > **mic**; **caileag** > **caileige**; **cailleach** > **caillich(e)**; **ceòl** > **ciùil**, etc. Watch out for examples below.

TYPE 1: + SLENDERISATION

Masculine nouns only

NOMINATIVE	GENITIVE	EXAMPLE	
cat cat	**cait**	**biadh cait**	cat or cat's food
ministear minister	**ministeir**	**taigh ministeir**	a minister's house
balach boy	**balaich**	**ad balaich**	a boy's hat
bòrd table	**bùird**	**cas bùird**	leg of a table
ceòl music	**ciùil**	**fear-ciùil**	a music man, musician

TYPE 2: + SLENDERISATION + E

Feminine nouns only

NOMINATIVE	GENITIVE	EXAMPLE	
cluas ear	**cluaise**	**fàinne cluaise**	an earring
cas foot, leg	**coise**	**ball-coise**	football
sgoil school	**sgoile**	**maighstear-sgoile**	school teacher
caileag girl	**caileig(e)**	**còta caileig(e)**	a girl's coat
cailleach old woman	**caillich(e)**	**taigh caillich(e)**	an old woman's house

In type 2, the addition of -**e** in polysyllabic nouns can be described as conservative literary Gaelic, and the use of '+slenderisation' as traditional / conservative spoken Gaelic. The masculine noun **taigh** 'house' irregularly forms its genitive by adding -**e** (**taighe**).

TYPE 3: + A

Masculine and feminine nouns

NOMINATIVE	GENITIVE	EXAMPLE	
pìob (*f*) pipe	**pìoba**	**ceòl pìoba**	pipe music
loch (*m*) lake	**locha**	**uisge locha**	lake water
fiodh (*m*) wood	**fiodha**	**each fiodha**	a wooden horse

A subtype de-slenderises the final consonant before adding **-a**, and in some instances the root vowel may change:

NOMINATIVE	GENITIVE	EXAMPLE	
feòil (*f*) meat	**feòla**	**pìos feòla**	a piece of meat
sùil (*f*) eye	**sùla**	**galar sùla**	eye disease
fuil (*f*) blood	**fala**	**dòrtadh fala**	bloodshed
muir (*f*) sea	**mara**	**iasg mara**	sea-fish

7

TYPE 4: (+ SYNCOPE) + (E)ACH

Feminine nouns only
Note that the final syllable is lost (called *syncope*) when **(e)ach** is added.

NOMINATIVE	GENITIVE	EXAMPLE	
obair work	**obrach**	**latha obrach**	a work day
litir letter	**litreach**	**bogsa-litreach**	a letter-box
cathair city	**cathrach**	**bus cathrach**	a city bus

TYPE 5: NO CHANGE

Masculine and feminine nouns

NOMINATIVE	GENITIVE	EXAMPLE	
baile (*m*) town	**baile**	**meadhan baile**	middle of a town
duine (*m*) man	**duine**	**ad duine**	a man's hat
bus (*m*) bus	**bus**	**dràibhear bus**	a bus driver
bainne (*m*) milk	**bainne**	**gloine bainne**	a glass of milk
tì (*f*) tea	**tì**	**cupa tì**	a cup of tea
colaiste (*f*) college	**colaiste**	**cùrsa colaiste**	a college course
naidheachd (*f*) news	**naidheachd**	**pàipear-naidheachd**	a newspaper

Types 1 and 2 are by far the most commonly used. Type 5 is used for all nouns with final vowels or final **-chd**, and also for the majority of recent loan-words from English. In what may be termed progressive spoken Gaelic, type 5 (i.e. the use of nominative for genitive) is often used as a variant in types 1–4. Note: all subsequent nouns in this lesson will have a number attached to indicate which genitive formation they have. For irregular genitive formations, see **Section 58a**.

57b The article in the genitive case

The article changes form in the genitive. We must distinguish between masculine and feminine forms. The masculine forms are **an*** which we have met before (see nominative feminine singular and prepositional singular forms of the article, **Lessons 2** and **6**). The feminine forms are **na** which are discussed below.

MASCULINE: *an**

a' + lenition	before all lenitable consonants (except **d t s f**; see **Appendix 7**), i.e. **b c g m p**
an t-	before **s** (**sl sr sn**), NOT **sg sp st sm**
an + lenition	before **f** (which becomes **fh**)
an	otherwise, i.e. before **d n t l r** and all vowels

FEMININE: *na*

na h-	before all vowels
na	otherwise

Some examples:

NOMINATIVE	GENITIVE	
am bainne (*m*, 5)	**a' bhainne**	of the milk
an t-uisge (*m*, 5)	**an uisge**	of the water
am fear (*m*, 1)	**an fhir**	of the man
an leabhar (*m*, 1)	**an leabhair**	of the book
a' chluas (*f*, 2)	**na cluaise**	of the ear
an obair (*f*, 4)	**na h-obrach**	of the work

Note: numbers indicating genitive type are given in **Lessons 7** and **8** only.

58 Double definite article

We have seen that when two nouns come together in the same noun phrase where the second noun is adjectival or attibutive with respect to the first (e.g. **leabhar Sheumais** 'James' book', **sgian-arain** 'a bread-knife'), the second noun appears in the genitive case. When the second noun is a definite noun (i.e. a proper noun or a noun preceded by the article or a possessive pronoun, see **Section 20**) the first noun may NOT be preceded by the definite article.

Am mac 'the son' and **am ministear** 'the minister' combine to give **mac a' mhinisteir** (with only one article) which means 'the son of the minister' or 'the minister's son' (note that the English counterpart contains only one article also). The definiteness of such noun phrases is marked by the definiteness of the second noun only. Here are some more examples:

MASCULINE

fear an taighe	the man of the house, compère
fear a' bhainne	the man of the milk, the milkman
ceann a' chait	the head of the cat, the cat's head
meadhan a' bhaile	the centre of the town
leabhar a' ghille	the book of the boy, the boy's book

FEMININE

gloine na h-uinneig(e)	the glass of the window
mac na caileig(e)	the son of the girl, the girl's son
solas na grèine	the light of the sun, the sunlight
duilleagan na craoibhe	the leaves of the tree

Note that **grèine** is the genitive singular of **grian** (f).

> ### DDA RULE
> The DDA rule (the Double Definite Article rule) states that if the 'possessor' is a definite noun the preceding noun (the 'possessee') will not be preceded by the article.

In a string of nouns connected in a genitival relation only the last noun (the possessor) appears in the genitive, e.g.

bràthair a' bhalaich (*gen*)	the boy's brother
taigh bràthair a' bhalaich (*gen*)	the boy's brother's house
doras taigh bràthair a' bhalaich (*gen*)	the door of the boy's brother's house

58a Genitive of irregular nouns

NOMINATIVE		GENITIVE		EXAMPLE
athair (*m*)	father	**athar**	**càr a h-athar**	her father's car
bean (*f*)	wife	**mnà/ mnatha**	**còta na mnà/ mnatha**	the wife's coat
biadh (*m*)	food	**bidhe**	**taigh-bidhe**	a restaurant
bò (*f*)	cow	**bà**	**bainne na bà**	the cow's milk
bràthair (*m*)	brother	**bràthar**	**taigh do bhràthar**	your brother's house
ceòl (*m*)	music	**ciùil**	**fear-ciùil**	a man of music, a musician
cù (*m*)	dog	**coin**	**biadh a' choin**	the dog's food
deoch (*f*)	drink	**dighe/ dibhe**	**buaidh na dighe/ dibhe**	the influence of drink
leabaidh (*f*)	bed	**leapa**	**aodach leapa**	bed clothes
mac (*m*)	son	**mic**	**bean do mhic**	your son's wife

màthair (f)	mother	màthar	athair mo mhàthar	my mother's father
piuthar (f)	sister	peathar	caraid mo pheathar	my sister's friend
sgian (f)	knife	sgine/ sgèine	bàrr na sgine/sgèine	the top of the knife
taigh (m)	house	taighe	doras an taighe	the door of the house

Vocabulary

biadh (m, irreg)	/biəɣ/	food
cnoc (m, 1), **cnuic** (gen)	/krɔ̃xk/, /krũɛ̃çkʲ/	hill
dath (m, 3)	/d̪a/	colour
doras (m, 1)	/d̪ɔrəs/	door
leabhar (m, 1)	/ʎɔ-ər/	book
mac (m, irreg)	/mãhk/, /mãxk/	son
mullach (m)	/mũʈəx/	top
sagart (m, 1)	/sagər(s)t̪/	priest
sgoil (f, 2)	/skɔl/	school
sneachd(a) (m, 5)	/ʃnɛxk(ə)/	snow

Exercise 7.1

Translate

1   the son of the priest
2   the colour of the snow
3   the top of the hill
4   the door of the school
5   my brother's sister
6   the key of the house
7   my sister's car
8   the cat's food
9   James' father
10 Catherine's book

59 Surnames

In surnames the element following **Mac** is usually a noun in the genitive, e.g.

MacDhòmhnaill	MacDonald	(*lit* 'the son of Donald')
MacAonghais	MacInnes	(*lit* 'the son of Angus')
Mac a' Ghobhainn	Smith	(*lit* 'the son of the smith')
Mac an t-Saoir	MacIntyre	(*lit* 'the son of the carpenter')

Nic rather than **Mac** is used for females; **Nic** derives from **nighean** 'daughter' + **mhic** (*gen* of **mac** 'son'). Examples:

NicDhòmhnaill	MacDonald
NicAonghais	MacInnes
Nic a' Ghobhainn	Smith
Nic an t-Saoir	MacIntyre

60 Adverbs of quantity

On occasions you will need to talk about quantities; you may have too much, too little, a lot or not enough of something, etc.

Study the following:

mòran	much, many
beagan	little, small amount
tòrr	a lot
cus	too much, too many (very many)
gu leòr/pailteas	enough, plenty
tuilleadh	more (in sense 'additional amount')
barrachd	more (in sense of 'surplus')

These words can be used on their own as nouns, e.g.

Chan eil mòran an seo.	There is not much here.
Tha beagan agam.	I have a little.
Tha tòrr an sin.	There is a lot there.
Dh'òl Dòmhnall cus a-raoir.	Donald drank too much last night.
A bheil gu leòr agad?	Do you have enough?
Tha mi ag iarraidh tuilleadh.	I want more.

These words can also be used with a following noun in which case the following noun appears in the genitive:

mòran airgid (G)	much money
beagan salainn (G)	a little salt
tòrr siùcair (G)	a lot of sugar
cus feòla (G)	too much meat
gu leòr/pailteas càise (G)	enough/plenty of cheese
tuilleadh bidhe (G)	more food
barrachd airgid (G)	more money

However, **mòran** and **beagan** may also be used with the preposition **de** 'of':

mòran de dh'airgead	much money
beagan de shalann	a little salt

On the use of partitive **de** 'of', see **Section 83**.

61 The verbal noun and the genitive case

In **Lesson 3**, we discussed the periphrastic construction involving the verb **tha** and verbal nouns. The direct object of this periphrastic construction normally appears in the genitive when the object is a definite noun (see **Section 20**), e.g.

Tha mi a' leughadh <u>an leabhair</u> (G).	I am reading the book.
Tha e a' seinn <u>an òrain</u> (G).	He is singing the song.
Tha i ag ithe <u>na feòla</u> (G).	She is eating the meat.

The use of the genitive is easily understood when we consider a literal translation of the above examples:

I am at the reading of the book.

He is at the singing of the song.

She is at the eating of the meat.

The genitive is generally not used when the noun in indefinite, e.g.

Tha mi a' leughadh <u>leabhar</u>.	I am reading a book.
Tha e a' gabhail <u>òran</u>.	He is singing a song.
Tha i ag ithe <u>feòil</u>.	She is eating meat.

If the verbal noun in question is complemented by a preposition, the (indirect) object of such verbs does not appear in the genitive since it follows a preposition, in which case the prepositional (P) form may be used. Here are some examples:

Bha mi a' bruidhinn ri Seumas.	I was talking to James.
Tha Calum a' toirt pòg dhan a' chaileig (P).	Calum is giving a kiss to the girl/Calum is kissing the girl
Bha mi ag innse naidheachd dhan a' chaillich (P).	I was telling a story to the old woman.
Bha an cèilidh a' còrdadh ris a' chloinn (P).	The children were enjoying the ceilidh (*lit* the ceilidh was according with the children).

Vocabulary

ceannach (*vn*)	/kʲaɳəx/	buying
ceòl (*m*, 1)	/kʲɔːɫ/	music
doras (*m*, 1)	/d̪ɔrəs/	door
dùnadh (*vn*)	/d̪uːnəɣ/	closing
èisteachd (*vn*) **ri**	/eːʃtʲəxk rʲi/	listening to
fàgail (*vn*)	/faːgal/	leaving
fosgladh (*vn*)	/fɔsgɫəɣ/	opening
gabhail (*vn*)	/ga-al/	singing (when used with **òran** 'song')
Gàidhlig (*f*, 5)	/gaːligʲ/	Gaelic
innse (*vn*) **do**	/ĩːʃə d̪ə/	telling to, relating to
ithe (*vn*)	/içə/	eating
leabhar (*m*, 1)	/ʎɔ-ər/	book
naidheachd (*f*, 5)	/ɳɛ̃-əxk/	news
òran (*m*, 1)	/ɔːran/	song
tì (*f*, 5)	/tiː/	tea
tuigsinn (*vn*)	/t̪ugʲʃiɲ/	understanding
uinneag (*f*, 2)	/ũɲag/	window

7

Exercise 7.2

Translate

1 We are leaving the house today.
2 Are they eating the food?
3 Who is singing the song?
4 They are not listening to the music.
5 We were drinking the tea.
6 Were you telling the news to Ann?
7 She understands (the) Gaelic.
8 They are buying the book.
9 I am opening the door.
10 She is closing the window.

62 Composite prepositions

The prepositions which we have met so far have been simple prepositions consisting of monosyllabic words. These prepositions are followed by the prepositional form (of the article and of feminine nouns) in Gaelic. There are, however, other prepositions which we may call **composite prepositions** which consist of two words, one of which is a simple preposition. There are two types, the distinction between them depending upon the position of the simple preposition; the simple preposition may be (A) the second element or (B) the first element.

Type A: word + preposition = new composite preposition

coltach ri	like
còmhla ri	along with
timcheall air	around
tarsainn air	across, over
seachad air	past
faisg air	near, close to

The prepositional form of the article and of feminine nouns are used following these composite prepositions since their final element is a simple preposition:

coltach ri seann chù	like an old dog
còmhla ri mo phiuthair (P)	(along) with my sister
timcheall air a' chladach	around the shore
tarsainn air a' bhalla	over the wall
seachad air a' chaillich (P)	past the old woman
faisg air a' chathair	near the city

Type B: preposition + noun = new composite preposition

air cùl	behind
air beulaibh	in front
(air) feadh	throughout
an aghaidh	against
an dèidh	after
mu dheidhinn	about, concerning
os cionn	over, above
ri taobh	beside
a dh'ionnsaigh	to, towards
às aonais	without, in the absence of
airson (=**air** + **son**)	for (the sake of)

A noun following these composite prepositions appears in the genitive. This is illustrated by the following example:

ri taobh a' chait (G)	beside the cat

Ri taobh means literally 'by side'. When a noun, e.g. **an cat** 'the cat' follows, this becomes 'by the side of the cat', hence the need for the genitive. Most of the above composite (type B) prepositions can be translated by using two words in English which would use 'of' before a following noun, e.g. **air cùl** 'on back (of)', **air beulaibh** 'in front (of)', **an aghaidh** 'in face (of)', etc. Traditionally **air** + **son** is written as one word, **airson**.

Some examples:

airson do mhàthar (G)	for your mother
air cùl an taighe (G)	behind the house
air feadh na h-Alba (G)	throughout Scotland
an aghaidh na gaoithe (G)	against the wind

an dèidh a' gheama (G)	after the game
mu dheidhinn a' ghaoil (G)	about love
os cionn an dorais (G)	above the door
ri taobh a' bhalaich (G)	beside the boy
a dh'ionnsaigh a' bhaile (G)	towards the town
às aonais mo pheathar (G)	without my sister

62a Prepositions followed by the genitive

There is a small number of **simple prepositions** which are followed by the genitive:

chun	to
far	off
rè	during
tarsainn	across

Here are some examples:

chun a' bhaile (G)	to the town
far a' bhùird (G)	off the table
rè na h-oidhche (G)	during the night
tarsainn na pàirce (G)	across the park

Do not confuse **far** 'off' which is a preposition and therefore only used before nouns, with **far an** 'where' which is a verbal particle and is therefore only used before verbs.

Fad 'length' acts with the force of a preposition, e.g.

fad na h-oidhche	all night, *lit* the length / duration of the night
fad na h-ùine	all the time, *lit* the length / duration of the time
fad an latha	all day, *lit* the length / duration of the day

Composite prepositions with pronouns

Type A

Pronoun objects of type A composite pronouns combine in the usual way with the final preposition:

coltach rium	like me
còmhla riut	along with you
timcheall oirnn	around us
tarsainn orra	across them
seachad oirbh	past you (*pl*)

Type B

Pronoun objects of type B composite prepositions do not follow the preposition as expected. Instead the pronoun appears as a possessive pronoun and precedes the noun part of the composite preposition. 'Behind me' is not **air cùl mi** but **air mo chùlaibh**, literally 'on my back(s)'. Here are other examples:

AIR CÙL		AIR BEULAIBH	
air mo chùlaibh	behind me	air mo bheulaibh	in front of me
air do chùlaibh	behind you	air do bheulaibh	in front of you
air a chùlaibh	behind him/it	air a bheulaibh	in front of him/it
air a cùlaibh	behind her/it	air a beulaibh	in front of her/it
air ar cùlaibh	behind us	air ar beulaibh	in front of us
air ur cùlaibh	behind you	air ur beulaibh	in front of you
air an cùlaibh	behind them	air am beulaibh	in front of them
AN AGHAIDH		AN DÈIDH	
nam aghaidh	against me	nam dhèidh	after me
nad aghaidh	against you	nad dhèidh	after you
na aghaidh	against him/it	na dhèidh	after him/it
na h-aghaidh	against her/it	na dèidh	after her/it
nar n-aghaidh	against us	nar dèidh	after us
nur n-aghaidh	against you	nur dèidh	after you
nan aghaidh	against them	nan dèidh	after them
MU DHEIDHINN		RI TAOBH	
mu mo dheidhinn	about me	ri mo thaobh	beside me
mu do dheidhinn	about you	ri do thaobh	beside you
mu a dheidhinn	about him/it	ri a thaobh	beside him/it
mu a deidhinn	about her/it	ri a taobh	beside her/it
mu ar deidhinn	about us	ri ar taobh	beside us
mu ur deidhinn	about you	ri ur taobh	beside you
mu an deidhinn	about them	ri an taobh	beside them
AIRSON		OS CIONN	
air mo shon	for me	os mo chionn	over me
air do shon	for you	os do chionn	over you
air a shon	for him/it	os a chionn	over him/it
air a son	for her/it	os a cionn	over her/it
air ar son	for us	os ar cionn	over us
air ur son	for you	os ur cionn	over you
air an son	for them	os an cionn	over them
A DH'IONNSAIGH		ÀS AONAIS	
gam ionnsaigh	towards me	às m' aonais	without me
gad ionnsaigh	towards you	às d' aonais	without you
ga ionnsaigh	towards him/it	às a aonais	without him/it
ga h-ionnsaigh	towards her/it	às a h-aonais	without her/it
gar n-ionnsaigh	towards us	às ar n-aonais	without us
gur n-ionnsaigh	towards you	às ur n-aonais	without you
gan ionnsaigh	towards them	às an aonais	without them

Exercise 7.3

Translate

1 behind me
2 in front of you
3 above him
4 beside her
5 without us
6 like them
7 along with me
8 around us
9 past it (*m*)
10 to the door

63 More on time

We have already learnt how to tell the time in simple hours. We will now learn how to tell other times. The word for 'after/past' is **an dèidh** and the word for 'to' is **gu**. The counting form of the numerals follows both **gu** and **an dèidh** i.e. **a** precedes the numerals from two to ten e.g. **a dhà, a trì, ..., a h-ochd** etc. However, the **a** is generally elided in speech and usually in writing following **gu**; it will be retained here for reasons of clarity. The word for 'quarter' is **cairteal** (**ceathramh** in some dialects) and the word for 'half' is **lethuair**.

cairteal an dèidh a deich	quarter past ten
cairteal gu a sia	quarter to six
lethuair an dèidh a h-ochd	half past eight
cairteal gu a h-ochd	quarter to eight
cairteal gu aon uair deug	quarter to eleven
lethuair an dèidh dà uair dheug	half past twelve

You will note that **uair**, **uairean** are usually omitted in the above examples, except in the case of **aon uair deug**, 'eleven o'clock', and **dà uair dheug**, 'twelve o'clock'.

When using minutes the appropriate form of the word **mionaid** 'minute' is used, i.e. singular after **dà** and plural, **mionaidean**, after numerals from three to ten. The singular form of **mionaid** is always used with **fichead** 'twenty'.

mionaid an dèidh uair	a minute past one
dà mhionaid an dèidh a h-ochd	two minutes past eight
trì mionaidean gu a deich	three minutes to ten
còig mionaidean gu meadhan latha	five (minutes) to midday
deich mionaidean an dèidh a trì	ten (minutes) past three
fichead mionaid gu a ceithir	twenty (minutes) to four
còig mionaidean fichead gu a seachd	twenty-five to seven

Note that **mionaidean** is generally <u>not</u> omitted in Scottish Gaelic as 'minute(s)' is in English.

Vocabulary

abhainn (*f*)	/ā-iɲ/, /āviɲ/, /āwiɲ/ etc	river
àite (*m*)	/aːhtʲə/	place
an Sìdhean (*m*)	/əɲ ʃiː-ɛn/, /ə ʃiː-an/	the Fairy Mound
an-uiridh (*adv*)	/ə n̪urʲi/, /ə n̪uri/	last year
Beinn (*f*) **na h-Iolaire**	/beiɲ nə çul̪ərʲə/	the Mountain of the Eagle
Càrn (*m*) **Sheumais**	/kaːn̪ heːmiʃ/	the Cairn of James
Cnoc (*m*) **a' Chapaill**	/krɔ̃xk ə xahpəʎ/	the Hill of the Horse
coibhneil (*adj*)	/kỹn̪ɛl/	kind
coltas (*m*)	/kol̪t̪əs/, /kol̪əs/	appearance
còrd ri (*vb*)	/kɔːʀ(s)t̪ rʲi/	enjoy, be pleasing to
dùthaich (*f*), **dùthcha** (G)	/d̪uː-iç/, /d̪uːxə/	country, district
eachdraidh (*f*)	/ɛxd̪ri/	history
geamair (*m*)	/gʲɛmɛrʲ/	gamekeeper
gu sònraichte (*adv*)	/gə sɔːriçt̪ʲə/	especially
gu tric (*adv*)	/gə t̪riçkʲ/	often
iasgach (*vn*)	/iəskəx/	fishing
lathaichean saora (*m*)	/l̪a-içən suːrə/	holidays
le chèile (*adv*)	/lɛ çeːlə/	both, together
Linne (*f*) **na Ciste**	/ʎiɲə nə kʲiʃt̪ʲə/	the Pool of the Chest
Loch (*m* **na Creige**	/l̪ɔx nə krʲegʲə/	the Loch of the Crag
muir (*f*), **mara** (G)	/murʲ/, /marə/	sea
rathad (*m*)	/ʀa-əd̪/	road
riamh (*adv*)	/rʲiəv/	ever
roimhe (*adv*)	/rɔ̃jə/, /rẽjə/	before
shreap (*vb*)	/hrɛhp/	climbed
sreap (*vb*)	/st̪rɛhp/	climb
tachair ri (*vb*)	/t̪axərʲ rʲi/	meet with
taobh (*f*)	/t̪ɯːv/	side, part
uabhasach (*adv*)	/ũãvasəx/	terribly (intensifier), very much

CÒMHRADH (CONVERSATION)

Lathaichean saora faisg air Beinn na h-Iolaire †

Dòmhnall	Tha mac mo pheathar agus bràthair m' athar a' tighinn gar n-ionnsaigh air an lathaichean saora.
Iain	An robh iad an taobh seo riamh roimhe?
Dòmhnall	O bha gu dearbh. Bha iad an seo an-uiridh còmhla ruinn.
Iain	Agus dè a rinn sibh?
Dòmhnall	Sheall sinn Beinn na h-Iolaire dhaibh agus shreap sinn Cnoc a' Chapaill.
Iain	An do chòrd sin riutha?
Dòmhnall	Chòrd, agus gu sònraichte chòrd coltas an àite riutha uabhasach math.
Iain	An robh sibh ag iasgach còmhla riutha?
Dòmhnall	Bha gu tric air Loch na Creige agus aig Linne na Ciste.
Iain	An deach sibh tarsainn air an abhainn no seachad air Càrn Sheumais?
Dòmhnall	Chaidh, le chèile, agus timcheall air an t-Sìdhean agus ri taobh na mara air an rathad dhachaigh.
Iain	An do thachair geamair na dùthcha ruibh?
Dòmhnall	Thachair agus dh'innis e eachdraidh an àite dhaibh. Bha e uabhasach coibhneil.

TRANSLATION

Holidays near Beinn na h-Iolaire

Donald	My nephew (sister's son) and my uncle (father's brother) are coming (to visit us) on their holidays.
John	Were they ever in these parts before?
Donald	Oh yes indeed. They were here last year with us.
John	And what did you do?
Donald	We showed them Beinn na h-Iolaire and we climbed Cnoc a' Chapaill.
John	Did they enjoy that?
Donald	They did, and especially they enjoyed the appearance of the place very much.
John	Were you fishing along with them?
Donald	Yes, often on Loch na Creige and at Linne na Ciste.
John	Did you go across the river or past Càrn Sheumais?
Donald	Yes we did, both of them, and round the Sìdhean and beside the sea on the way home.
John	Did the gamekeeper of the district meet you?
Donald	Yes, he did and he told them the history of the place. He was terribly kind.

† A not uncommon place-name throughout the Highlands and Islands.

Lesson 8

64 'Tha': future

You will recall that Gaelic differentiates between independent and dependent verbal forms. Independent forms are used (i) independently and (ii) following independent verbal particles. Dependent forms are used following dependent verbal particles. In the future tense (of regular verbs) there are two independent verbal forms, the first of which is used independently and the second, following independent verbal particles. Here are the future forms of **tha**:

INDEPENDENT (i)	INDEPENDENT (ii) =Relative	DEPENDENT	
bidh	bhios	bi	will be
bidh mi	bhios mi	bi mi	I will be
bidh tu	bhios tu	bi thu	you will be
bidh e/i	bhios e/i	bi e/i	he, she will be
bidh sinn	bhios sinn	bi sinn	we will be
bidh sibh	bhios sibh	bi sibh	you will be
bidh iad	bhios iad	bi iad	they will be

Note also that **tu** is used with the independent forms and **thu** is used with the dependent form.

The future forms of **tha** may also be used to denote habitual actions, particularly when adverbs implying habit are present, e.g.

| **Bidh mi ann an Glaschu a h-uile latha.** | I am in Glasgow every day. |
| **Bidh mi a' snàmh a h-uile madainn.** | I swim every morning. |

Disyllabic forms of the independent forms are sometimes used, particularly in answers and in emphatic speech; these are often spelled with (silent) **-th-**, e.g. **bithidh, bhitheas**.

64a Regular verbs: future

The periphrastic construction involving **tha** and the verbal noun, when used in the future usually refers only to the continuous future, e.g. **bidh mi ag òl** 'I will be drinking'. The simple future consists of short verbal forms derived from the verbal root. We must distinguish once again between independent and dependent forms in the future tense. Moreover, we must distinguish between **two** independent forms in the future. You will recall that independent forms occur:

    (i)   in utterance initial position and
    (ii) following independent particles.

The future uses separate verbal forms for each. We will refer to the first independent form as the independent form of the future and to the second independent form as the relative form of the future.

The independent form is made by adding **-(a)idh** to the verbal root e.g. **cuiridh** 'will put'. The relative form is made by adding **-(e)as** to the verbal root and leniting the verbal root, e.g. **chuireas**; if the verbal root begins with a vowel or **f** + vowel, **dh'** is prefixed to the verbal root, e.g. **dh'òlas, dh'fhalbhas**.

The endings **-aidh** and **-as** are used following verbal roots with final broad consonants in accordance with the fundamental spelling rule of Gaelic: **Leathann ri Leathann is Caol ri Caol** 'Broad with broad and slender with slender'. Similarly, **-idh** and **-eas** are used following verbal roots with final slender consonants.

The dependent form of the future is the verbal root itself. Here are some examples:

Imperative/ Verbal Root	Independent (i)	Independent (ii) =Relative	Dependent
cuir put	**cuiridh**	**chuireas**	**cuir**
gabh eat, etc.	**gabhaidh**	**ghabhas**	**gabh**
brist break	**bristidh**	**bhristeas**	**brist**
ceannaich buy	**ceannaichidh**	**cheannaicheas**	**ceannaich**
leugh read	**leughaidh**	**leughas**	**leugh**
òl drink	**òlaidh**	**dh'òlas**	**òl**
falbh go away	**falbhaidh**	**dh'fhalbhas**	**falbh**

8

Examples:

<u>**Cuiridh**</u> **mi a-mach an cat.**	Independent	I will put the cat out.
Cò a <u>chuireas</u> a-mach an cat?	Relative	Who will put the cat out?
Cha <u>chuir</u> Seumas a-mach e.	Dependent	James won't put him/it out.
<u>**Gabhaidh**</u> **mi buntàta is ìm.**	Independent	I will eat potatoes and butter.
Dè a <u>ghabhas</u> Anna?	Relative	What will Ann eat?
Nach <u>gabh</u> i an aon rud?	Dependent	Will she not have/take the same (thing)?
<u>**Òlaidh**</u> **mi uisge beatha.**	Independent	I will drink whisky.
Nuair a <u>dh'òlas</u> mi lionn.	Relative	When I drink ale.
An <u>òl</u> thu balgam beag?	Dependent	Will you drink a little drop?

64b Pronouns

The personal pronouns **mi, t(h)u, e, i, sinn, sibh, iad** are used with all future forms. However, **tu** is used with the independent forms **-(a)idh** and **-(e)as** and **thu** is used with the dependent forms, e.g.

Bristidh tu a' ghloine.	You will break the glass.
Dè a sheinneas tu?	What will you sing?
An ceannaich thu am pàipear?	Will you buy the paper?

Note that **cha** normally lenites a following consonant (except **d, t** and **s**) and becomes **chan** before vowels and **f** + vowels, e.g.

Cha chuir mi a-mach an cù.	I will not put the dog out.
Cha ghabh e sìon.	He will not eat anything.
Chan òl mi uisge beatha.	I will not drink whisky.
Chan fhalbh iad gu bràch.	They will never leave.

IMPORTANT

Verbs with two syllables usually ending in **-r, -l, -n, -ng** lose their second syllable when the future endings are added; this is referred to as syncope. Here is a list of the most important examples, illustrated with the endings **idh, as**:

tachair	**tachraidh, thachras**	will happen
fosgail	**fosglaidh, dh'fhosglas**	will open
bruidhinn	**bruidhnidh, bhruidhneas**	will speak
tarraing	**tàirrnidh, thàirrneas**	will pull

Note also:

innis	**innsidh, dh'innseas**	will tell

Note: final **-nn** and **-ng** are reduced to **-n** when an ending is added. When the future independent endings **-idh, -eas** are added to the verb **èirich** 'rise, get up', the **-ich** is dropped, i.e. **èiridh, dh'èireas**.

In English in sentences where the main clause is in the future tense, subordinate clauses introduced by 'when' and 'if' usually appear in the present tense. In Gaelic the future tense is retained throughout in both clauses, e.g.

Leughaidh mi an leabhar nuair a bhios an ùine agam.
I will read the book when I have the time.

Òlaidh mise tè ma ghabhas tu fhèin tè.
I will drink one (a drink) if you take one.

64c Present habitual use of future tense

The future tense forms may, as in English, be used to denote present habitual actions, particularly when adverbs implying habit are present, e.g.

Ceannaichidh Iain am pàipear a h-uile latha.	John buys the paper every day.
Falbhaidh iad gach seachdain.	They go away every week.
Bidh mi an Glaschu gu math tric.	I am in Glasgow fairly frequently.

65 Ability

The future tense can imply 'ability', e.g.

seinnidh Anna	Ann can sing
cluichidh Iain camanachd	John can play shinty

Vocabulary

airgead (*m*, 1)	/[arʲa]gʲəd̪/, /[ɛrʲɛ]gʲəd̪/	money
anns a' mhadainn	/as ə vãd̪iɲ/	in the morning
aran (*m*, 1)	/aran/	bread
cuidich (*vb*)	/kud̪ʲiç/	help
doras (*m*, 1)	/d̪ɔrəs/	door
dùin (*vb*)	/d̪uːɲ/	close
dùisg (*vb*)	/d̪uːʃkʲ/	wake up
fàg (*vb*)	/faːg/	leave
falbh (*vb*)	/f[aɫa]v/	go away, leave
geal (*adj*)	/gʲaɫ/	white
gu moch (*adv*)	/gə mɔx/	early
ionnsaich (*vb*)	/jũːsiç/	learn
òran (*m*, 1)	/ɔːran/	song
pàipear (*m*, 1)	/pɛːhpɛrʲ/	paper
gabh (*vb*)	/gav/	sing
till (*vb*)	/tʲiːʎ/	return
uair sam bith (*adv*)	/uərʲ səm bi/	any time

Exercise 8.1

Translate

1   Ann will drink her tea.
2   I will learn Gaelic.
3   When will you sing the song?
4   She will not buy white bread any time.
5   Will they go away early in the morning?

6   I will speak to him if he returns.
7   Where will we leave the money?
8   Who will help me?
9   I will read the paper when I wake up.
10   How will you close the door?

Note: **gabh** 'sing' is used with **òran** 'song', and **seinn** 'sing' is used with **salm** 'psalm'; both **gabh** and **seinn** can be used with **laoidh** 'lay'.

66 Answering questions (future)

As usual, we repeat the main verb of the question:

An òl thu am bainne?	Will you drink the milk?
Òlaidh.	Yes.
Chan òl.	No.

An dùin thu an doras?	Will you close the door?
Dùinidh.	Yes.
Cha dùin.	No.

Note: **cha** does not usually lenite **d t s** but can lenite in some dialects, e.g. **cha dhùin** occurs as a variant for the **cha dùin** in the last example.

67 Conjunctions

Conjunctions are words that join two clauses together. There are two types of conjunctions:

(a)   co-ordinating conjunctions
(b)   subordinate conjunctions

(a) Co-ordinating conjunctions

Co-ordinating conjunctions join two sentences or clauses together which are of *equal* importance. **Agus** 'and', **ach** 'but' and **no** 'or' are examples of co-ordinating conjunctions. Co-ordinating conjunctions are not strictly speaking either independent or dependent particles. This is clearly seen when they are used in future sentences where the independent (i) form of a following verb is used, not the independent (ii) = relative form. Here are some examples:

Bidh Iain ann <u>agus</u> bidh Anna ann cuideachd.
John will be there and Ann will be there also.

Chan eil am pathadh orm <u>ach</u> òlaidh mi fion.
I am not thirsty but I will drink some wine.

Seinnidh e òran <u>no</u> innsidh e sgeulachd.
He will sing a song or he will tell a story.

(b) Subordinate conjunctions

Subordinate conjunctions introduce subordinate clauses, i.e. clauses that are dependent on a main clause. Subordinate clauses are often marked in Gaelic either by the presence of the relative particle **a** 'that' or a dependent verbal form. The subordinate nature of independent verbal particles is shown by the presence of the relative pronoun **a** 'that'; see **Lesson 6, Section 52** where it was pointed out that most independent particles contain the relative particle **a** 'that'. Here are some examples of subordinate conjunctions:

Tha iad a' ràdh gun tàinig Iain.
They say that John came.

An aithne dhut an t-àite far a bheil Anna a' fuireach?
Do you know the place where Ann lives?

Cha tèid Màiri air lathaichean saora ged a bhios an t-airgead aice.
Mary will not go on holiday even though she will have the money.

67a 'Because', 'since'

There are many words in Gaelic which may be roughly translated as 'because', which can be classified into two types:

TYPE 1		TYPE 2	
a chionn is gun	because	**a chionn**	because, since
a thoradh is gun	because	**a thoradh**	because, since
		airson	because, since
		oir	because, since
		bhon	because, since
		a thaobh	because, since

Type 1 conjunctions are the norm and are dependent verbal particles; as such they are followed by dependent verbal forms. Type 2 conjunctions are neither followed by the relative pronoun nor by dependent verbal forms. They act, in effect, like co-ordinating conjunctions and are followed by independent (non-relative) verbal forms. It is as if a break in syntax occurs following type 2 conjunctions. Here is an example of both:

Chaidh mi a Pheairt <u>a chionn is gun robh</u> mo charaid a' fuireach ann.
I went to Perth because my friend was living there.

Chaidh mi a Pheairt <u>a chionn bha</u> mo charaid a' fuireach ann.
I went to Perth since my friend was living there.

67b 'Never', 'ever'

The Gaelic word **gu bràch** is used with the future and conditional.

Chan fhàg mi an t-Eilean Sgitheanach gu bràch.
I will never leave the Isle of Skye.

Chan òl mi lionn gu bràch.
I will never drink beer.

An ceannaich thu taigh ùr gu bràch?
Will you ever buy a new house?

Mairidh sin gu bràch.
That will last forever.

Gu bràch can be emphasised by adding **tuilleadh**, e.g.

Cha cheannaich mi aran geal gu bràch tuilleadh.
I will never again buy white bread.

See also **Section 51a**.

68 The nominative plural

The majority of nouns have one plural form only which is used for all forms, the nominative, prepositional and genitive. The nominative and prepositional plural forms are identical for **all** nouns. Some nouns, however, have a different genitive plural form as we will see below. It is important to note that the plural form of any noun may vary according to dialect, e.g. **àiteachan** and **àitichean** are both used as the plural form of **àite** (*m*) 'place'. There are two main ways of forming the plural in Scottish Gaelic:

(A) by adding a suffix ending in **-(e)an**
(B) by slenderising the final consonant

There is no easy way of predicting what the plural form for any given noun will be. Plural forms must be learnt as vocabulary items.

> ### TYPE A SUFFIXES ENDING IN -(E)AN
> 1 **(e)an**
> 2 **t(e)an**
> 3 **(e)achan**
> 4 **(a)ichean**
> 5 **(e)annan**
> 6 **slenderisation + ean**

Examples

TYPE A1

	Singular	Plural	
(e)an	caileag	caileagan	girls
	uinneag	uinneagan	windows
	gille	gillean	boys
	craobh	craobhan	trees

TYPE A2

t(e)an	sgoil	sgoiltean	schools
	baile	bailtean	towns
	teine	teintean	fires
	coille	coilltean	woods

TYPE A3

(e)achan	gloine	gloineachan	glasses
	balla	ballachan	walls
	àite	àiteachan	places
	deise	deiseachan	suits

Balla and **àite** also have plural forms **ballaichean** and **àitichean** respectively.

TYPE A4

(a)ichean	bliadhna	bliadhnaichean	years
	càr	càraichean	cars
	clas	clasaichean	classes
	latha	lathaichean	days
	nurs	nursaichean	nurses

TYPE A5

(e)annan	àm	amannan	times
	oidhche	oidhcheannan	nights
	dealbh	dealbhannan†	pictures
	ainm	ainmeannan	names

Note: Learners can expect to find the type A1 ending -**an** in place of the type 5 -**annan** ending in some nouns both in writing and speech, e.g. **dealbhan** and **ainmean**.

† A type 1 plural, **deilbh**, is used in some dialects.

TYPE A6

Slenderisation + ean	cladach	cladaichean	sea shores
	anart	anairtean	linens
	ugh	uighean	eggs
	aodann	aodainnean	faces
	moladh	moladhean	recommendations

TYPE B SLENDERISATION
This applies to masculine nouns only. The process of slenderisation can affect the preceding vowel, as before. See **Appendix 1**.

Examples

SINGULAR	NOMINATIVE PLURAL	
bodach	bodaich	old men
òran	òrain	songs
cat	cait	cats
boireannach	boireannaich	women
Gàidheal	Gàidheil	Gaels
bòrd	bùird	tables
fiadh	fèidh	deer
cnoc	cnuic	hills
Gall	Goill	Lowlanders
ceann	cinn	heads

8

68a The genitive plural

For type A suffix plurals (i.e. all plurals ending in **-an**), the genitive plural is for most nouns the same as the nominative plural. For type B plurals, the genitive plural in Gaelic is different from the nominative plural and is in fact the same as the nominative singular.

Note that nouns with suffix plurals (i.e. type A) can also have genitive plural forms which are identical to the nominative singular, e.g. **clachan** or **clach** 'stones' (*gen pl*). The shorter forms are particularly common in higher registers of the language but are not uncommon in local dialects.

Here are some examples which illustrate the two types of genitive plural formation:

NOM. SING.		NOM. PL.		GEN. PL.	
TYPE A					
caileag	girl	caileagan	girls	caileagan	girls'
sgoil	school	sgoiltean	schools	sgoiltean	schools'
càr	car	càraichean	cars	càraichean	cars'
dealbh	picture	dealbhannan	pictures	dealbhannan	pictures'
craobh	tree	craobhan	trees	craobhan	trees'
TYPE B					
bodach	old man	bodaich	old men	bodach	old men's
òran	song	òrain	songs	òran	songs'
boireannach	woman	boireannaich	women	boireannach	women's
Gàidheal	Gael	Gàidheil	Gaels	Gàidheal	Gaels'
cat	cat	cait	cats	cat	cats'

68b The plural article

As with nouns, the nominative and prepositional plural form of the article is identical; it is **na**. (This, you will recall, is also the form of the feminine singular genitive article; see **Lesson 7, Section 57b**.)

> **Nominative (= prepositional) article (*pl*): na**
> **na h-** before vowels
> **na**   otherwise

The genitive plural form of the article is **nan:**

> **Genitive article: nan**
> **nam** before the labials **b p f m**
> **nan** otherwise

NOM. SING.		NOM. PL.	GEN. PL.
uinneag	window	**na h-uinneagan**	**nan uinneagan**
caileag	girl	**na caileagan**	**nan caileagan**
pìob	pipe	**na pìoban**	**nam pìoban**
cat	cat	**na cait**	**nan cat**
bodach	old man	**na bodaich**	**nam bodach**

Note that the Double Definite Article (**Section 58**) rule applies here also, e.g.

gloine nan uinneagan	the glass of the windows
biadh nan cat	the food of the cats

68c The indefinite genitive plural

When the article does not precede a genitive plural noun, the noun is automatically lenited. In other words indefinite genitive plurals are automatically lenited, e.g.

mòran ghillean (G, *pl*)	a large number of boys, many boys
mòran bhrògan (G, *pl*)	many shoes
beagan choileach (G, *pl*)	a small number of cockerels
beagan chlach(an)(G, *pl*)	a small number of stones

69 Prepositions before the article

We have already noted that the prepositional plural is always the same as the nominative plural. You will recall that most prepositions change form when they precede the singular article by adding **-n** or **-s**. Those prepositions which add **-s** before the singular article also add **-s** before the plural article. All other prepositions do *not* change form before the plural article except **do** and **de** which may become **dha** and **dhe** respectively. Here are some examples:

anns na craobhan	in the trees
leis na gillean	with the boys
bruidhinn ris na nursaichean	speak to the nurses
às na càraichean	out of the cars
bho na lathaichean sin	since those days
tro na dorsan	through the doorways
do/dha na bodaich	to the old men
tro na h-uinneagan	through the windows

8

Vocabulary

airgead (*m*, 1)	/[ɛrʲɛ]gʲəd̪/	money
an dèidh (+ *genitive*)	/ən dʲeː/, /ən dʲɤ-i/	after
cànan (*m*) (**cànain** (*f*) in some dialects)	/kaːnan/	language

Exercise 8.2

Translate

1 the girls and the boys
2 in the towns
3 under the tables
4 from the Gaels
5 on the hills
6 the teachers of the schools
7 the boys' books
8 the language of the Gaels
9 the women's money
10 after the nights

70 Irregular nouns: plural

There is a small handful of nouns whose plural formations are irregular and as such should be learnt separately:

NOMINATIVE SING.		NOMINATIVE PL.	GENITIVE PL.
athair (*m*)	father	**athraichean**	**athraichean**
bean (*f*)	wife	**mnathan**	**ban**
beinn (*f*)	mountain	**beanntan**	**beann(tan)**
bò (*f*)	cow	**bà** or more commonly **crodh** (*m*), which is a singular collective noun	**bò**
bràthair (*m*)	brother	**bràithrean**	**bràithrean**
caora (*f*)	sheep	**caoraich**	**caorach**
cù (*m*)	dog	**coin**	**con**
duine (*m*)	man	**daoine**	**daoine**
leabaidh (*f*)	bed	**leapannan**	**leapannan**
mac (*m*)	son	**mic**	**mac**
màthair (*f*)	mother	**màthraichean**	**màthraichean**
piuthar (*f*)	sister	**peathraichean**	**peathraichean**
sgian (*f*)	knife	**sgeinean**	**sgeinean**

8

70a Other plural forms

Prepositional plural

The prepositional plural form in modern Scottish Gaelic is identical with the nominative plural. The older prepositional (dative) plural ending **-(a)ibh** is no longer used productively but survives in composite prepositions such as **air beulaibh**, **air cùl(aibh)** (see **Section 62**) and in the vocative plural form -(a)ibh described in the next paragraph. It is also found occasionally in verse and song as a plural.

Vocative plural

In **Section 33** we discussed the vocative of personal names. In theory, all nouns can have vocative forms. The vocative singular of most masculine nouns is formed by slenderisation, e.g. **a chait** 'cat!', **a bhradain** 'salmon!'. The vocative singular of most other nouns is identical with the nominative singular, e.g. **a chailleach** 'old woman!'. The noun **cù** 'dog' is irregular: its vocative form is **a choin** 'dog!'.

The vocative plural is **-(e)an** for most nouns with nominative plural ending -(e)an (i.e. for type A above). For nouns that form their nominative plural by slenderisation (i.e. type B above), the vocative plural is formed by adding **-a** or

-aibh to the nominative singular form, e.g. **a bhàrda** or **a bhàrdaibh** 'poets!', **a fhearaibh** 'men!', **a bhalchaibh** 'boys!' (with syncope from balach), etc.; in practice, however, such vocative plural forms rarely occur.

71 Numerals with nouns

We saw in **Section 23** how the basic numerals are preceded by **a** when counting. When the numerals are used with nouns, the **a** is usually dropped. The numerals from three to ten are normally followed by the plural form of the noun. **Aon** and **dà** are followed by the singular form of the noun which is lenited; note **aon** does not lenite a noun beginning with **d** or **t**: see **Appendix 7**. The noun always precedes **deug**.

1	**aon chat**	one cat	11	**aon chat deug**	eleven cats
2	**dà chat**	two cats	12	**dà chat dheug**	twelve cats
3	**trì cait**	three cats	13	**trì cait d(h)eug**	thirteen cats
4	**ceithir cait**	four cats	14	**ceithir cait d(h)eug**	fourteen cats
5	**còig cait**	five cats	15	**còig cait d(h)eug**	fifteen cats
6	**sia cait**	six cats	16	**sia cait d(h)eug**	sixteen cats
7	**seachd cait**	seven cats	17	**seachd cait d(h)eug**	seventeen cats
8	**ochd cait**	eight cats	18	**ochd cait d(h)eug**	eighteen cats
9	**naoi cait**	nine cats	19	**naoi cait d(h)eug**	nineteen cats
10	**deich cait**	ten cats			

Deug is sometimes lenited when it follows a plural noun with final slenderised consonant but is always lenited following **d(h)à** + noun, e.g.

trì cait d(h)eug	thirteen cats
naoi cnuic dheug	nineteen hills
dà chat dheug	twelve cats

71a Dual number

There are remnants of a dual form in Scottish Gaelic. Only feminine nouns have a dual form which is formed by slenderising the final consonant. This is in effect the same form as the prepositional form (see **Section 46**).

dà bhròig	two shoes
dà chluais	two ears
dà uinneig	two windows

Recall that slenderisation can, in some instances, affect the preceding vowel (see **Appendix 1**), e.g.

dà chois	two feet	(from **dà** + **cas**)
dà chloich	two stones	(from **dà** + **clach**)
dà chirc	two hens	(from **dà** + **cearc**)

The singular rather than the plural form of the noun **bliadhna** 'year' is used with all numerals, e.g.

dà bhliadhna	two years
trì bliadhna	three years
deich bliadhna	ten years

Note: There is a tendency for younger speakers to use the plural form **bliadhnaichean** after numbers in the range 3 to 19.

Vocabulary

pìob (*f*), **pìoban** (*pl*)	/piːb/, /piːbən/	pipe, pipes

Exercise 8.3

Translate, writing the numerals in words:

(a)	3 windows	(f)	12 cars
(b)	10 schools	(g)	15 pipes
(c)	7 shoes	(h)	18 songs
(d)	2 classes	(i)	2 feet
(e)	8 trees	(j)	12 windows

72 Verbal nouns with pronoun objects

Verbs which are complemented by prepositions are straightforward; the object combines with the preposition in the usual way. Here are some examples:

Bha mi a' bruidhinn <u>ris</u> an-dè.	I was speaking to him yesterday.
Thachair iad <u>rithe</u> an-uiridh.	They met her last year.
An do chòrd an oidhche <u>riut</u>?	Did you enjoy the night?
An tug Iain an t-airgead sin <u>dhut</u>?	Did John give you that money?

When the verb is not followed by a preposition, things are not so straightforward. If we want to say 'he is making bread', we say: **tha e a' dèanamh aran**. If we want to say 'he is making it', we might expect to be able to say: **tha e a' dèanamh e**, where the pronoun object simply follows the verbal noun; the latter is possible for some dialects but is not recommended in textbooks. While this has been a possibility in some dialects since the nineteenth century at least, the majority would say, **tha e ga dhèanamh**, literally 'he is at its making', where **ga** = **ag** 'at' + **a** 'its'. The pronoun object becomes the corresponding possessive pronoun.

Here is the full paradigm:

gam* (me)   + lenition
gad* (you)   + lenition
ga* (him, it)   + lenition
ga (her, it)   prefixes **h-** to vowels
gar (our)   prefixes **n-** to vowels
gur (your)   prefixes **n-** to vowels
gan/gam (them)

Examples

Tha Iain gam bhualadh.	John is hitting me.
Tha sinn gad fhaicinn.	We see you.
A bheil thu ga chluinntinn?	Do you hear him/it?
Tha iad ga cluinntinn.	They hear her/it.
Tha Màiri gar coinneachadh.	Mary is meeting us.
Tha na balaich gur faighneachd.	The boys are asking for you.
Bha Anna gan iarraidh.	Ann wanted them.
Bha Seumas ga h-iarraidh.	James wanted her/it.
An robh sibh gar n-iarraidh?	Did you want us?

Vocabulary

ceannach (*vn*)	/kʲaɴəx/	buying
fàgail (*vn*)	/faːgal/	leaving
freagairt (*vn*)	/frʲegəɾ(s)tʲ/	answering
seinn (*vn*)	/ʃeiɲ/	singing

Exercise 8.4

Translate

1   Do you hear me?
2   Do you (*pl*) see it?
3   John is meeting them.
4   Were the boys hitting you (*pl*)?
5   Who wants us?
6   Ann was asking for you.
7   I am answering him now.
8   Are you leaving us here?
9   Are you buying it (*fem*)?
10 They were singing it (*masc*).

73 'Duine'

Duine (*plural* **daoine**) can mean 'man', 'husband' or simply 'person'. Consider the following examples:

Tha duine ag obair anns a' gharaids.	A man is working in the garage.
Is e Seumas an duine agam.	James is my husband.
Bha daoine gu leòr ann.	There were a lot of people there.

Duine can also be used impersonally. Consider the following examples:

A bheil duine a-staigh?	Is there anyone in?
Chan eil f(h)ios aig duine.	Nobody knows.

Vocabulary

a laochain (*m*)	/ə lɯːxaɲ/	good lad, friend (address form)
an-còmhnaidh (*adv*)	/əŋ kõːni/	always
an-dràsta (*advõ*)	/əɳ d̪õːst̪ə/	now, this minute
cairteal (*m*)	/karst̪ʲaɫ/	quarter
co-là-breith sona dhut	/kɔ t̪aː brʲe sɔnə ɣuht̪/	happy birthday (to you)
dìnnear/dinnear (*f*)	/d̪ʲiːɲɛrʲ/	dinner
fidhlear (*m*)	/fiːlɛrʲ/	fiddler
fiughair (*m*)	/fju-ərʲ/	hope, expectation, looking forward to
freagarrach (*adj*)	/fregərəx/	suitable
gu mì-fhortanach (*adv*)	/gə miː ɔrst̪anəx/	unfortunately
idir (*adv*)	/id̪ʲərʲ/	at all
laochan (*m*)	/ɫɯːxan/	good lad, friend (used only of males)
math fhèin (*adv*)	/ma heːn/	great, splendid
ma-thà (*interj*)	/mə haː/	then! so!
meal do naidheachd	/mjaɫ d̪ə nẽ-əxk/	congratulations (informal)
mus (*cjn*)	/mas/	before
pìobaire (*m*)	/piːbərʲə/	piper
seinneadair (*m*)	/ʃeɲəd̪ɛrʲ/	singer
sìon (*m*)†	/ʃĩan/, /ʃĩən/	a particle, a small bit
sìon (*m*) **a dh'fhios**	/ʃĩan ə jis/	a bit of knowledge, not a clue, no idea
taghta (*adj*)	/t̪ɯːht̪ə/	fine, great
taigh-òsta (*m*)	/t̪ɤj ɔːst̪ə/	hotel, pub
timcheall air (*cmp prp*)	/t̪ʲ[imi]çaɫ ɛrʲ/	around, about
tràth (*adv*)	/t̪raː/	early

† Recall that **sìon** is used only with negative and interrogative verbs.

CÒMHRADH (CONVERSATION)

Co-là-breith Anna

Iain	Hallo, a bheil Anna a-staigh?
Anna	Is e Anna a tha a' bruidhinn. Cò a tha agam an seo?
Iain	Is e Iain a tha ann.
Anna	Hallo, a Iain.
Iain	Co-là-breith sona dhut, a Anna, agus meal do naidheachd.
Anna	Tapadh leat, a Iain. Càite am bi sinn a' dol a-nochd?
Iain	Bidh chun a' chèilidh.
Anna	Cò a bhios a' seinn aig a' chèilidh?
Iain	Chan eil sìon a dh'fhios agamsa ach tha seinneadairean is pìobairean is fidhleirean às an àite seo fhèin a' dol ann. Seinnidh Pàdraig agus Catrìona co-dhiù. Tha òrain gu leòr acasan. Bidh iad gan seinn an-còmhnaidh.
Anna	A bheil thu ag iarraidh dìnnear anns an taigh-òsta mus fhalbh sinn?
Iain	Bidh sin math fhèin. Cuin a ghabhas sinn ar dìnnear, ma-thà?
Anna	Timcheall air ochd uairean. Am bi sin freagarrach leatsa?
Iain	Cha bhi gu mì-fhortanach. Am bi seachd uairean ro thràth dhuibh?
Anna	Cha bhi idir. Tha sin taghta.
Iain	Glè mhath ma-thà. Bidh mise gad fhàgail an-dràsta ach bidh mi gad fhaicinn ann an taigh-òsta Dhòmhnaill timcheall air cairteal gu a seachd.
Anna	Bidh fiughair agam ri sin ma-thà, a laochain.

TRANSLATION

Ann's birthday

John	Hello, is Ann in?
Ann	It's Ann who is speaking. Who is this?
John	It's John.
Ann	Hello, John.
John	Happy birthday, Ann, and congratulations.
Ann	Thank you, John. Where will we be going tonight?
John	To the ceilidh.
Ann	Who will be singing at the ceilidh?
John	I've no idea, but there are plenty of singers and pipers and fiddlers from this place itself going there. Patrick and Catriona will sing anyway. They have songs galore. They're always singing them.
Ann	Do you want dinner in the hotel before we go?
John	That will be great. When will we have dinner then?
Ann	About eight o'clock. Will that be suitable for you?
John	No, unfortunately. Will seven o'clock be too early for you?
Ann	Not at all. That will be splendid.
John	Very good then. I'll be leaving you just now but I'll be seeing you in Donald's Hotel about quarter to seven.
Ann	I look forward to that then, my good friend.

Lesson 9

74 Irregular verbs: future

We learnt the past tense forms of the irregular verbs in **Lesson 4**. We will now look at the (simple) future forms. As with the past tense, most irregular verbs distinguish between an independent and dependent form. We will see that the future forms are very different from the past forms. It is possible to group the future tense formation of irregular verbs into the following three groups:

(i) Verbs whose independent and dependent forms differ substantially:

INDEPENDENT	DEPENDENT	
their	**abair**	will say
nì	**dèan**	will do, make
chì	**faic**	will see
gheibh	**faigh**	will get
bheir	**toir**	will bring, give

(ii) Verbs whose independent and dependent forms begin with **th-** and **t-** respectively:

INDEPENDENT	DEPENDENT	
thèid	**tèid**	will go
thig	**tig**	will come

Note: the dependent forms **toir**, **tèid** and **tig** are all pronounced with initial **d-**. Some prefer to spell these forms with an initial **d-** or even **d'th-**.

(iii) Verbs whose future formation is regular

INDEPENDENT	DEPENDENT	
beiridh	**beir**	will catch
bheireas (*rel*)		
cluinnidh	**cluinn**	will hear
chluinneas (*rel*)		
ruigidh	**ruig**	will reach
ruigeas (*rel*)		

Notes

1. The personal pronouns are used as usual with these verbal forms except that **tu** rather than **thu** is used after **-idh** and **-as** with group (iii) verbs as with regular verbs.

2. Negative **cha*** becomes **chan*** before **faic** and **faigh**, e.g. **chan fhaic mi** 'I will not see', **chan fhaigh thu** 'you will not get'. **Nach** also lenites **faic** and **faigh**, e.g. **nach fhaic thu i?** 'will you not see her?', **nach fhaigh e e?** 'will he not get it?'. **Cha** without lenition is used with **dèan**, **toir**, **tèid**, **tig**, **ruig** (although the variant **cha dhèan** can also occur in some dialects); **cha*** is used with **beir**, and **chan** with **abair**.

3. The future forms can express capability. This is particularly true of the verbs **faic** 'see' and **cluinn** 'hear'. Here are some examples:

Cluinnidh mi an t-eun.	I can hear the bird.
Chì thu a' bheinn.	You can see the mountain.

Note that the regular verb **can** is used for **abair** in the future tense, the imperative and, as we will see, in the conditional also.

Examples
Their e riut a-màireach, nach abair? †
He will say to you tomorrow, won't he?

Cha bheir sinn air a' mheàirleach a-nis.
We will not get hold of the robber now.

Cluinnidh tu na h-eòin.
You will hear the birds.

Nì mi mo dhìcheall.
I will do my best.

Dè a chì thu? Chan fhaic sìon.
What do you see? Nothing.

Cuin a gheibh iad am plèan?
When will they get the plane?

Thèid sinn a Ghlaschu.
We will go to Glasgow.

An ruig sibh an taigh a-nochd?
Will you reach home (*lit* the house) tonight?

An tig thu a chèilidh orm a-nochd? Thig.
Will you come to visit me tonight? Yes.

Nach toir thu an t-airgead aige air ais?
Will you not give back his money?

† Commonly = **Canaidh e riut a-màireach, nach can?**

In English in sentences where the main clause is in the future tense, subordinate clauses introduced by 'when' and 'if' usually appear in the present tense. In Gaelic the future tense is retained throughout in both clauses, e.g.

Chì sinn thu nuair a thig thu.
We will see you when you come.

Dè nì sinn ma thèid sinn air chall?
What will we do if we get lost?

Vocabulary

bean an taighe (*f*)	/bɛn əŋ ţɛhə/	the woman of the house
dìcheall (*m*)	/dʲiːçəɫ̃/	utmost, best
dìreach (*adv*)	/dʲiːrʲəx/	directly
eun (*m*), **eòin** (*pl*)	/ian/, /jɔːɲ/	bird, birds
lathaichean saora (*m, pl*)	/ɫa-içən suːrə/	holidays
obair (*f*4)	/obərʲ/	work
seinn (*vn*)	/ʃeiɲ/	singing
sìon (*m*)	/ʃĩãn/	anything
trèan (*f*)	/trɛːn/	train

Exercise 9.1

Translate

1   I will not say anything to him.
2   What will you give to the woman of the house?
3   Do you hear the birds singing?
4   Will you do the work for me?
5   Will they get their holidays tomorrow?
6   We will see them when they reach Glasgow.
7   Will your brother go to the ceilidh?
8   They will not come home directly after school.
9   He will get the train when it comes.
10   Will you do your best this time John?

75 Answering questions

As usual, we repeat the main verb of the question:

An dèan thu e?	Will you do it?
Nì.	Yes.
Cha dèan.	No.

An cluinn thu an ceòl?	Do you hear the music?
Cluinnidh.	Yes.
Cha chluinn.	No.

An tig iad?	Will they come?
Thig.	Yes.
Cha tig.	No.

76 Present habitual use of the future tense

As with the regular verbs, the future tense forms may, as in English, be used to denote habitual actions, particularly when adverbs implying habit are present, e.g.

Chì mi Iain a h-uile latha.
I see John every day.

Thèid Anna a Ghlaschu a h-uile Dimàirt.
Ann goes to Glasgow every Tuesday.

77 The relative

We have already met the relative (= independent form (ii)) of the future tense of regular verbs (**Sections 64** and **64a**). In a typical relative construction we have the following elements in the following order:

ANTECEDENT	+	RELATIVE PRONOUN	+	RELATIVE CLAUSE
na balaich		**a**		**chluich**
the boys		who		played

The antecedent may be the object or the subject of a preceding verb, e.g.

VERB	+	SUBJECT	+	OBJECT = ANTECEDENT	+	RELATIVE
chunnaic		**Iain**		**na balaich**		**a chluich**
saw		John		the boys		who played

John saw the boys who played

VERB	+	SUBJECT = ANTECEDENT	+	RELATIVE
dh'fhalbh		**na balaich**		**a chluich**
left		the boys		who played

the boys who played left

We will be concerned only with the relative construction itself and so our discussion below will be restricted to the relative clause and the order of its elements.

The relative pronoun is an independent particle and as such is followed by independent verbal forms (independent (ii) = relative in the case of the future). Here are some examples:

an duine a dh'fhalbh	the man who left
na caileagan a sheinneas	the girls who will sing
an sgioba a bhuannaicheas	the team that will win

The relative clause has the following elements in the following order:

VERB	+	SUBJECT OR OBJECT OF RELATIVE VERB	+	ADVERB

To sum up, a relative construction consists of the following elements in the following order:

ANTECEDENT	REL PRON	VERB	SUBJ *OR* OBJ OF REL VERB	ADVERB
a' chaileag	**a**	**chaidh**		**a-mach**
the girl	who	went		out

the girl who went out

an t-òran	**a**	**sheinn**	**Iain** (subj)	
the song	that	sang	John	

the song that John sang

am boireannach	**a**	**dh'fhàg**	**an taigh** (obj)	**a-raoir**
the woman	who	left	the house	last night

the woman who left the house last night

am ministear	**a**	**sheinneas**	**na sailm** (obj)	
the minister	who	will sing	the psalms	

the minister who will sing the psalms

It will be clear from the above examples that Gaelic unlike English does not distinguish between relative clauses which contain the subject or the object of the relative verb. In other words, phrases like 'the boy who hit the teacher (*obj*)' and 'the boy that the teacher (*subj*) hit' are identical in Gaelic: **an gille a bhuail an tidsear.** This does not lead to ambiguities as it is usually clear from the context which noun is the subject and which is the object of the relative verb.

77a Relative 'whose'

There is no one word in Gaelic to translate relative 'whose'. Instead Gaelic uses both the relative pronoun **a** and the third person possessive pronoun which agrees in gender and number with the antecedent. A typical sentence like 'the teacher whose son went to Perth', would in Gaelic become literally 'the teacher that his son went to Perth':

An tidsear a chaidh <u>a</u> mhac a Pheairt.   The teacher whose son went to Perth.

Here are some further examples:

A' chaileag a tha <u>a</u> màthair tinn.   The girl whose mother is ill.

Na tidsearan a tha <u>na</u> clasaichean aca math.   The teachers whose classes are good.

Note: Circumlocutions are often used in 'whose' sentences. For instance, the first example might also be translated as:

(Siud) An tidsear agus chaidh a mac a Pheairt.

(There's) The teacher and her son went to Perth.

77b Relative 'in which', 'with whom', etc.

Gaelic has two relative pronouns which both precede the following 'relative' verb:

(i) **a**   direct relative pronoun
(ii) **an/am**   indirect relative pronoun

We have just met the direct relative pronoun **a** in the relative clauses discussed above. When the relative clause, however, contains a preposition, the indirect relative pronoun **an/am** is used. **Am** is used before verbs beginning with the labials **b, p, f, m. An/am** is a dependent particle and as such is followed by dependent verbal forms. The order of elements in indirect relative constructions is as follows:

ANTECEDENT	+	PREPOSITION	+	AN/AM	+	VERB (DEPENDENT)	+	SUBJECT
an sèithear		**air**		**an**		**do shuidh**		**Ailean**
the chair		on		which		sat		Alan

the chair on which Alan sat

an duine	**aig**	**an**	**robh**	**an t-airgead**
the person	at	whom	was	the money

the person who had the money

All prepositions (other than **air, aig**) change form slightly before the indirect relative pronoun **an/am.** We have learnt these forms already; they are exactly the same as the forms of the prepositions which occur before the singular article. See **Section 46**

Prepositions which add **-s:**

PREPOSITION		FORM OF PREPOSITION BEFORE INDIRECT RELATIVE PRONOUN
à	→	**às**
ann an	→	**anns**
le	→	**leis**
ri	→	**ris**
gu	→	**gus**

Prepositions which add **-n:**

PREPOSITION		PREPOSITION BEFORE INDIRECT RELATIVE PRONOUN:
bho	→	**bhon**
fo	→	**fon**
do	→	**dhan**
de	→	**dhen**
mu	→	**mun**
ro	→	**ron**
tro	→	**tron**

Here are some further examples:

na daoine ris an do bhruidhinn mi
the men to whom I spoke

am baile anns an robh sinn
the town in which we were

an rùm às an do theich iad
the room out of which they fled

an toll dhan an do thuit an t-uaireadair
the hole into which the watch fell

a' chraobh fon a bheil/am bheil an taigh aca
the tree under which their house is

am baile tron an deach sinn
the town through which we went

77c Relative 'in which', 'with whom': alternative construction

Like English, Gaelic has an alternative relative construction for relative clauses containing prepositions. The alternative to our first example above 'the chair on which Alan sat' would in English be 'the chair that Alan sat on'. The alternative construction in Gaelic is similar to the English alternative construction except that a prepositional pronoun, agreeing in person and number with the antecedent, appears instead of a simple preposition. The above example would in Gaelic literally be 'the chair that Alan sat on-it':

ANTECEDENT	+	REL PRON (DIRECT)	+	VERB	+	SUBJECT	+	PREPOSITIONAL PRONOUN
an sèithear		**a**		**shuidh**		**Ailean**		**air**
the chair		that		sat		Alan		on-it (*m*)

the chair that Alan sat on

Here are some further examples:

na daoine a bhruidhinn mi **riutha**	the people that I spoke to (them)
am baile a bha sinn **ann**	the town that we were in (it)
an rùm a theich iad **às**	the room that they walked out of (it)
a' chraobh a tha an taigh aca **foidhpe**	the tree that their house is under (it)
am baile a chaidh sinn **troimhe**	the town that we went through (it)

78 Negative relative clauses

To negate any of the above relative clauses (i.e. both direct and indirect), we replace **a** and **an/am** with **nach** which is a dependent particle and as such is always followed by a dependent verbal form.

Here are some examples:

am boireannach nach do dh'fhàg an taigh	the woman who did not leave the house
a' chaileag nach deach a-mach	the girl who did not go out
am balach nach robh a' bruidhinn	the boy that was not speaking
am ministear nach seinn na sailm	the minister who will not sing the psalms
an uinneag nach fhosgail Màiri	the window that Mary will not open
sin leabhar nach do leugh mi anns an sgoil	that's a book that I didn't read at school
am boireannach nach eil a màthair tinn	the woman whose mother is not ill
na daoine ris nach do bhruidhinn mi	the men to whom I did not speak
am baile anns nach robh sinn	the town in which we were not
an rùm às nach do theich iad	the room out of which they did not flee
na daoine nach do bhruidhinn mi riutha	the men that I did not speak to
am baile nach robh sinn ann	the town that we were not in
an rùm nach do theich iad às	the room that they did not flee from

Note that the relative pronoun is sometimes left out in English but never in Gaelic, e.g. 'the man (that) I saw' **an duine a̠ chunnaic mi.**

Vocabulary

an-uiridh (*adv*)	/ə n̠ urʲi/	last year
bruidhinn (*vb*) **mu dheidhinn**	/bruːiɲ ma je-iɲ/	speak about
ceòl (*m*)	/kʲɔːɫ/	music
ceum (*m*)	/kʲeːm/	degree
clach (*f*)	/kɫ̠ax/	stone
cluich (*vb*)	/kɫ̠uiç/	play
èisteachd (*f*) **ri**	/eːʃtʲəxk/	listening to
innis do (*vb*)	/ʃiːʃ d̠ə/	tell to
iuchair (*f*)	/juxərʲ/	key
naidheachd (*f*)	/n̠ɛ̃-əxk/, /n̠ãjəxk/	news, story
rathad (*m*)	/ra-əd̠/	road
sgioba (*m*)	/skʲibə/	team
tachair ri (*vb*)	/t̠axirʲ rʲi/	meet (with)
tilg (*vb*)	/tʲ[ili]gʲ/	throw

Exercise 9.2

Translate

1   Do you know the boy who threw the stone?
2   There is the woman who sang that beautiful song last night.
3   Where is the book that you did not read?
4   This is the room that I left the key in.
5   Is that the woman to whom you told the news?
6   I like the team with which I played.
7   Do you like the music that Donald was listening to?
8   The road that we were speaking about.
9   Is that the man you met?
10 Do you know the lawyer whose son got his degree last year?

79 Interrogatives involving prepositions

We will now learn how to ask questions involving verbs which are complemented by prepositions, i.e. how to say in Gaelic 'to whom did you speak?'. In **Lesson 5** we learnt how to say in Gaelic 'who owns the book?', which as you will recall was:

Cò leis a tha an leabhar?

This can be literally translated as 'who with-him is the book'. This gives us the model for other interrogatives involving prepositions:

CÒ	+	PREP PRON, 3RD SING	+	REL PRON	+	VERB	+	SUBJECT	+	DIR OBJ

cò	**ris**	**a**	**bhruidhinn**	**Iain**	
who	to-him	that	spoke	John	

To whom did John speak?

cò	**dha**	**a**	**dh'innis**	**Anna**	**an naidheachd**
who	to-him	that	told	Ann	the news

To whom did Ann tell the news?

cò	**aige**	**a**	**tha**	**an iuchair**	
who	at-him	that	is	the key	

At whom is the key?, who has the key?

The last example gives us an example of an idiom which involves a preposition in Gaelic but not in English. Watch out for others. Here is one further example:

cò	**dheth**	**a**	**dh'fhaighnich**	**thu**
who	of-him	that	asked	you

Of whom did you ask?, Who did you ask?

Because of the merger of the prepositions **de** and **do** in speech, the last example can also occur as:

Cò dha a dh'fhaighnich thu?   Who did you ask?

Note: Some northern dialects use the indirect relative pronoun **an** + dependent verb in the above examples, e.g.

Cò ris an do bhruidhinn Iain?   To whom did John speak?
Cò aige a bheil an iuchair?   Who has the key?

80 Relative form of '*is*'

Is usually combines with the relative pronoun **a** to give **as.** The written forms **is** and **as** are pronounced identically.

an rud <u>as</u> toil leam	the thing that I like
sin an fheadhainn <u>as</u> fheàrr leamsa	these are the ones which <u>I</u> prefer
dè <u>as</u> fheàrr leat?	what do you prefer?
ged <u>as</u> e droch oidhche a tha ann	although it is a bad night
nuair <u>as</u> ann a' dol dhachaigh a bhios tu	when it is going home that you will be

Note: the **s** in **as fheàrr** is pronounced as a slender **s**, i.e. like the **sh** in 'shoe'.

The relative pronoun **a** does not combine with the past/conditional forms of **is**:

an rud <u>a</u> bu toil leam	the thing that I would like
an rathad <u>a</u> b' aithne dhomh	the road that I knew

80a Negative relative forms of '*is*'

The negative relative form of **is** is **nach** in the present tense (which lenites **f**); in the past/conditional it is **nach bu.** Here are some examples:

an fheadhainn nach toil leam	the ones that I don't like
sin am fear nach fheàrr le Anna	that's the one that Ann does not prefer
ged nach e Seumas a tha ann	although it's not James
sin rud nach bu toil leam	that's a thing that I wouldn't like
balach nach b' aithne dhomh	a boy whom I didn't know

81 Adjectives: singular

(a) Nominative

We have already learnt that adjectives are lenited when they follow feminine nouns in the nominative singular but are not lenited when they follow masculine nouns:

MASCULINE		FEMININE	
cat mòr	a big cat	**bròg bheag**	a small shoe
càr dearg	a red car	**cas mhòr**	a big foot
leabhar geal	a white book	**deise dhubh**	a black suit

(b) Prepositional

Adjectives are lenited when they follow (singular) nouns which are preceded by a preposition and the article. Adjectives are in addition also slenderised when they follow (singular) feminine nouns; however, the use of slenderisation in such instances often does not occur in colloquial Gaelic:

MASCULINE	FEMININE	FEMININE (COLLOQUIAL)
air a' chat mhòr	**anns a' bhròig bhig**	**anns a' bhròg bheag**
on the big cat	in the small shoe	in the small shoe
fon a' chàr dhearg	**air a' chois mhòir**	**air a' chois/chas mhòr**
under the red car	on the big foot	on the big foot
anns an leabhar gheal	**leis an deise dhuibh**	**leis an deise dhubh**
in the white book	with the black suit	with the black suit

Note: Adjectives following masculine nouns which are not preceded by the article are not lenited, e.g. **fo chàr dearg** 'under a red car', **air bòrd mòr** 'on a big table'.

(c) Genitive

Adjectives are lenited and slenderised when they follow a masculine noun in the genitive:

MASCULINE	
a' chait mhòir	of the big cat
a' chàir dheirg	of the red car
an leabhair ghil	of the white book

Adjectives are slenderised and add **-e** when they follow a feminine noun in the genitive:

FEMININE	
na bròige bige	of the small shoe
na coise mòire	of the big foot
na deise duibhe	of the black suit

There is a tendency in colloquial Gaelic to use the lenited and slenderised form of the adjective following feminine nouns in the genitive, especially when disyllabic feminine nouns drop the final **-e** of the genitive. Compare:

na caileige mòire	OR	**na caileig mhòir**	of the big girl
na cailliche bige		**na caillich bhig**	of the small old woman
na bròige bige		**na bròig bhig**	of the small shoe

Vocabulary

camara (*m*)	/kamərə/	camera
càraid (*f*)	/ka:rɛdʲ/	couple
ceàrr (*adj*)	/kʲa:ɾ/	wrong
ceòl (*m*)	/kʲɔ:ɫ/	music
cosgais (*f*)	/kɔskəʃ/	cost
daor (*adj*)	/duːr/	dear, expensive
dath (*m*)	/da̪/	colour
deise (*f*)	/dʲeʃə/	suit
facal (*m*), **faclan** (*pl*)	/fahkəɫ/, /faxkəɫ/, /fahk̪ən/, /faxk̪ən/	word, words
geal (*adj*)	/gʲaɫ/	bright, white
laghach (*adj*)	/ɫɤ-əx/	kind
òran (*m*)	/ɔːran/	song
pìob-mhòr (*f*)	/piːb voːr/	bagpipe
rathad (*m*)	/ɾa-əd̪/	road
solas (*m*)	/sɔɫ̪əs/	light

Exercise 9.3

Translate

1. with the small cat
2. on the white table
3. to the big girl
4. in the bright light
5. the colour of the new suit
6. the words of the beautiful song
7. the music of the bagpipe
8. the cost of the expensive camera
9. with the kind couple
10. on the wrong road

82 More on numerals: 20–99

For numerals over 20, there are two ways of counting in Gaelic. The traditional system of counting operates with 20 as its base (hence it is called the vigesimal system) as in French. The Gaelic for 30 is **deich air fhichead** which means literally 'ten on twenty'. A more modern, decimal system has been introduced into schools in very recent times. Both systems are given below:

	VIGESIMAL	DECIMAL
20	fichead	fichead
30	deich air fhichead	trithead
40	dà fhichead	ceathrad
50	dà fhichead is a deich	caogad
60	trì fichead	seasgad
70	trì fichead is a deich	seachdad
80	ceithir fichead	ochdad
90	ceithir fichead is a deich	naochad
100	ceud	ceud

Leth-cheud is also used for 50. **Is** (pronounced and often written **'s**) is short for **agus** 'and' in the above and following lists of numbers.

The other numbers are formed as follows:

	VIGESIMAL	DECIMAL
21	a h-aon air fhichead	fichead is a h-aon
22	a dhà air fhichead	fichead is a dhà
29	a naoi air fhichead	fichead is a naoi
31	a h-aon-deug air fhichead	trithead is a h-aon
38	a h-ochd-deug air fhichead	trithead is a h-ochd
41	dà fhichead is a h-aon	ceathrad is a h-aon
49	dà fhichead is a naoi	ceathrad is a naoi
51	dà fhichead is a h-aon-deug	caogad is a h-aon
52	dà fhichead is a dhà-dheug	caogad is a dhà
66	trì fichead is a sia	seasgad is a sia
77	trì fichead is a seachd-deug	seachdad is a seachd
88	ceithir fichead is a h-ochd	ochdad is a h-ochd
99	ceithir fichead is a naoi-deug	naochad is a naoi

You will see that multiples of **fichead** usually precede other numerals in such phrases; but between 21 and 39, in the vigesimal system, **fichead** comes last in the phrase. The forms given above are those which are used when counting, i.e. without a following noun.

82a Numerals with nouns

VIGESIMAL

When these numbers are used with a noun, the noun follows multiples of **fichead** but precedes **fichead** in the numbers from 21 to 39. Note that singular forms of the noun are used with **fichead** and multiples of **fichead**, and also with **dà** (see **Section 71a**). Otherwise, the plural form is used as before. Note that **a** is not used when a noun follows the numeral:

21 cats	**aon chat air fhichead**
22 cats	**dà chat air fhichead**
29 cats	**naoi cait air fhichead**
31 cats	**aon chat deug air fhichead**
38 cats	**ochd cait deug air fhichead**
41 cats	**dà fhichead cat is a h-aon**
49 cats	**dà fhichead cat is a naoi**
51 cats	**dà fhichead cat is a h-aon-deug**
52 cats	**dà fhichead cat is a dhà-dheug**
66 cats	**trì fichead cat is a sia**
77 cats	**trì fichead cat is a seachd-deug**
88 cats	**ceithir fichead cat is a h-ochd**
99 cats	**ceithir fichead cat is a naoi-deug**

Decimal

The singular form of the noun is used with the decimal forms. The noun may either come right at the end or it may follow the numeral which is a multiple of ten as follows:

21 cats	**fichead is a h-aon cat**	**fichead cat is a h-aon**
22 cats	**fichead is a dhà cat**	**fichead cat is a dhà**
29 cats	**fichead is a naoi cat**	**fichead cat is a naoi**
31 cats	**trithead is a h-aon cat**	**trithead cat is a h-aon**
38 cats	**trithead is a h-ochd cat**	**trithead cat is a h-ochd**
41 cats	**ceathrad is a h-aon cat**	**ceathrad cat is a h-aon**
49 cats	**ceathrad is a naoi cat**	**ceathrad cat is a naoi**
51 cats	**caogad is a h-aon cat**	**caogad cat is a h-aon**
52 cats	**caogad is a dhà cat**	**caogad cat is a dhà**
66 cats	**seasgad is a sia cat**	**seasgad cat is a sia**
77 cats	**seachdad is a seachd cat**	**seachdad cat is a seachd**
88 cats	**ochdad is a h-ochd cat**	**ochdad cat is a h-ochd**
99 cats	**naochad is a naoi cat**	**naochad cat is a naoi**

The singular form of nouns is used with **ceud** '100' and multiples of **ceud**. This also applies for **mìle** '1,000' and **muillean** '1,000,000'.

Here are some examples involving the higher numbers:

1,040	**mìle is dà fhichead**
3,789	**trì mìle, seachd ceud, ceithir fichead is a naoi**
80,453	**ceithir fichead mìle, ceithir ceud, dà fhichead is a trì-deug**

The vigesimal system is used for years and dates. Note how years are normally broken up into two numbers as in English:

1990	**naoi-deug, ceithir fichead is a deich**
1996	**naoi-deug, ceithir fichead is a sia-deug**

82b Age; 'How old are you?'

Study the following phrases. Note that **a dh'aois** 'of age' is optional:

Dè an aois a tha thu?	How old are you?
Tha mi deich bliadhna a dh'aois.	I am ten years of age.
Tha mi còig bliadhna deug a dh'aois.	I am fifteen years of age.
Tha mi fichead bliadhna a dh'aois.	I am twenty years of age.
Tha mi bhliadhna air fhichead.	I am twenty one years of age.
Tha mi dà fhichead bliadhna is a ceithir.	I am forty four years of age.

9

Exercise 9.4

Translate

- (a) 45 books
- (b) 76 horses
- (c) 87 chairs
- (d) 39 years of age
- (e) 62 years of age
- (f) 70 years of age

83 Use of '*de*' ('of')

In **Lesson 7** we saw that the genitive corresponds in many cases to the use of the preposition 'of' in English or 'de' in French. Generally speaking, the corresponding Gaelic preposition **de** 'of' is not used in possessive contexts. However, **de** 'of' is used, particularly in partitive contexts. Here are some examples:

tè de na boireannaich	one of the women
fear de na balaich	one of the boys
aon de na tidsearan	one of the teachers
cuid de na daoine	some of the people
punnd de shiùcar	a pound of sugar

84 Countries

In Gaelic, most countries are feminine in gender and are preceded by the article:

a' Bheilg	Belgium
a' Bhreatainn Bheag	Brittany
a' Chuimrigh	Wales
an Danmhairg	Denmark
an Eadailt	Italy
an Eilbheis	Switzerland
an Fhraing	France
an Fhionnlainn	Finland
a' Ghearmailt	Germany
a' Ghrèig	Greece
an Òlaind	Holland
a' Phòlainn	Poland
a' Phortaigeil	Portugal
an Ruis	Russia
an Roinn-Eòrpa	Europe
an t-Seapan (also **Iapan**)	Japan
an Spàinn(t)	Spain
an t-Suain	Sweden

Note: the article is also written in upper case, e.g. **An**, **A'**, etc

Ruisia without the article is also used for 'Russia'.

The following countries are not normally preceded by the article:

Alba or **Albainn**	Scotland
Breata(i)nn	Britain

Canada (*m*)	Canada
Èirinn	Ireland
Lucsamburg	Luxemburg
Lochla(i)nn/Nirribhidh	Norway
Sasa(i)nn	England
Sìna	China
an Rìoghachd Aonaichte	the United Kingdom
na Stàitean Aonaichte	the United States

Some dialects use **na Staidean** for the 'United States'.

In the genitive **Alba** and **Èirinn** may be preceded by the article, e.g.

muinntir na h-Alba	the people of Scotland
ceòl na h-Èireann (G)	the music of Ireland

In literary Gaelic, **Alba** also has the following case forms:

Albainn (prepositional)

Albann (genitive)

Vocabulary

nur comain	/nar komɛɲ/	in your debt, indebted to you
aiseag (*m*)	/aʃəg/	ferry
àm (*m*), **amannan** (*pl*)	/aum/, /aman̪ən/	time, times
an comain	/əŋ komɛɲ/	indebted, obliged
an-iar	/ə ɲiər/	western
bàta (*m*)	/baːht̪ə/	boat
bòrd-sanais (*m*)	/bɔːɼ(s)t̪ saniʃ/	notice board
caismeachd (*f*)	/kaʃmaxk/	signal, announcement
deagh* (*adj*)	/dʲoː/	good
duilich (*adj*)	/d̪uliç/	sorry
eilean (*m*)	/elan/, /elɛn/, /elaɲ/	island
gabhaibh (*vb*) **mo lethsgeul**	/ga-əv mə leʃkʲal̪/	excuse me (polite, formal form)
rathad (*m*), **rathaid** (G)	/ɼa-əd̪/, /ɼa-idʲ/	road
stèisean (*m*)	/stɛːʃən/	station
tiocaid (*f*)	/tɤgʲɛdʲ/	ticket
trèan (*m*)	/trɛːn/	train

CÒMHRADH (CONVERSATION)

Anns an stèisean

Torcal	Gabhaibh mo lethsgeul. Càite an tèid mi airson nan tiocaidean?
Anna	Thèid chun an dorais anns a bheil fear an stèisein na sheasamh.
Torcal	Mòran taing dhuibh.

Torcal a' bruidhinn ri fear an stèisein

Torcal	Am faigh mi tiocaid a bheir à seo gu ruige na h-Eileanan An-iar mi?
Fear an Stèisein	Gheibh, agus bidh sin còig notaichean air fhichead, a' dol taobh an Òbain.
Torcal	An toir an tiocaid fad an rathaid mi?
Fear an Stèisein	Tha mi duilich. Cha toir. Gheibh thu tiocaid eile airson an aiseig nuair a ruigeas tu an t-Òban.
Torcal	Am beir an ath thrèan air a' bhàta?
Fear an Stèisein	Beiridh, agus ann an deagh àm. Chì thu amannan nan trèanaichean air a' bhòrd-shanais ach cluinnidh tu caismeachd mus tig an trèan a-staigh dhan an stèisean.
Torcal	Tapadh leibhse. Tha mi fada nur comain.

TRANSLATION

In the station

Torquil	Excuse me. Where can I go for the tickets?
Ann	To the door where the station-master is standing.
Torquil	Many thanks to you.

Torquil speaking to the station-master

Torquil	Can I get a ticket that will take me from here to the Western Isles?
Station-master	Yes, and that will be £25, going via Oban.
Torquil	Will the ticket take me the whole way?
Station-master	I'm sorry. No. You will get another ticket for the ferry when you get to Oban.
Torquil	Will the next train catch the boat?
Station-master	Yes, and in good time. You will see the train times on the notice-board but you will hear an announcement before the train comes into the station.
Torquil	Thank you. I'm much obliged to you.

9

Lesson 10

85 Regular verbs: conditional/past habitual: independent forms

The forms of the conditional and the past habitual are identical in Scottish Gaelic. The conditional/past habitual is based on the verbal root as with the simple past and future. The difference between independent and dependent conditional/past habitual forms is slight. They both share the same endings and differ only in that independent forms are lenited; dependent forms are not lenited unless lenition is caused by a preceding leniting particle such as **cha** 'not'. The independent forms of the conditional/past habitual are formed as follows:

> ### CONDITIONAL/PAST HABITUAL:
> ### REGULAR VERBS: INDEPENDENT
>
> 1   Lenite the initial consonant of verbal root
> 2   Prefix **dh'** to vowels and **f** + vowel
> 3   Add the following suffixes:
>
> | Singular | Plural |
> |---|---|
> | 1 **(a)inn** | 1 **(e)amaid** or **(e)adh sinn** |
> | 2 **(e)adh tu** | 2 **(e)adh sibh** |
> | 3 **(e)adh e/i** | 3 **(e)adh iad** |

Here are examples based on the verbs **cuir** put and **òl** drink:

chuirinn	I would put; I used to put
chuireadh tu	you would put; you used to put
chuireadh e/i	he/she/it would put; he/she/it used to put
chuireamaid	we would put; we used to put
chuireadh sibh	you would put; you used to put
chuireadh iad	they would put; they used to put
dh'òlainn	I would drink; I used to drink
dh'òladh tu	you would drink; you used to drink
dh'òladh e/i	he/she/it would drink; he/she/it used to drink
dh'òlamaid	we would drink; we used to drink
dh'òladh sibh	you would drink; you used to drink
dh'òladh iad	they would drink; they used to drink

To form the conditional/past habitual, we lenite the initial consonant of the verb or prefix **dh'** to vowels and **f** + vowel and add the following endings to the verbal root: **(a)inn** and **(e)amaid** for the first person singular and plural respectively; **(e)adh** + the appropriate pronoun for the other persons. Note **tu** rather than **thu** is used with the conditional/past habitual ending **(e)adh**. The ending **(e)adh** is the form used with all noun subjects.

The pronouns **mi** and **sinn** are 'inbuilt' in the endings **(a)inn** and **(e)amaid** respectively. We refer to these as <u>synthetic</u> verbal forms. Verbal forms where the pronouns appear separated from or affixed to the verb are called <u>analytic</u> forms. Some dialects use analytic forms instead of **(e)amaid** for the first person plural e.g. **chuireadh sinn** instead of **chuireamaid**.

IMPORTANT

Verbs with two syllables usually ending in **-r, -l, -n, -ng** lose their second syllable when the conditional endings are added. Here is a list of the most important examples, illustrated with the ending **(e)adh**:

tachair	**thachradh**	would happen
fosgail	**dh'fhosgladh**	would open
bruidhinn	**bhruidhneadh**	would speak
tarraing	**thàirrneadh**	would pull

Note also:

innis	**dh'innseadh**	would tell

Note: final **-nn** and **-ng** are reduced to **-n** when an ending is added

Note that **-ich** is dropped in the verb **èirich** when a conditional ending is added, e.g. **dh'èirinn, dh'èireadh**

85a Regular verbs: conditional/past habitual: dependent forms

The independent and dependent forms of the conditional/past habitual are the same except that dependent forms are not lenited and that **dh'** is not prefixed to vowels or **f** + vowel. Note, however, the exceptions of **cha***, and **nach** which lenites **f**; **cha** becomes **chan** before **f**. Here are some examples:

Nach canadh tu sin a Sheumais?
Would you not say that, James?

Càite an cuireadh iad na beathaichean?
Where would they put the animals?

Cha ghlasainn an doras a h-uile h-oidhche.
I used not to lock the door every night.

Nach fhalbhadh Anna aig dà uair?
Wouldn't Ann leave at two o'clock?

The dependent froms **glasainn** and **falbhadh** in the last two examples are lenited by **cha** and **nach** respectively.

85b 'Tha': conditional/past habitual

The independent conditional/past habitual forms of the verb **tha** are:

bhinn	I would be; I used to be
bhiodh tu	you would be; you used to be
bhiodh e/i	he/she/it would be; he/she/it used to be
bhiomaid or **bhiodh sinn**	we would be; we used to be
bhiodh sibh	you would be; you used to be
bhiodh iad	they would be; they used to be

The dependent forms are exactly the same except that they are unlenited unless preceded by a leniting particle (e.g. **cha bhinn** 'I would not be'):

binn
biodh tu
biodh e/i
biomaid or **biodh sinn**
biodh sibh
biodh iad

When the conditional/past habitual forms of **tha** are used in the periphrastic (long) construction involving verbal nouns, the sense is usually continuous conditional/past habitual and not simple conditional/past habitual, e.g.

bhinn ag òl	I would be drinking; I used to be drinking
bhiodh Anna a' seinn	Ann would be singing; Ann used to be singing

Disyllabic forms are sometimes used, particularly in answers and in emphatic speech; these are often spelled with (silent) **-th-**, e.g. **b(h)ithinn**, **b(h)itheadh**, etc.

85c Answering questions

As usual, we repeat the main verb of the question:

Am biodh tu toilichte?	Would you be happy?
Bhiodh.	Yes.
Cha bhiodh.	No.
An òladh sibh seo?	Would you drink this?
Dh'òladh.	Yes.
Chan òladh.	No.
An glasadh Iain an doras?	Would John lock the door?
Ghlasadh.	Yes.
Cha ghlasadh.	No.

10

86 'If'

Gaelic has two words for 'if', namely **ma** and **nan**. **Nan** is only used with the conditional/past habitual. **Ma** is used with all other tenses, i.e. past, present and future. **Nan** in a dependent particle; **ma** is an independent particle.

86a 'Ma'

Ma dh'fhàg thu an sin e, càite a bheil e? (Past)
If you left it there, where is it?

Tha mise a' dol ann ma tha Anna a' tighinn. (Present)
I am going (there) if Ann is coming.

Chì mi thu ma bhios tu ann. (Future)
I will see you if you are (will be) there.

The clause containing 'if' is referred to as the <u>subordinate clause</u>; the remainder of the sentence is referred to as the <u>main clause</u>. When the main clause is in the past, present or future, the subordinate 'if' clause has the same tense as the main clause and 'if' is translated as **ma**.

86b 'Nan'

In Gaelic, if the main clause of an 'if' sentence is in the conditional, then the 'if' clause is also in the conditional and 'if' is translated as **nan**. Note that in English the 'if' clause appears in the past tense in such instances. Consider the following examples:

Sheinneadh Iain nan seinneadh tusa.
John would sing if you sang.

Cha ghlasadh iad an doras nam biodh fios aca.
They wouldn't lock the door if they knew.

Thogainn an iuchair nam fàgadh tu ann i.
I would pick up the key if you left it there.

Nan becomes **nam** before labials **b, p, f, m**.

86c '*Robh*' and conditional use of past tense

The form **robh** is often used instead of the conditional form, **bhiodh/b(h)itheadh**, of the verb **tha**. The form **robh** represents an old subjunctive form (see **Section 110**) though formally it is the same as the dependent past tense form. Examples:

Nam biodh tu ann aig deich uairean dh'fhalbhadh sinn còmhla.
If you were there at ten o'clock we would leave together.

OR

Nan robh thu ann aig deich uairean dh'fhalbhadh sinn còmhla.
If you were there at ten o'clock we would leave together.

The past tense is sometimes used in place of the conditional to introduce more certainty into conditional sentences: see **Section 98a**.

87 '*Mura*' ('if not')

English uses two words to express 'if not'. Gaelic uses one word: **mura**, which is a dependent particle. We have seen that Gaelic has two words for 'if, **ma** and **nan**, the latter form used with the conditional. **Mura** serves as the negative form for both **ma** and **nan**. Examples:

Innis dhomh mura bheil thu a' tighinn.
Tell me if you aren't coming.

Chan fhaic mi thu mura bi thu ann.
I will not see you if you aren't there.

Cha s(h)einneadh Iain mura seinneadh tusa.
John wouldn't sing if you didn't.

Leughainn am pàipear mura binn sgìth.
I would read the paper if I wasn't tired.

Mura becomes **mur** before **do** in the past tense of regular verbs and those irregular verbs which have **do** in their dependent forms:

Dèan an obair agad a Sheumais mur do rinn thu fhathast i.
Do your work James if you haven't done it yet.

Tha Dòmhnall ann an taigh Anna mur do dh'fhalbh e.
Donald is in Ann's house if he hasn't left (unless he has left).

87a 'If it were not for...'

'If it were not for' is translated in Gaelic as **mura b' e**. Consider the following examples:

Dh'fhalbhamaid a-mach an-diugh mura b' e an droch shìde.
We would go out today if it weren't for the bad weather.

Bhiodh Anna toilichte mura b' e Seumas.
Ann would be happy if it weren't for James.

88 'If' meaning 'whether'

When 'if' is used in a non-conditional sense in English, i.e. when it means 'whether', neither **ma** nor **nan** is used; instead we use the interrogative particle **an**. Consider the following examples:

Chan eil f(h)ios agam <u>an</u> tàinig Seumas.
I don't know if/whether James has come.

Chì sinn <u>an</u> tig e a-nochd.
We will see if/whether he comes tonight.

Saoil <u>an</u> e Anna a tha ann.
I wonder if/whether it's Ann.

Faighnich do Shìle <u>a bheil</u> i a' tighinn.
Ask Sheila if/whether she is coming.

Vocabulary

ach (*cjn*)	/ax/	only
abhainn (*f*)	/ãviɲ/, /ã-iɲ/, /ãũ-iɲ/, etc.	river
àite (*m*)	/aːhtʲə/	place
cuid (*f*) **mhath**	/kudʲ vã/	a fair amount
cuir (*vb*) **suas ri**	/kurʲ suəs rʲi/	put up with
dhomh (*adv*)	/ɣõ/	for me
dùisg (*vb*)	/d̪uːʃgʲ/	wake
dìreach (*adv*)	/dʲiːrʲəx/	just
druthag (*f*)	/d̪ru-ag/	drop
gabh (*vb*) **anail**	/gav anal/	rest, take a breather
grèim (*m*)	/grʲeim/	a bite
gu dearbh (*adv*)	/gə dʲ[ɛrɛ]v/	certainly
ith (*vb*)	/i/, /iç/	eat
litir (*f*)	/ʎihtʲərʲ/	letter
lorg (*vb*)	/ɫ̪[ɔrɔ]g/	find
madainn (*f*)	/mãd̪iɲ/	morning
nigh (*vb*)	/ɲi/	wash
post (*vb*)	/pɔst̪/	post
tha (*vb*) **f(h)ios agam**	/ha (f)is agəm/, /ha (f)isəm/	I know

Exercise 10.1

Translate

1   I wouldn't put up with that.
2   When did you used to wake up in the morning?
3   Why would John believe that?
4   They used to wash themselves in the river.
5   We found a place where we could draw breath.
6   They wouldn't eat a bite.
7   I would only take a small drop.
8   Would you post this letter for me?
9   They would understand a fair amount of it, certainly.
10   I would open the door for you if I knew you were there.

89 Adjectives: equative, comparative and superlative

(a) Equative

The pattern is as follows:

CHO	+	ADJECTIVE	+	RI	+	NOUN
cho		**sgìth** **ri**				**seann chù**
as		tired as				an old dog

Here are some other examples:

Tha Anna cho làidir ri Iain.	Ann is as strong as John.
Tha Màiri cho seòlta ri sionnach.	Mary is as cunning as a fox.

The equative forms can be used adverbially:

Tha an latha cho brèagha.	The day is so beautiful.
Tha e cho fuar.	It is so cold.
Tha a' chlann cho modhail.	The children are so well-behaved.

(b) Comparative and superlative of adjectives

The comparative and superlative forms of adjectives are identical in Gaelic and are differentiated only by the particle which precedes them, **nas** in the case of the comparative and **as** in the case of the superlative. For regular adjectives, the comparative/superlative is formed by slenderising the final consonant of the adjective and adding **e**. Slenderisation may affect the preceding vowel in the usual manner. (See **Appendix 1**.) **Nas** and **as** both lenite **f**. Here are some examples:

òg	young	**òige**
àrd	high, tall	**àirde**
dearg	red	**deirge**
sean	old	**sine**
trom	heavy	**truime**
brònach	sad	**brònaiche**
tiugh	thick	**tighe**
fliuch	wet	**fliche**
geur	sharp	**gèire**

Some adjectives drop their second syllable when the final **-e** is added:

ìseal	low	**ìsle**
uasal	high, noble	**uaisle**
dìleas	loyal	**dìlse**
milis	sweet	**mìlse**

Adjectives ending in a vowel show no change in the comparative/superlative:

brèagha	beautiful, lovely	**brèagha**
buidhe	yellow	**buidhe**
toilichte	happy	**toilichte**

90 Irregular adjectives

Here are some of the most important adjectives whose comparative/ superlative forms are irregular:

beag	small	**lugha**
bochd	poor	**bochda**
dona, olc	bad	**miosa**
doirbh	hard, difficult	**dorra**
duilich	hard	**duilghe**
fada	long	**faide**
furasda	easy	**fasa**
gearr, goirid	short	**giorra**
làidir	strong	**treasa** (or **làidire**)
math	good	**feàrr**
mòr	big	**motha, mò**
teth	hot	**teotha**

(b1) Comparative

NAS + ADJECTIVE + SLENDERISATION + E +   NA 'THAN'

nas   **òige**   **na**

younger than

Examples:

Tha mi nas fheàrr a-nis, tapadh leat.	I am better now, thank you.
Tha na balaich sin a' fàs nas miosa.	Those boys are getting worse.
Tha Anna nas sine na Catrìona.	Ann is older than Catherine.
A bheil Iain nas òige na Peigi?	Is John younger than Peggy?
Tha stàilinn nas treasa na fiodh.	Steel is stronger than wood.

(b2) Superlative

AS +   ADJECTIVE + SLENDERISATION + E

as   **òige**

youngest

Examples:

an gille as òige	the youngest boy
an taigh as motha	the biggest house
Sin a' chèic as mìlse a bhlais mi riamh oirre.	That is the sweetest cake I ever tasted.
Is e Iain as miosa.	John is the worst.

Nas and **as** are used when the main verb of the clause in which they occur is in the present or future tense. When the main verb of the clause is in the past or conditional/past habitual, the forms **na bu*** and **a bu*** (**na b'** and **a b'** before vowels and **f** + vowel) are used respectively. However, there is a tendency among younger speakers to use **nas** and **as** in all contexts. Here are some examples:

Bha na balaich na bu mhiosa.	The boys were worse.
Bhiodh Anna na bu mhotha an uair sin.	Ann would be bigger at that time.
Bha Màiri na bu shine na Iain.	Mary was older than John.
Bhinn na bu t(h)oilichte ri sin.	I would be happier with that.
Thàinig an nighean a bu bhrèagha.	The most beautiful girl came.
Sin an ceòl a b' fheàrr a chuala mi riamh.	That is the best music that I ever heard.
Sin an taigh a bu mhotha a chunnaic mi riamh	That is the the biggest house I ever saw.
Is e Iain a bu mhiosa.	John was the worst.

10

Vocabulary

a' Bheurla (f)	/ə vjɤːɾɫ̪ə/	English
a' Ghàidhlig (f)	/ə ɣaːligʲ/	Gaelic
Ailean	/alan/, /ɛlan/, /ɛlɛɲ/, etc.	Alan
an t-Òban (m)	/ən̪ t̪ɔːban/	Oban
beairteach (adj)	/bɛɾst̪ʲəx/, /bjaɾst̪ʲəx/	rich
buinig (vb)	/buɲigʲ/	win
can (vb)	/kan/	say
craobh (f)	/krɯːv/	tree
doirbh, duilich (adj)	/d̪[ɤrʲɤ]v/, /d̪uliç/	difficult
duais (f)	/d̪uəʃ/	prize
fear (m) **lagha**	/fɛr ɫ̪ɤɣə/	lawyer
riamh (adv)	/rʲiəv/	ever
sgian (f)	/skʲiən/	knife
sìde (m,f)	/ʃiːdʲə/	weather
suidh (vb)	/sɯj/	sit
teaghlach (m)	/tʲɤːɫ̪əx/	family

Exercise 10.2

Translate

1   I would say that John is older than Mary.
2   If the weather were better we would sit outside.
3   I told you that you would win the biggest prize.
4   William lived in Oban when he was younger.
5   James is the eldest in his family.
6   It is easier when the knife is sharper.
7   Peggy is stronger than Alan although she is smaller than him.
8   That is the highest tree that I ever saw.
9   Gaelic is as difficult as English. (say: *the* Gaelic and *the* English)
10   The teacher is not as rich as the lawyer.

91 'That': linking clauses and reported speech

It is important to distinguish between **a** 'that/which' and **gun** 'that' in Gaelic. Both **a** and **gun** correspond to different functions of 'that' in English and there can be some confusion amongst learners about when to use **a** and when to use **gun**. The difference between them is this: **a** is a relative pronoun and **gun** is a conjunction. **A** is used following nouns, adverbs and independent particles and is followed by an independent verbal form. **Gun** always follows a verbal clause, usually containing one of the verbs meaning 'say, tell, hear, think, promise, etc.' (i.e. in reported speech), and is followed by a dependent verbal form. Consider the following examples:

Relative **a**

Cò <u>a</u> rinn seo?	Who did this?
Dè <u>a</u> dh'òl thu?	What did you drink?
an t-òran <u>a</u> sheinn Seumas	the song that James sang
am bàta <u>a</u> thàinig a-steach	the boat that came in
Is ann fliuch <u>a</u> tha an latha.	It is wet that the day is.
Is ann an-dè <u>a</u> chaidh Iain a Ghlaschu.	It is yesterday that John went to Glasgow.

Conjunction **gun**

Thuirt Iain <u>gun</u> robh sneachd an Glaschu.	John said that there was snow in Glasgow.
Chuala mi <u>gun</u> do dh'fhalbh Anna.	I heard that Ann left.
Thuirt iad rium <u>gun</u> tigeadh iad.	They told me that they would come.
Gheall Màiri <u>gun</u> tilleadh i a dh'aithghearr.	Mary promised that she would return soon.
Tha mi a' smaoineachadh <u>gun</u> tàinig Iain.	I think that John came.

Note: 'that' may be left out in English but never in Gaelic, e.g.

an t-òran <u>a</u> sheinn Iain   the song (that) John sang
Chuala mi <u>gun</u> tàinig Anna.   I heard (that) Ann came.

Note also that **nach** serves as the negative form of both **a** and **gun** (see **Section 52**), e.g.

an t-òran <u>nach</u> do sheinn Seumas (*rel*)
the song that James didn't sing

Chuala mi <u>nach</u> do dh'fhalbh Anna. (conj)
I heard that Ann didn't leave.

91a *'Gun'*, *'gur'*: linking *'is'* sentences

When **gun** is used to link an **is/is e** and **is ann** clause/sentence to a preceding clause/sentence, **gun** and **is** combine to give **gur** when **is** is followed by a pronoun or **ann**; **gur** prefixes **h** to **e/i/iad** and **ann**. Note that some dialects use **gun** in preference to **gur**, in which case **gun** does not prefix **h-**. In idioms involving **is** (**Section 32a** and **42c**), **gun** combines with **is** to give **gun**.

Thuirt Iain + is e tidsear a tha ann an Anna becomes:
Thuirt Iain <u>gur h-e</u> tidsear a tha ann an Anna.
John said that Ann is a teacher.

Here are some other examples:

Tha mi a' smaoineachadh <u>gur h-e</u> damhan-allaidh a tha ann.
I think that it is a spider.

Dh'innis Iain dhomh <u>gur h-e</u> Màiri a sheinn aig a' chèilidh.
John told me that it was Mary who sang at the ceilidh.

Chuala mi <u>gur h-e</u> co-là-breith Sìle a tha ann an-diugh.
I heard that it is Sheila's birthday today.

Thuirt Anna <u>gur h-e</u> a piuthar a bha a' seinn aig a' chèilidh.
Ann said that it was her sister that was singing at the ceilidh.

Gheall Iain <u>gur sibhse</u> a ghlasadh an doras.
John promised that you would lock the door.

Tha Dòmhnall ag ràdh <u>gun</u> aithne dha piuthar Sheumais.
Donald says that he knows James' sister.

Tha mi a' smaoineachadh <u>gun</u> toil le Peigi suiteas.
I think that Peggy likes sweets.

Thuirt Mòrag <u>gun</u> fheàrr leatha fion dearg na fion geal.
Morag said she prefers red wine to white wine.

Note: **gun** lenites **f**.

10

91b Linking '*is ann*' sentences

As before, **gun** combines with **is** to give **gur** which prefixes **h-** to **ann**. Some dialects use **gun** which does not prefix **h-** to **ann**.

Dh'innis Iain dhomh + is ann air a' bhus a chunnaic e Catrìona becomes:
Dh'innis Iain dhomh <u>gur h-ann</u> air a' bhus a chunnaic e Catrìona.
John told me that it was on the bus that he saw Catherine.

Here are some other examples:

Chuala mi <u>gur h-ann</u> an-diugh a tha an clas.
I heard that it is today that the class is, i.e. that the class is (on) today.

Leugh mi <u>gur h-ann</u> ann an Dùn Èideann a bha Donnchadh Bàn a' fuireach.
I read that it was in Edinburgh that Duncan Bàn lived.

(See **Reading Practice**, **Texts 2** and **3**.)

Vocabulary		
Gàidhealtachd (*f*)	/gɛ:-ə̪t̪əxk/	Highlands, Gaelic-speaking area

Exercise 10.3

*Link the following clauses using **gun (gur)** or **a** where appropriate and translate:*

1 Thuirt Iain + bha e a-muigh a-raoir.
2 Chuala mi + thàinig Seumas.
3 An rud + chunnaic mi.
4 An naidheachd + chuala tu.
5 Thuirt Anna + is e ministear a tha ann.
6 Tha mi a' smaoineachadh + is e co-là-breith Sheumais a tha ann an-diugh.
7 Leugh mi + is ann an-diugh a thachair e.
8 Tha iad a' ràdh + is ann air a' Ghàidhealtachd a bha iad a' fuireach.

92 Adjectives: plural

Only adjectives with one syllable used attributively (**Section 16**) have plural forms. Attributive adjectives with more than one syllable do not change form in the plural. (Predicative adjectives never have plural forms.) Nominative, prepositional and genitive plural forms are identical. To form the plural of adjectives, we add **-a** or **-e** to final consonants; **-a** is added to adjectives which end in broad consonants; **-e** is added to adjectives which end in slender consonants. In colloquial Scottish Gaelic there is a tendency to use singular in place of plural adjectives with many monosyllabic adjectives. Consider the following examples:

SINGULAR	PLURAL	
mòr	mòra	big
beag	beaga	small
dubh	dubha	black
math	matha	good
glic	glice	clever
mìn	mìne	smooth
tinn	tinne	sick
marbh	marbha	dead

Plural adjectives are lenited if they follow a plural noun which ends in a slender consonant (i.e. Type B plurals; see **Lesson 8, Section 68**). Consider the following examples:

TYPE A PLURALS

na caileagan òga	the young girls
na bùthan ùra	the new shops
na leabhraichean matha	the good books

TYPE B PLURALS

na balaich bheaga	the small boys
na cait dhubha	the black cats
na boireannaich ghlice	the clever/wise women

Note that the lenited plural form of adjectives is used with the indefinite pronoun **feadhainn** 'some', e.g.

an fheadhainn bheaga	the small ones, the small children
an fheadhainn mhòra	the big ones

Vocabulary

inntinneach	/iː ɲdʲiɲəx/	interesting

Exercise 10.4

Remove the brackets and make the necessary adjustments and translate the following phrases:

1 caileagan (òg)
2 an fheadhainn (geal)
3 cait (dubh)
4 clasaichean (mòr)
5 balaich (modhail)
6 daoine (làidir)
7 bùird (glan)
8 pàistean (math)
9 leabhraichean (inntinneach)
10 boireannaich (beairteach)

93 Personal numerals

When referring to people, the following numerals are used:

dithis/dithis(t)	two people, a twosome
triùir	three people, a threesome
ceathrar	four people
còignear	five people
sianar	six people
seachdnar	seven people
ochdnar	eight people
naonar	nine people
deichnear	ten people

These numerals, unlike the other numerals we have met so far, are nouns and may be used on their own without a following noun, e.g.

Bha dithis(t) aca ann.	There were two of them there.
Thàinig ceathrar a-steach dhan an t-seòmar.	Four (people) came into the room.

All are masculine except **dithis(t)** and **triùir** which are feminine. The lenited plural form of adjectives is generally used with the personal numbers, e.g.

an dithis(t) mhòra	the two big people
an triùir bheaga	the three small people

Qualifying nouns may follow these numerals, in which case they appear in the genitive plural. Recall that genitive plurals are automatically lenited when the definite article does not precede (**Section 68c**). Here are some examples:

dithis(t) dhaoine	two people	**dithis(t) ghillean**	two boys
triùir dhaoine	three people	**triùir ghillean**	three boys
ceathrar dhaoine	four people	**ceathrar ghillean**	four boys
còignear dhaoine	five people	**còignear ghillean**	five boys
sianar dhaoine	six people	**sianar ghillean**	six boys
seachdnar dhaoine	seven people	**seachdnar ghillean**	seven boys
ochdnar dhaoine	eight people	**ochdnar ghillean**	eight boys
naonar dhaoine	nine people	**naonar ghillean**	nine boys
deichnear dhaoine	ten people	**deichnear ghillean**	ten boys

In each case it is possible to translate as 'a twosome of ...', 'a threesome of ...', etc.

Vocabulary

air neo (*cjn*)	/əɾ ɲɔː/	or, alternatively
Alba (*f*)	/[aɫa]bə/	Scotland
an dà chuid (*f*)	/ən̪ daː xudʲ/	both
an lorg sin (*adv*)	/ən̪ ɫ[ɔrɔ]g ʃin/	after that, following that
an toiseach (*adv*)	/ən̪ t̪ɔʃəx/	firstly
an uair sin (*adv*)	/ən̪ uərʲ ʃin/	that time, then
beachd (*m*)	/bɛxk/, /bjaxk/	opinion
beò (*adj*)	/bjɔː/	alive
boin (*vb*)	/bɔɲ/	belong to, relate to
clas-oidhche (*m*)	/klas ɤiçə/	night-class, evening-class
cò dhiubh?	/koː juː/	which of?
cuingichte (*adj*)	/kuiɲʲigʲniçtʲə/	restricted, limited to
cuir (*vb*) **air bhonn**	/kurʲ ɛrʲ voun̪/	set up, found
cuir (*vb*) **air dòigh**	/kurʲ ɛrʲ d̪ɔːj/	arrange, set up, organise
cùrsa-taic (*m*)	/kuːɾsə taçkʲ/	support-course, back-up course
cùm (*vb*)	/kuːm/	keep
dealbh (*vb*)	/dʲ[aɫa]v/	create, shape, construct, design
deireadh-sheachdain (*m*)	/dʲɛrʲə hɛxkɛn/	weekend
dian-chùrsa (*m*)	/dʲian xuːɾsə/, /dʲiən xuːɾsə/	intensive course
dualchainnt (*f*)	/d̪uəɫxaiɲdʲ/	dialect
fa leth (*adj*)	/fa le/	particular
fileanta (*adj*)	/filan̪t̪ə/	fluent
fuasgailte (*adj*)	/fuəsgiʎtʲə/	fluent, active
Gàidhealtachd (*f*)	/geː-əɫd̪əxk/, /geː-əɫd̪axg/	Highlands, Gaelic-speaking area
Galltachd (*f*)	/gauɫt̪axk/	Lowlands
iarr (*vb*)	/iəɾ/	want, ask
is dòcha	/əs d̪ɔːxə/	probably, perhaps
labhairt (*f*)	/ɫavər(s)tʲ/	speaking
lean (*vb*)	/ʎɛn/	follow
leig fios gu (*vb*)	/ʎegʲ fis gə/	inform
leudaich (*vb*)	/ʎiad̪iç/	expand
luchd-ionnsachaidh (*m*)	/ɫuxk jũːn̪sxəxi/	learners
mair (*vb*)	/marʲ/	live, last
mìos (*f*)	/mĩəs/, /mĩəs/	month
modh (*m*) **cainnte**	/mõɣ kaiɲdʲə/	mode of speaking, speech
plana (*m*), **planaichean** (*pl*)	/planə/, /planiçən/	plan, plans
seòrsa (*m*)	/ʃɔːɾsə/	type
sgoil (*f*)	/skɔl/	school
suidhich (*vb*)	/sui-iç/	situate
tairg (*vb*)	/t̪[ɛrʲɛ]gʲ/	offer
teagasg (*vn*)	/tʲegəsk/	teaching
tì (*f*)	/tiː/	tea

CÒMHRADH (CONVERSATION)

Iain a' dèanamh agallamh airson obair mar oifigear cànain le Comann Luchd Ionnsachaidh

Màiri Thig a-staigh agus suidh an seo. Cò dhiubh a b' fheàrr leat tì no cofaidh?

Iain Cofaidh as fheàrr leamsa, gun bhainne, gun siùcar.

Màiri Ceart gu leòr. A-nis, nan gabhadh tu an obair seo – nan tairgeamaid dhut i – dè na planaichean a bhiodh agad airson luchd-ionnsachaidh na Gàidhlig ann an Alba an-diugh?

Iain An toiseach, chuirinn air dòigh dian-chùrsa labhairt a mhaireadh mìos no dà mhìos. Dhealbhainn an uair sin, an lorg sin, cùrsaichean-taic a bhiodh na bu ghiorra a ghabhadh iad ann an clasaichean-oidhche air neo ann an sgoiltean deireadh-sheachdain. Chumadh sin a' Ghàidhlig aca fileanta fuasgailte.

Màiri Càite an suidhicheadh tu na cùrsaichean sin? An ann air a' Ghàidhealtachd air neo air a' Ghalltachd a chuireadh tu iad?

Iain An dà chuid. Anns an dà àite.

Màiri An leudaicheadh tu air sin dhuinn?

Iain Dh'iarrainn gum biodh cuid aca air a' Ghàidhealtachd a chionn is gur h-ann an sin as motha a tha a' Ghàidhlig beò. Ach air an làimh eile, bhiodh e na b' fhasa do mhòran luchd-ionnsachaidh air a' Ghalltachd nam biodh cothrom aca air cùrsaichean a bhiodh na b' fhaisge orra.

Màiri Nan cuireadh tu na cùrsaichean sin air bhonn, am boineadh an seòrsa Gàidhlig a bhiodh tu a' teagasg do dh'àite sam bith fa leth?

Iain Air a' Ghàidhealtachd, is dòcha gum biodh e na b' fheàrr nan leanamaid ri dualchainnt an àite. Ach air a' Ghalltachd, chanainn gum biodh e na b' fhasa nan taghamaid modh cainnte nach robh cho cuingichte.

Màiri Tapadh leat airson do bheachdan. Leigidh sinn fios thugad uaireigin air an ath-sheachdain ciamar a chaidh dhut anns an agallamh. Beannachd leat.

Iain Mar sin leibh.

10

TRANSLATION

John doing an interview for a job as a language officer with Comann Luchd Ionnsachaidh (Learners' Society)

Mary   Come in and sit here. Which would you prefer, tea or coffee?

John   I prefer coffee, without milk or sugar.

Mary   Very well. Now, if you should accept this job – if we were to offer it to you – what plans would you have for Gaelic learners in Scotland today?

John   First, I would set up an intensive course of speaking that would last for a month or two months. Then, after that, I would design back-up courses that were shorter that they could take in night-classes or in weekend-schools. That would keep their Gaelic fluent and active.

Mary   Where would you situate these courses? Is it in the Gaelic-speaking areas you would put them or in the Lowlands?

John   Both. In the two places.

Mary   Would you expand on that for us?

John   I would want some of them to be in the Gaelic speaking area since that is where Gaelic is most alive. But on the other hand, it would be easier for most of the learners in the Lowlands if they had an opportunity to have courses that were nearer them.

Mary   If you should set up these courses, would the kind of Gaelic you would be teaching belong to any particular place?

John   In the Gaelic-speaking areas, perhaps it would be better if we followed the dialect of the place. But in the Lowlands, I would say it would be easier if we selected a mode of speech that wasn't so restricted.

Mary   Thank you for your opinions. We'll let you know sometime next week how you fared in the interview. Goodbye.

John   Goodbye.

10

Lesson 11

94 Modal verbs 'feum' and 'faod'

The modal verbs **feum** 'must' and **faod** 'may' are defective verbs, which usually appear in the future and conditional only.

Future:

feumaidh mi	I must
faodaidh tu	you may/can

Conditional:

dh'fheumadh Iain	John would have to
dh'fheumainn	I would have to
dh'fhaodadh Anna	Ann could
dh'fhaodamaid/dh'fhaodadh sinn	we could

95 Infinitives

The infinitive form of a verb in Gaelic is the same as that of the verbal noun: see **Section 17**. The infinitive forms of the irregular verbs **rach** and **thig** are normally **a dhol** and **a thighinn**, although **dol** and **tighinn** are also used respectively. Infinitives are used with the following auxiliary verbs and idioms:

  (a)   the modal verbs **feum** and **faod**
  (b)   modal idioms expressing obligation
  (c)   a number of idioms expressing 'wanting, liking, hoping, capability, remembering, obligation, managing'
  (d)   verbs expressing motion or intent
  (e)   the verb **sguir** 'cease'

Consider the following examples:

VERBAL NOUN/INFINITIVE

(a)

feumaidh tu	**falbh**	you must leave
faodaidh tu	**tighinn/a thighinn**	you may come
dh'fheumadh Anna	**tilleadh**	Ann would have to return
dh'fhaodainn	**dol/a dhol**	I could go
(b)		
is fheàrr dhut	**sgur**	you had better stop, cease

bu chòir dhut	seinn	you should sing
tha còir agad	falbh	you should leave

(c)

tha mi airson	seinn	I want to sing
tha mi ag iarraidh	tilleadh	I want to return
bu toil le Iain	suidhe	John would like to sit
tha dùil aig Màiri	siubhal	Mary expects to travel
is urrainn do Sheumas	dràibheadh	James can drive
tha cuimhne agam air	dùsgadh	I remember wakening
tha/bha aig Iain ri	falbh	John has/had to leave/go away
chaidh aig Anna air	fònadh	Ann managed to phone

(d)

chaidh Iain	a cheannach	John went to buy
tha Seumas a' dol	a bhruidhinn	James is going to speak
thàinig Anna	a dh'fhaicinn	Ann came to see

(e)

sguir iad	a chaoineadh	they stopped crying

Leaving aside the irregular variants **a thighinn** and **a dhol**, you will see from the above examples that **a** 'to' occurs before an infinitive only when the preceding verb is a verb of motion or a verb implying intent, and after the verb **sguir** 'cease':

a* occurs before consonants and

a dh' occurs before vowels and **f** + vowel

95a Indirect objects of infinitives

Noun objects of infinitive verbs complemented by prepositions follow the preposition; pronoun objects combine with the preposition to form the appropriate prepositional pronoun:

Bu toil leam bruidhinn ri Seumas.
I would like to speak to James.

An urrainn dhut faighneachd de dh'Anna?
Are you able to ask Ann?

Bu chòir dhut fuireach ruinn.
You should wait for us.†

Thàinig Iain a bhruidhinn ris a' chlas.
John came to talk to the class.

Chaidh Anna a dh'fhuireach còmhla ri Peigi.
Ann went to stay with Peggy.

Tha Ailean a' dol a dh'innse dhuinn.
Alan is going to tell (to) us.

† Note the contrast with **Bu chòir dhut fuireach againn** 'You should stay with us (i.e. you should lodge with us)'.

Vocabulary

a-nis (*adv*)	/ə niʃ/	now
Baile Àtha Cliath	/bal a kliə/	Dublin
coimhead (*vn*)	/kɔjəd̪/, /kɛ̃-əd̪/	watching
cuideachadh (*vn*)	/kud̪ʲəxəɣ/	helping
dol (*vn*)	/d̪ɔl̪/	going
duilich (*adj*)	/d̪uliç/	sorry
èisteachd (*vn*)	/eːʃd̪ʲəxk/	listening
falbh (*vn*)	/f[al̪a]v]	leaving
fuireach (*vn*)	/furʲəx/	living
ithe (*vn*)	/i-ə/, /içə/	eating
snàmh (*vn*)	/sn̪ãːv/	swimming
tighinn (*vn*)	/tʲi-iɲ/, tʲi-ən/	coming

Exercise 11.1

Translate

1 I like to eat.
2 I have to leave.
3 He would like to help.
4 She wants to speak.
5 He was going to come.
6 She came to watch.
7 They expect to live in Oban.
8 You should go to Dublin.
9 Aren't you going to listen?
10 Peggy can swim.

11

95b Direct objects of infinitives: nouns

When the infinitive is preceded by **a***/**a dh'** 'to' (i.e. types (d) and (e) above), noun objects follow the infinitive directly. A following noun object usually appears in the genitive only when the object is a definite noun: see **Section 20**.

Thàinig Seumas a dh'ithe <u>biadh</u>.
James came to eat food.

Chaidh iad a cheannach <u>leabhraichean</u>.
They went to buy books.

Dh'fhalbh na gillean a chluich <u>ball-coise</u>.
The boys went off to play football.

Thàinig Anna a dhèanamh <u>na h-obrach</u>. (G)
Ann came to do the work.

Tha Peigi a' dol a leughadh <u>a' phàipeir</u>. (G)
Peggy is going to read the paper.

Sguir a' chlann a bhruidhinn <u>na Beurla</u>. (G)
The children ceased to speak English.

95c Inversion

When the infinitive is not preceded by **a*/a dh'**, i.e. when 'to' is not translated (i.e. types (a), (b), (c) above), the noun object of the infinitive comes before the infinitive. In other words the normal order is inverted, and **a*** is inserted between the object and the infinitive. When this **a*** precedes a vowel or **fh-** it is usually not written in order to reflect pronunciation but it is retained here for reasons of clarity. Here are some examples:

Bu toil leam <u>bruidhinn</u>.	I would like to speak.
Bu toil leam <u>Gàidhlig a bhruidhinn</u>.	I would like to speak Gaelic.
Bu chòir dhut <u>ionnsachadh</u>.	You should learn.
Bu chòir dhut <u>Gàidhlig a ionnsachadh</u>.†	You should learn Gaelic.

† 'a ionnsachadh' pronounced as 'ionnsachadh'.

Some other examples:

Tha Alasdair ag iarraidh <u>leabhar a cheannach</u>.
Alasdair wants to buy a book.

Bha dùil aig Anna <u>Iain a fhaicinn</u> a-màireach.††
Ann hoped to see John tomorrow.

Dh'iarr an tidsear orm <u>an doras a fhosgladh</u>.
The teacher asked me to open the door.

11

An urrainn dhut <u>Gàidhlig a bhruidhinn</u>?
Can you speak Gaelic?

†† 'a fhaicinn' pronounced as 'fhaicinn'.

Vocabulary

bainne (*m*)	/baɲə/	milk
dotair (*m*)	/dɔhtɛrʲ/	doctor
faighinn (*vn*)	/fɛ̃-iɲ/, /fɛ̃-in/, /fãjiɲ/	getting
obair (*f*)	/obərʲ/	work
pàigheadh (*vn*)	/pɛ:-əɣ/	paying
togail (*vn*)	/togal/	raise, pick up, etc.

Exercise 11.2

Translate

1   I must do my work.
2   She can speak Gaelic.
3   You should buy a new car.

4   John wants to write a book.
5   You had better close the door after you.
6   We couldn't pay the doctor.
7   We are going to get milk.
8   Ann came to pick up her son.
9   Donald remembers reading that book.
10   Peggy could speak Gaelic.

96 Direct objects of infinitives: pronouns

Direct object pronouns of infinitives do not follow the infinitive. Possessive pronouns are used instead of the ordinary pronouns to denote the objects of infinitives; they precede the infinitive. 'I would like to do it' becomes in Gaelic 'I would like its doing': **bu toil leam a dhèanamh**.

Here are other examples:

Bu toil leam <u>a faicinn</u>.	I would like to see her.
Tha Iain ag iarraidh <u>a cheannach</u>.	John wants to buy it.
Tha dùil aig Seumas <u>mo phòsadh</u>.	James expects to marry me.
Dh'iarr iad orm <u>an dùnadh</u>.	They asked me to close them.
Tha mi airson <u>ur coinneachadh</u>.	I would like to meet you.
An urrainn dhuibh <u>ar faicinn</u> an-diugh?	Can you see us today?

When **a*/a dh'** precedes the infinitive (i.e. types (d) and (e) above), the possessive pronouns combine with it to give the following forms (cf. **Section 72**):

gam*	**gar**
gad*	**gur**
ga*	**gan/gam**
ga	

Examples:

Tha sinn a' dol <u>ga choimhead</u>.	We are going to watch him/it.
Thàinig na caileagan <u>ga dùsgadh</u>.	The girls came to wake her/it.
Chaidh Iain <u>gan iarraidh</u>.	John went to get them.

96a Demonstrative pronouns as objects of infinitives

The demonstrative pronouns **seo, sin, siud** are treated like nouns, e.g.

Thàinig Anna a dhèanamh <u>sin</u>.	Ann came to do that.
Bu toil leam <u>sin a dhèanamh</u>.	I would like to do that.
Feumaidh mi <u>seo a ràdh</u>.	I must say this.

97 'A bhith' ('to be')

The infinitive form of the verb **tha** is **a bhith**. (It cannot be used with the periphrastic construction involving **tha**, unlike other infinitives/verbal nouns.) Here are some examples:

Bu toil leam <u>a bhith</u> an Glaschu.	I would like to be in Glasgow.
Tha mi a' dol <u>a bhith</u> an Dùn Èideann.	I am going to be in Edinburgh.
Tha dùil aca <u>a bhith</u> a' falbh.	They expect to be leaving.
Bu chòir dhut <u>a bhith</u> modhail.	You should be well behaved.
Tha Dòmhnall a' dol <u>a bhith</u> ag obair.	Donald is going to be working.

Vocabulary

coimhead (*vn*)	/kɔ̃jəd/, /kɛ̃-əd̪/	watching, seeing (of visit)
creidsinn (*vn*)	/krʲedʲʃiɲ/	believing
cuideachadh (*vn*)	/kudʲəxəɣ/	helping
dùsgadh (*vn*)	/d̪uːskəɣ/	wakening
glanadh (*vn*)	/gɫanəɣ/	cleaning
is fheàrr le Màiri	/ʃaːr lɛ mãːrʲi/	Mary prefers
òran (*m*)	/ɔːran/	song
ràdh (*vn*)	/raː(ɣ)/	saying
tarraing (*vn*)	/t̪ariɲ/	pull
teagasg (*vn*)	/tʲegəsk/	teaching
tha an t-eagal air Iain	/ha əṇ tʲegəɫ ɛrʲ i-aɲ/	John is afraid

11

Exercise 11.3

Translate

1. He likes to eat it (*m*).
2. Ann hoped to sing it (*m*) at the ceilidh.
3. John was afraid to pull it (*f*).
4. The young boys have to clean them.
5. Calum went to watch her.
6. Mary prefers to teach it (*f*).
7. You should believe us.
8. Ann is going to waken them.
9. We would like to help you.
10. James remembers saying that.

98 The perfect

A periphrastic construction is used to form the perfect in Gaelic. It is similar to that which we learnt for the present tense except that **air** 'after' replaces **aig** 'at'. Compare:

The Iain a' tighinn.	John is coming.
Tha Iain air tighinn.	John has come, *lit* 'John is after coming'.

Here are some other examples:

Tha Anna air falbh.	Ann has left.
Tha Uilleam air tilleadh.	William has returned.
Tha iad air a dhol a-mach.	They have gone out.
Tha Màiri air seinn.	Mary has sung.

Direct objects are inverted and placed before the verbal noun/infinitive as before (see **Section 95c**):

Tha Calum air <u>leabhar a cheannach</u>.	Calum has bought a book.
Tha Niall air <u>Gàidhlig a ionnsachadh</u>.	Neil has learnt Gaelic.
Tha Dàibhidh air <u>an doras a pheantadh</u>.	David has painted the door.

Note: when the object is preceded by the definite article, it does not take the prepositional form after **air**, e.g.

Tha Anna air <u>an t-uisge a òl</u>.	Ann has drunk the water.
Tha Raibeart air <u>an cù a bhiadhadh</u> mar-thà.	Robert has fed the dog already.
Tha Anna air <u>am borbair a phàigheadh</u>.	Ann has paid the hairdresser.

11

98a The pluperfect

The pluperfect is formed by replacing **tha** with the past form, **bha** in the periphrastic perfect construction:

Bha Anna air tighinn.	Ann had come.
Bha Uilleam air tilleadh.	William had returned.
Bha iad air a dhol a-mach.	They had gone out.
Bha Màiri air seinn.	Mary had sung.
Bha Calum air leabhar a cheannach.	Calum had bought a book.
Bha Niall air Gàidhlig a ionnsachadh.	Neil had learnt Gaelic.
Bha Dàibhidh air an doras a pheantadh.	David had painted the door.

Note: The pluperfect is sometimes used in place of the conditional to introduce more certainty into conditional sentences (see **Section 86b**), e.g.

Nan robh thu/nam biodh tu ann aig deich uairean bha sinn air falbh còmhla.
If you had been/were there at ten o'clock we would (definitely) have left together.

98b The future perfect

The future perfect is formed by replacing **tha** with the future form **bidh** in the periphrastic perfect construction:

Bidh Anna air falbh.	Ann will have left.
Bidh Uilleam air tilleadh.	William will have returned.
Bidh iad air a dhol a-mach.	They will have gone out.
Bidh Màiri air seinn.	Mary will have sung.
Bidh Calum air leabhar a cheannach.	Calum will have bought a book.
Bidh Niall air Gàidhlig a ionnsachadh.	Neil will have learnt Gaelic.
Bidh Dàibhidh air an doras a pheantadh.	David will have painted the door.

98c The conditional perfect

The conditional perfect is formed by replacing **tha** with the conditional form **bhiodh** in the periphrastic perfect construction:

Bhiodh Anna air falbh.	Ann would have left.
Bhiodh Uilleam air tilleadh.	William would have returned.
Bhiodh iad air a dhol a-mach.	They would have gone out.
Bhiodh Màiri air seinn.	Mary would have sung.
Bhiodh Calum air leabhar a cheannach.	Calum would have bought a book.
Bhiodh Niall air Gàidhlig a ionnsachadh.	Neil would have learnt Gaelic.
Bhiodh Dàibhidh air an doras a pheantadh.	David would have painted the door.

11

The pluperfect is also formed with **an dèidh** and the infinitive/verbal noun as follows:

an dèidh do Sheumas tilleadh
after/when James had returned (*lit* 'after returning by James')

an dèidh do Chatrìona an cat a chur a-mach
after/when Catherine had put out the cat

an dèidh dhomh mo bhracaist a ghabhail
after/when I had taken my breakfast/after/when I had had my breakfast

an dèidh dhi an sgoil a fhàgail
after/when she had left the school

an dèidh dhuinn an obair againn a dhèanamh
after/when we had done our work

98d The immediate perfect

The immediate perfect is formed by inserting **dìreach** 'just' before **air** in the ordinary perfect construction.

Tha Màiri dìreach air tighinn.	Mary has just arrived.
Tha iad dìreach air falbh.	They have just left.
Tha mi dìreach air an doras a dhùnadh.	I have just closed the door.

Vocabulary

an t-seachdain seo tighinn (*adv*)	/əɲ tʲɛxkɛn ʃɔ tʲi-iɲ/	next week
cruinneachadh (*vn*)	/kruɲəxəɣ/	gathering
cuideam (*m*)	/kudʲəm/	weight
cuir air (*vb*)	/kurʲ erʲ/	to put on (of weight)
cus (*adv*)	/kus/	too much
fiosrachadh (*m*)	/fisrəxəɣ/	information
gu lèir (*adv*) (follows the noun)	/gə ʎeːrʲ/	all
ionnsaich (*vb*)	/jũːn̪siç/, /jũːsiç/	learn
litir (*f*)	/ʎihtʲərʲ/	letter
mu dheireadh (*adv*)	/ma jerʲəɣ/	at last
oilthigh (*m*)	/ɔlhɣi/	university
reic (*vb*)	/reckʲ/	selling
tòisich (*vb*)	/t̪ɔːʃiç/	begin, start

Exercise 11.4

Translate

1. Robert has just gone.
2. Joan has come.
3. John has written the letter.
4. He has put on weight.
5. They have gone out.
6. Mary will have started in the university next week.
7. Ann has sold the old house at last.
8. James would have learnt Gaelic.
9. John has eaten too much already.
10. After Neil had gathered all of the information...

99 '*Ri*' + noun

Ri followed by a noun (mostly verbal nouns) can imply:
  (i)   being engaged in something, often in connection with an occupation or continuous behaviour
  (ii)   that something is to be done

Consider the following example:
(i) being engaged in something

Bha na balaich ri èigheachd.	The boys were screaming.
Tha Iain ri sgrìobhadh an-còmhnaidh.	John is writing always.
Bha Anna ri ceòl fad a beatha.	Ann was at music all her life.
Bidh iad ri iasgach as t-earrach.	They will be at fishing in the Spring time.

Ri can also be used with the definite article in similar contexts, e.g.

Tha Seumas ris an òl.	James is constantly drinking.
Tha iad ris an iasgach.	They are at the fishing, i.e. they are engaged with fishing or they are fishermen.
Tha Iain ris a' mhuir.	John is at the sea, i.e. John is working at sea or John is a sailor.

(ii) something is to be done
The formula is:

THA + SUBJECT + RI + POSSESSIVE PRONOUN A* + VERBAL NOUN/INFINITIVE
Tha   obair   ri   a   dhèanamh
there is work to be done

11

Here are some further examples:

Tha gu leòr ri a ràdh.	There is much to be said.
Bha cus ri a ithe.	There was too much to eat.
Tha Iain ri a mholadh.	John is to be praised.

Note: **ri a** is pronounced **ri** here.

100 '*Gu*' + verbal noun/infinitive

Gu followed by a verbal noun/infinitive implies 'about to, on the point of, almost':

Tha mi gu spreadhadh.	I am almost bursting (with food).
Tha e gu bristeadh.	It is about to break.
Tha iad gu bhith deiseil.	They are almost ready.
	(*lit* 'about to be ready')

100a Colours

The colour systems used in Gaelic are slightly different to those used in English, most notably with the colours grey, green, and blue.

bàn	/baːn/	fair (of hair), pale
buidhe	/buɪjə/	yellow
dearg	/dʲ[ara]g/	(bright) red
donn	/dōũn̪/	brown
dubh	/d̪u/	black
geal	/gʲal̪/	white, bright
glas	/gl̪as/	grey, grey-green
gorm	/g[ɔrɔ]m/	(dark) blue, green
liath	/ʎiə/	(light) blue, grey
orains	/ɔrəɲʃ/	orange
pinc	/piŋʲgʲ/	pink
ruadh	/ɾuəɣ/	(darker) red (also 'red' of hair)
uaine	/uəɲə/	green
fionn	/fjuːn̪/	blond (of hair)

There is some variation in the grey-green and grey-blue spectrum between **liath** and **glas**, and between **liath** and **gorm** respectively in Scottish Gaelic dialects. For instance, **liath** and / or **glas** can be used of 'grey' hair, and **liath** and / or **gorm** can be used of 'blue' sky.

101 Ordinal numbers (first, second ...)

Most ordinal numbers are formed by adding **-th(e)amh** or **-(e)amh** to the basic numeral except in the case of 'first, second, third' which have special forms. The ordinal numbers are normally preceded by the article. The following examples are illustrated with the word **fear**, here meaning 'one':

1st	**a' chiad* fhear**	the first one
2nd	**an dàrna/dara fear**	the second one
3rd	**an treas/trìtheamh/treasamh fear**	the third one
4th	**an ceathramh fear**	the fourth one
5th	**an còigeamh fear**	the fifth one
6th	**an siathamh fear**	the sixth one
7th	**an seachdamh fear**	the seventh one
8th	**an t-ochdamh fear**	the eighth one
9th	**an naoitheamh fear**	the ninth one
10th	**an deicheamh fear**	the tenth one
11th	**an t-aonamh fear deug**	the eleventh one
12th	**an dàrna/dara fear deug**	the twelfth one
13th	**an treas(amh)/trìtheamh fear deug**	the thirteenth one
18th	**an t-ochdamh fear deug**	the eighteenth one
20th	**am ficheadamh fear**	the twentieth one

The vigesimal and decimal systems pattern as follows:

	VIGESIMAL	DECIMAL
21st	an t-aonamh fear air fhichead	am ficheadamh fear is a h-aon
22nd	an dàrna/dara fear air fhichead	am ficheadamh fear is a dhà
29th	an naoitheamh fear air fhichead	am ficheadamh fear is a naoi
30th	an deicheamh fear air fhichead	an tritheadamh fear
31st	an t-aonamh fear deug air fhichead	an tritheadamh fear is a h-aon
35th	an còigeamh fear deug air fhichead	an tritheadamh fear is a còig
40th	an dà fhicheadamh fear	an ceathradamh fear
41st	an dà fhicheadamh fear is a h-aon	an ceathradamh fear is a h-aon
42nd	an dà fhicheadamh fear is a dhà	an ceathradamh fear is a dhà
49th	an dà fhicheadamh fear is a naoi	an ceathradamh fear is a naoi
50th	an dà fhicheadamh fear is a deich	an caogadamh fear
55th	an dà fhicheadamh fear is a còig-deug	an caogadamh fear is a còig
60th	an trì ficheadamh fear	an seasgadamh fear
61st	an trì ficheadamh fear is a h-aon	an seasgadamh fear is a h-aon

100th	an ceudamh fear
1,000th	an mìleamh fear
1,000,000th	an muilleanamh fear

Here are some examples involving **latha** 'day':

8th	an t-ochdamh latha
12th	an dàrna/dara latha deug
27th	an seachdamh latha air fhichead
31st	an t-aonamh latha deug air fhichead or a' chiad latha deug air fhichead

Note: In the vigesimal system numbers in the range 21–29 can also be expressed with **fichead** in place of **air fhichead**.

27th   an seachdamh latha fichead

Note: The form of the article preceding the oridinal numerals '6', '7', '8' and '11' depend on the gender of the following noun:

MASCULINE		FEMININE	
an siathamh leabhar	the sixth book	an t-siathamh sgoil	the sixth school
an seachdamh clas	the seventh class	an t-seachdamh nighean	the seventh girl
an t-ochdamh latha	the eighth day	an ochdamh oidhche	the eighth night
an t-aonamh càr deug	the eleventh car	an aonamh freagairt deug	the eleventh reply

Vocabulary

a leithid	/a lehidʲ/	its like, the same
a' chiad*	/ə çiəḏ/	the first
Bliadhna Mhath Ùr†	/bliən̪ə vã uːr/	Happy New Year
ceann (*m*)	/kʲau̯n̪/	head, end
cèiliche (*m*)	/kʲeːliçə/	visitor
cèilidh (*vn*)	/kʲeːli/	visit, visiting
di-beathte (*adj*)	/dʲə bɛhtʲə/	welcome
dòirt (*vb*)	/d̪ɔːɾ(s)tʲ/	pour
drama (*m*)	/d̪ramə/	a dram, a drink of whisky
fairich (*vb*)	/farʲiç/	perceive, feel (also 'hear')
fàs (*vb*)	/faːs/	growing
feuch (*vb*)	/fiax/	see, make sure
foghain (*vb*)	/fo-iɲ/	suffice
fòghnaidh (*vb*) **sin**	/foːni ʃin/	that will suffice
ged-thà (*adv*)	/gə t̪aː/	however
grian (*f*)	/grʲiən/	sun
grunn (*adv, m*)	/gruːn̪/	a good deal, a lot
làn dì do bheatha	/ɫaːn dʲi: d̪ə vɛhə/	you are very welcome
mear (*adj*)	/mɛr/	merry
nochdadh (*vn*)	/n̪ɔxkəy/	appearing, showing up
Oidhche na Bliadhna Ùire	/ɤiçə nə bl̪ən̪ uːrʲə/	Hogmanay, New Year's Eve
ruigheachd (*vn*)	/ruijəxk/	reaching, getting to
seachad (*adv*)	/ʃɛxad̪/	past
sgrìob (*f*)	/skrʲiːb/	trip
stiall ort (*vb*)	/stʲiəɫ ɔɾst̪/	on you go, continue
tadhal (*vn*)	/t̪ɤ-əɫ/	visiting
tog (*vb*)	/t̪og/	raise, lift
togail (*vn*)	/t̪ogal/	raising, taking

---

† Some use the order **Bliadhn' Ùr Mhath**.

CÒMHRADH (CONVERSATION)

Oidhche na Bliadhna Ùire

Donnchadh	Thig a-staigh, a Theàrlaich. Is math t' fhaicinn.†
Teàrlach	Bliadhna Mhath Ùr, a Dhonnchaidh. Bliadhna Mhath Ùr, a Mhàiri.
Donnchadh	A leithid eile dhuibh fhèin is mòran dhiubh.
Teàrlach	Feumaidh tu drama a ghabhail. Seo agad uisge-beatha math. Gloine dhut an seo.
Donnchadh	Tog, tog. Fòghnaidh sin.
Teàrlach	Do dheagh shlàinte. 'A h-uile latha a chì is nach fhaic.'†† An tàinig duine eile a chèilidh oirbh mar-thà?
Donnchadh	Cha tàinig. Is tu fhèin a' chiad chèiliche a tha air nochdadh gu ruige seo. Nach e a Mhàiri?
Màiri	Is e. Chan fhaca sinn duine eile fhathast.
Teàrlach	Seo an treas taigh a tha mise air a ruigheachd a-nochd.
Donnchadh	Is ann a bhios tu a' fàs mear, a Theàrlaich. Is dòcha gum bu chòir dhut beagan uisge a chur na cheann.
Teàrlach	B' fheàrr leamsa a ghabhail dìreach mar a tha e.
Donnchadh	Nach tusa a dh'fhaodas a bhalaich. Stiall ort – agus làn dì do bheatha.
Teàrlach	Chan fheum mi cus a òl ged-thà. Tha dùil agam tadhal ann an grunn thaighean eile mus èirich a' ghrian.
Donnchadh	Is ann a dh'fhaodainn fhìn a dhol còmhla riut. Tha mi air a bhith aig baile fad na h-oidhche. Is bu toil leam sgrìob a ghabhail a-mach.
Teàrlach	Dèan sin gu dearbh. Chan eil an oidhche ach òg fhathast. Ach aon drama eile mus fhalbh sinn, ma-thà.
Donnchadh	Tapadh leat fhèin, a Theàrlaich.
Teàrlach	Tha thu di-beathte – glè dhi-beathte. Slàinte mhath.
Donnchadh	Tha còir againn a bhith a' togail oirnn. Seall an uair a tha e.
Teàrlach	Oidhche mhath, a bhean an taighe.
Màiri	Oidhche mhath, a Theàrlaich, agus tapadh leat airson do chèilidh. Cha do dh'fhairich sinn an oidhche a' dol seachad. A Dhonnchaidh, feuch nach bi thu ro anmoch a' tighinn dhachaigh!

† Recall that the possessive pronoun **do** is reduced to **d'** or **t'** before vowels: see **Section 15**.

†† 'Every day that (we) see (one another) or not.' The expression wishes good health at all times.

TRANSLATION

Hogmanay

Duncan	Come in, Charles. It's good to see you.
Charles	Happy New Year, Duncan. Happy New Year, Mary.
Duncan	The same to you and many of them.
Charles	You'll have to take a dram. Here's a good whisky for you. A glass for you here.
Duncan	Stop, stop.† That will do.
Charles	Your good health. 'Every day we see and don't.' Has anyone else visited you already?
Duncan	No one. You're the first visitor who has appeared until now. Isn't he, Mary?
Mary	He is. We haven't seen anybody else yet.
Charles	This is the third house I've got to tonight.
Duncan	Then you will be getting merry, Charles. Perhaps you should put a little water in it.
Charles	I would rather take it just as it is.
Duncan	And well you may, boy. On you go – and very welcome you are!
Charles	I mustn't drink too much, though. I expect to call in a number of other houses before the sun rises!
Duncan	Indeed, I could go with you myself. I've been at home all night. And I'd like to take a trip out.
Charles	Do that indeed. The night is but young yet. But one more dram before we go, then.
Duncan	Thank you, Charles.
Charles	You're welcome, very welcome. Good health.
Duncan	We ought to be setting off. Look at the time.
Charles	Good night, lady of the house!
Mary	Good night, Charles, and thank you for your visit. We didn't feel the night passing. Make sure you're not too late coming home, Duncan.

11

† *lit* lift (i.e. stop pouring).

Lesson 12

102 Irregular verbs: conditional/past habitual

It is possible to group irregular conditional/past habitual formation into two groups:

(i) Verbs whose formation is regular:

INDEPENDENT	DEPENDENT	
bheireadh	**beireadh**	would catch
chluinneadh	**cluinneadh**	would hear
dhèanadh†	**dèanadh**	would do/make
rachadh†	**rachadh**	would go
ruigeadh	**ruigeadh**	would reach

(ii) Verbs whose independent and dependent forms are different:

INDEPENDENT	DEPENDENT	
theireadh	**abradh**	would say
chitheadh	**faiceadh**	would see
gheibheadh††	**faigheadh**	would get, find
thigeadh	**tigeadh**	would come
bheireadh	**toireadh**	would give

† Dialect variants include **dheidheadh** and **reigheadh** (with **do reigheadh** as dependent form).
†† Pronounced as if **gheobhadh** in some dialects.

Note: the dependent forms **tigeadh** and **toireadh** are both pronounced with initial **d-**. Some prefer to spell these forms with an initial **d-** or even **d'th-**.

Note: the endings we learnt for the regular verbs are also used with the irregular verbs. Consider the following example:

chluinninn	I would hear
chluinneadh tu	you would hear
chluinneadh e/i	he/she would hear
chluinneamaid/chluinneadh sinn	we would hear
chluinneadh sibh	you (*pl*) would hear
chluinneadh iad	they would hear

The conditional/past habitual forms of the verbs **cluinn** and **faic** can imply 'capability' as with the future forms:

Chluinneadh tu na h-eòin a' seinn.
You could hear the birds singing.

Chitheadh tu na reultan anns an adhar.
You could see the stars in the sky.

Note: the regular verb **can** may be used for **abair** in the conditional/past habitual as in the future tense and imperative.

Examples

Theirinn ris gun robh e gòrach sin a dhèanamh.
I would say to him that he was silly to do that.

Bheireadh i air a' chupa mus ruigeadh e an làr.
She would catch the cup before it reached the floor.

Dè a chluinneadh a' chlann nuair a bhiodh iad a-muigh?
What would the children hear when they were out?

Dhèanadh iad an obair sin gun teagamh.
They would do that work without doubt.

Chitheamaid a' mhuir a-mach romhainn.
We could see the sea out before us.

Chan fhaigheadh tu mòran airgid air a shon.
You wouldn't get much money for it.

Rachainn ann nan tigeadh tusa còmhla rium.
I would go there if you came along with me.

Thigeadh Anna gam choimhead nam biodh an ùine aice.
Ann would come to see me if she had the time.

Cha toireadh iad sgillinn dhut.
They wouldn't give you a penny.

102a Answering questions

As usual, the verb is echoed:

An tigeadh tu còmhla rium?	Would you come with me?
Thigeadh.	Yes.
Cha tigeadh.	No.
An toireadh Anna an leabhar do Pheigi?	Would Ann give the book to Peggy?
Bheireadh.	Yes.
Cha toireadh.	No.

12

Vocabulary

a leithid sin	/ə lehid^j ʃin/	the likes of that
aiseag (*m*)	/aʃəg/	ferry
àite sam bith	/aːht^jə səm bi/	anywhere
balgam (*m*) **tì**	/b[aṯa]gəm tiː/	some tea (*lit* 'a mouthful')
cead (*m*)	/k^jed/	permission
ceart gu leòr (*adv*)	/k^jaɾsṯ gə ʎɔːr/	right enough, OK
càirdean, companaich (*m, pl*)	/kaːɾ(s)d^jən/, /koumbaniç/	friends
cùil (*f*)	/kuːl/	corner
dràma (*m*), **dealbh-chluich** (*f*)	/ḏraːma/, /d^j[aṯa]xḻuç/	drama (play)
eile (*adj*)	/elə/	other, else
mìos (*f*)	/mĩãs/, /mĩəs/	month
mu dheireadh (*adv*)	/ma jer^jəɣ/	last
plèan (*m*)	/plɛːn/	aeroplane
suidheachan (*m*)	/sɯjəxan/	seat
taigh-tasgaidh (*m*)	/ṯɤj ṯaski/	museum
toilichte (*adj*)	/ṯɔliçt^jə/	pleased
uabhasach toilichte (*adv*)	/ũãvasəx ṯɔliçt^jə/	very, terribly pleased
uisge (*m*)	/uʃk^jə/	rain

Exercise 12.1

Translate

1 I would be very pleased if they came.
2 He would drink some tea right enough.
3 They would see their friends at school.
4 We used to go to the museum every month.
5 You would not get a seat on the aeroplane now.
6 Would you say that John would go to the drama?
7 Would you get the bus at that corner?
8 You would catch the last ferry at nine o'clock.
9 You would not hear the likes of that anywhere else.
10 Donald's mother would not give him permission to go out.

103 'Usually'

If we want to say someone usually or frequently does something, we use the idiom **is àbhaist do** which means literally 'it is customary for' as follows:

IS + ÀBHAIST + DO* + SUBJECT + A BHITH + A' VERBAL NOUN (+ ADVERB)

Is àbhaist do Sheumas a bhith a' seinn.
James usually sings.

Here are some more examples:

Is àbhaist do Mhàiri a bhith a' dùsgadh tràth.
Mary usually wakes up early.

Is àbhaist dhomh a bhith a' dol a dh'Èirinn as t-samhradh.
I usually go to Ireland in the summer.

Negative forms:

Chan àbhaist do Mhòrag a bhith a' smocadh.
Morag doesn't usually smoke.

Chan àbhaist dhut a bhith a' dràibheadh.
You don't usually drive.

Interrogative (positive) forms:

An àbhaist do Dhòmhnall a bhith a' cluich ball-coise?
Does Donald usually play football?

An àbhaist dha a bhith a' dol a dh'Uibhist?
Does he usually go to Uist?

Interrogative (negative) forms:

Nach àbhaist do Ruairidh a bhith ag ithe feòil?
Doesn't Ruairi usually eat meat?

Nach àbhaist dhi a bhith a' dol a-mach feasgar?
Does she not usually go out in the evening?

In reply to these positive and negative interrogative forms **An/nach àbhaist ...?**, we find:

Is àbhaist.	Yes.
Chan àbhaist.	No.

104 'Used to'

Is àbhaist do becomes **b' àbhaist do** in the past tense and means 'used to'. It is frequently used instead of the past habitual. Here are some examples:

B' àbhaist do Mhàiri a bhith ag obair an Glaschu.
Mary used to work in Glasgow.

Cha b' àbhaist dha a bhith ag obair cho dian.
He didn't use to work so hard.

Nach b' àbhaist dhut a bhith ag ionnsachadh Gàidhlig? Cha b' àbhaist.
Didn't you use to learn Gaelic? No.

Nach b' àbhaist do Chatrìona a bhith a' teagasg? B' àbhaist.
Didn't Catherine use to be teaching? Yes.

105 Past participles and the perfective

Gaelic uses a small number of past participles. Here is a list of those which are most commonly used:

pòsta	married
sgrìobhte	written
reòite (from **reòidhte**)	frozen
stèidhichte / stèite (from **stèidhte**)	established
foghlaimte	learned, educated
caillte	lost (spiritually), damned (which contrasts with **air chall** 'lost, mislaid')

Examples:

Tha Iain pòsta.
John is married.

Tha Anna stèidhichte ann an Glaschu a-nis.
Ann is established/based in Glasgow now.

Bha an t-uisge reòite.
The water was frozen.

Some past participles have developed 'new' meanings:

seòlta	cunning, clever
sgiobalta	tidy, neat
gleusta	canny, prudent
do-dhèante	impossible

The periphrastic perfective is normally formed in a similar way as the perfect.
See **Lesson 11**, **Section 98.** The pattern is as follows:

THA + SUBJECT + AIR + POSS PRON (AGREEING WITH SUBJ)	+ VERBAL NOUN/ INFINITIVE
tha am feur air a*	**ghearradh**

the grass is cut

Here are some further examples:

Bha <u>am fiadh</u> air <u>a</u> mharbhadh.	The deer was killed.
An robh <u>Niall</u> air <u>a</u> bhualadh?	Was Neil hit?
Bha <u>an t-uisge beatha</u> air <u>a</u> òl uile gu lèir.	The whisky was all drunk.
Cha robh <u>na bàtaichean</u> air <u>an</u> càradh.	The boats were not fixed.
An robh <u>Mòrag</u> air <u>a</u> taghadh?	Was Morag (s)elected?

Note that these perfectives can also have passive meaning. See below.

106 The passive

In Gaelic a passive sentence like 'the door was closed' can be expressed in three ways:

(a) by using the auxiliary verb RACH 'GO' + SUBJECT + A* + VERBAL NOUN/ INFINITIVE:

Chaidh an doras a dhùnadh.   The door was closed.

(b) by using the perfective construction introduced above: THA + SUBJECT + AIR + POSSESSIVE PRONOUN (AGREEING WITH SUBJECT) + VERBAL NOUN/INFINITIVE

Bha Niall air a bhualadh.   Neil was hit.

(c) by using special impersonal forms of the verb:

Dhùineadh an doras.   The door was closed.

Type (a) is the most commonly used in modern Gaelic. Type (c) is frequently used in literary Gaelic although it also occurs in ordinary spoken Gaelic.

Here are some more examples of type (a):

Chaidh Iain a bhualadh.	John was hit.
Cha deach an telebhisean a ghoid.	The television was not stolen.
An deach am biadh a ithe?	Was the food eaten?
Thèid an càr a reic.	The car will be sold.

If the subject of a passive sentence of type (a) is a pronoun, possessive pronouns are used with the verb **rach** and the verbal noun/infinitive as follows:

Chaidh mo bhualadh.	I was hit. (*lit* 'my hitting went/passed')
Chaidh do mholadh.	You were recommended/praised.
Chaidh a dhèanamh.	It was done.
Chaidh a pòsadh.	She was married.
Chaidh ar stiùireadh.	We were directed.
An deach ur leantail?	Were you followed?
Cha deach an clò-bhualadh fhathast.	They were not printed yet.

Here are some examples of type (b):

Bha an càr air a ghoid.	The car was stolen.
Bha an t-àite air a lìonadh le uisge.	The place was filled with water.

The following phrase using type (c) is used in all dialects.

Rugadh is thogadh mi ann an Alba.
I was born and brought up in Scotland.

The agent of a passive sentence is introduced by the preposition **le** 'with' or in some cases by the preposition **aig** 'at' as follows:

Chaidh a' bhùth a cheannach le Iain.
The shop was bought by John.

Chaidh a' chaora a leagail le càr.
The sheep was knocked down by a car.

An deach Anna a bhreabadh leis an each?
Was Ann kicked by the horse?

Bha Iain air a bhualadh aca.
John was hit by them.

Note: In practice active sentences often occur in preference to passives with agents, e.g.

Cheannaich Iain a' bhùth.
John bought the shop.

107 Impersonal verbal forms

Type C

The past, future and conditional/past habitual all have impersonal forms. In each case, the impersonal forms consist of endings which are attached to the relevant tense form of the verb. Here are the impersonal forms illustrated with the verb **dùin** 'close' and **mol** 'praise':

dhùineadh an doras	the door was closed, someone closed the door
dùinear an doras	the door will be closed, someone will close the door, the door is closed, someone closes the door
dhùinte an doras	the door would be closed, the door used to be closed, someone would close the door, someone used to close the door
mholadh an nighean	the girl was praised, someone praised the girl
molar an nighean	the girl will be praised, someone will praise the girl/the girl is praised, someone praises the girl
mholte an nighean	the girl would be praised, someone would praise the girl, the girl used to be praised, someone used to praise the girl

12

The impersonal use of these forms is clearly seen with intransitive verbs, i.e. verbs which do not have objects, e.g.

Thathar a' dol ann a h-uile bliadhna.
One is/people are going there every year.

Thigear an seo a h-uile madainn.
One comes/people come here every morning.

Chan urrainnear tiocaid a cheannach an seo.
One cannot buy a ticket here.

Dh'fheumte a dhol ann.
One had to go there/people had to go there.

Note: some dialects use **-(a)iste/-(a)ist** in place of **-te** in the conditional/past habitual impersonal, e.g.

Sheinnist(e) an t-òran sin gu tric.
That song used to be sung often.

108 Independent and dependent impersonal forms

Independent and dependent forms are identical in the future. In the past tense the distinction between both forms is as with other regular forms in the past, i.e. dependent form = **do** + independent form. The difference in the conditional/ past habitual is as with other regular forms, i.e. the independent forms are lenited; the dependent forms are not lenited (unless lenited by a dependent leniting particle). This may be summarised as follows:

IMPERSONAL FORMS:

TENSE	INDEPENDENT	DEPENDENT
PAST	lenition + **(e)adh**	**do** + independent form
	dh' + **(fh)** vowel + **(e)adh**	
PRESENT	**(e)ar**	**(e)ar**
COND/PAST HAB	lenition + **te**	**te**
	dh' + **(fh)** vowel + **te**	vowel + **te**

Examples:
Dhùineadh an uinneag.
The window was closed/Someone closed the window.

Cha do dh'fhosgladh an uinneag.
The window was not opened./No one opened the window.

Seinnear an t-òran sin a h-uile bliadhna.
That song will be sung every year./Someone will sing that song every year.

An leughar e?
Will it be read?/Will someone read it?

Cheannaichte gu leòr salainn an uair ud.
A lot of salt used to be bought at that time./People used to buy a lot of salt at that time.

An cante sin an da-rìribh?
Was that said seriously?/Did people say that seriously?

Cha chuirte an cat a-mach a h-uile h-oidhche.
The cat used not to be put out every night/Someone used not to put out the cat every night.

Note: in the last example **cha** lenites the dependent form **cuirte**.

Here is a list of the most commonly used impersonal forms of irregular verbs:

VERB	PAST		FUTURE		COND/PAST HAB	
	INDEP	DEP	INDEP	DEP	INDEP	DEP
abair	thuirteadh	tuirteadh	theirear	teirear	theirte	teirte
beir	rugadh	do rugadh	beirear	beirear	bheirte	beirte
cluinn	chualas	cualas	cluinnear	cluinnear	chluinnte	cluinnte
dèan	rinneadh	do rinneadh	nithear	dèanar	dhèante	dèante
faic	chunncas	facas	chithear	faicear	chìte	faicte
faigh	fhuaradh/ fhuaireadh/fhuaras	d' fhuaradh/d' fhuaireadh/ d' fhuaras	gheibhear	faighear	gheibhte	faighte
thoir	thugadh	tugadh	bheirear	toirear	bheirte	toirte

Note: the dependent forms **tuirteadh, teirear, teirte, tugadh, toirear** and **toirte** are all pronounced with initial **d-**; some spell these forms with **d** or even **d'th**.

The impersonal forms of the verb **tha** are as follows:

PAST		PRESENT		FUTURE		COND/PAST HAB	
INDEP	DEP	INDEP	DEP	INDEP	DEP	INDEP	DEP
bhathar/ bhathas	robhar/ robhas	thathar/ thathas	(bh)eilear/ (bh)eileas	bithear	bithear	bhite	bite

109 Another passive construction

The periphrastic (long) construction involving the verb **tha** and **ag** can be used passively. The formula is as follows:

THA + SUBJECT + (AG + POSS PRON, AGREEING IN NUMBER AND GENDER WITH THE SUBJECT) + VERBAL NOUN

Recall from **Lesson 8**, **Section 72** that **ag** combines with the possessive pronouns as follows:

gam*   gar
gad*   gur
ga*   gan/gam
ga

Here are some examples:

Bha Gàidhlig ga bruidhinn air feadh Alba.
Gaelic was (being) spoken all over Scotland.

Tha leabhraichean gan reic anns a' bhùth sin.
Books are being sold in that shop.

Bhiodh an t-òran sin ga ghabhail gu math tric air an rèidio.
That song used to be sung fairly often on the radio.

Vocabulary

airgead (*m*)	/[arʲa]gʲəḑ], /[ɛrʲɛ]gʲəḑ/	money
bho (*prp*)	/ɔ/, /vɔ/	since
caill (*vb*)	/kaiʎ/	lose
feadh (+G)	/fjɤɣ/	(at some point) during
leag (*vb*)	/ʎeg/	knock down
lean (*vb*)	/ʎɛn/	follow
marbh (*vb*)	/m[ara]v/	kill
nigh (*vb*)	/ɲi/	wash

Exercise 12.2

Translate the following using the impersonal forms of the verbs:

1 The song will be sung.
2 The window was opened.
3 The old house was pulled down/demolished.
4 Money is lost every year.
5 John was followed home yesterday.
6 It used to be washed every day.
7 The bird has not been seen or heard since last week.
8 It is said that he lived in Edinburgh when he was younger.
9 He was killed during the night.
10 I was born and brought up in Ireland.

110 The subjunctive

Scottish Gaelic does not have special subjunctive verbal forms which express desire or uncertainty. Normally the conditional form corresponds to the subjunctive in other languages.

> **Rachainn a Ghlaschu nan tigeadh Anna còmhla rium.**
> I would go to Glasgow if Ann came with me.

Subjunctive forms do survive, however, in higher registers of the language, particularly in the Bible, e.g.

> **Tog do shùil is gum faic thu a-nis am mùthadh mòr.**
> Lift thine eye that thou may now see the great change.

> **Gun tige do rìoghachd.** (**tige** pronounced as if **dige**)
> May Thy kingdom come.

Special 'wish' forms once common also survive in some phrases. These 'wish' forms are preceded by **gun** and **guma** '(would) that', '(wish) that', 'may'. Here are some examples:

Gu robh math agad.
'Thank you', *lit* 'may you have good', which is used in some south-western dialects for 'thank you' as in Irish Gaelic.

Gun tèid (gu math) leat!
May it go (well) with you/Good luck!

Guma math a thèid leat! *or* **Gur math a thèid leat!**
May it go well with you/Good luck!

Guma fada beò thu is ceò às do thaigh.
Long may you live and may there be smoke from your house!

111 Defective verbs

Defective verbs are verbs which do not appear in all tenses. We've already met the defective verbs **faod** 'may', **feum** 'must' and **is** 'be'. Here are some more:

(a) **Arsa** 'says, said'

Arsa means 'says' or 'said' and is used in quotative speech. When pronouns are used with **arsa**, they appear in the emphatic form. **Ars** is used before vowels and **arsa** before consonants.

"Dè a tha a' dol?" ars Iain.	"What's doing?" says/said John.
"Ciamar a tha sibh?" ars esan.	"How are you?" says/said he.
"Dè an t-ainm a tha ort?" arsa Seumas.	"What's your name?" says/said James.

(b) **Theab** 'almost'

Theab is used in the past tense. It is always followed by an infinitive/verbal noun:

Theab mi tuiteam.	I almost fell.
Theab i a dhol às a ciall.	She almost went out of her mind.

The verbal noun **teabachadh/teabachdainn** also occurs, e.g.

Bha mi a' teabachadh/ teabachdainn leum.
I was on the verge of / almost jumping (i.e. hesitating).

Bha Anna a' teabachadh/ teabachdainn a dhol a-mach air.
Ann was on the verge of falling out with him.

12

(c) **Dh'fhidir** 'know'/'sense'

Dh'fhidir is used in the past tense and present/future.

Dh'fhidir mi.	I know, I have heard.
Ma dh'fhidireas mi.	If I know.
Fidiridh / Fid(i)richidh an cù sin.	The dog will sense that.

The verbal noun **fidreachadh/fidreachdainn** also occurs, e.g.

Tha na coin a' fidreachadh/fidreachdainn rudeigin.
The dogs sense something.

(d) **Trobhad** 'come along'; **thugainn/thiugainn/tiugainn** 'let's go'; **siubhad** 'go on, continue'

Trobhad, thugainn (with dialect variants, e.g. **t(h)iugainn**) and **siubhad** are only used in the imperative (singular and plural):

Trobhad, a Sheumais!	Come along, James!
Trobhadaibh, an seo!	Come here!
Thugainn, a Mhàiri!	Let's go, Mary!
Thugnaibh, a ghillean!	Let's go, boys!
Siubhad, a Dhòmhnaill!	Go on, Donald!
Siubhdaibh, a nigheanan!	Continue, girls!

112 Interjections

Here is a list of some commonly used interjections:

A chiall!	/ə çiəɫ/	Oh dear!
A thiarna!	/ə hiərn̪(ə)/	Oh lord!
A dhiamh!	/ə jĩã/	Yuck!
A dhuine!	/ə ɣuɲə/	Dear man!
A thia(r)cais fhèin!	/ə hiə(r)kiʃ heːn/	Goodness me!
Mo chreach!	/mə xrɛx/	Alas!
Mo chreach-sa thàinig!	/mə xrʎɛxsə haːnigʲ/	Woe is me (*lit* my plundering has come)
Obh obh!	/o vo-əv/	Dear me!
(Dè a) b' àill leibh!	/(dʲeː) ba(ː)ʎ lu/	Excuse me! (I didn't hear)
ò thì!	/oː hiː/	'O God!'
fhalbh!/ thalla!	/h[aɫ]a/	go away!
fhalbh is tog ort!	/h[aɫ]a əs tog ɔrsṭ/	go away out of that!

113 Remaining prepositional pronouns

gu 'to'	bho 'from'	fo 'under'	à 'out of'
thugam	bhuam	fodham	asam
thugad	bhuat	fodhad	asad
thuige	bhuaidhe	fodha	às
thuice	bhuaipe	foidhpe	aiste
thugainn	bhuainn	fodhainn	asainn
thugaibh	bhuaibh	fodhaibh	asaibh
thuca	bhuapa	fodhpa	asta

de 'of'	ro 'before'	tro 'through'	mu 'about'
dhìom	**romham**	**tromham**	**umam**
dhìot	**romhad**	**tromhad**	**umad**
dheth	**roimhe**	**troimhe**	**uime**
dhith	**roimpe**	**troimpe**	**uimpe**
dhinn	**romhainn**	**tromhainn**	**umainn**
dhibh	**romhaibh**	**tromhaibh**	**umaibh**
dhiubh	**rompa**	**trompa**	**umpa**

Vocabulary

adhbhar (*m*)	/ɣːvər/	reason
ainmeil (*adj*)	/[ɛnɛ]mɛl/	famous
àrd-sgoil (*f*)	/aːʀ(s)d̪ skɔl/	secondary school
bàrd (*m*)	/baːʀ(s)d̪/	poet
bàrdachd (*f*)	/baːʀ(s)d̪axk/	poetry
builich (*vb*)	/buliç/	grant, bestow, confer
ceasnaiche (*m*)	/kʲesn̪içə/	interviewer
cèilidh (*vn*)	/kʲeːli/	visiting
ceum (*m*)	/kʲeːm/	degree
comharradh (*m*)	/kɔ̃hərəɣ/	sign
cuideachd (*adv*)	/kud̪ʲəxk/	also, too
cuspair (*m*)	/kuspɛrʲ/	subject
dreuchd (*f*)	/driaxk/	post, job
fad an t-siubhail (*adv*)	/fad̪ ən tʲu-əl/	all the time
fàilte (*f*) **air**	/faːʎtʲə ɛrʲ/	welcome to
feadhainn (*f*)	/fjoː-iɲ/	some
fhathast (*adv*)	/ha-əst̪/	still
foghlam (*m*)	/fɣːɫ̪əm/	education
foillsich (*vb*)	/fɣiʎʃiç/	publish
ge bè air bith gu dè an t-adhbhar	/ga be ər bi gə dʲeː ən̪ t̪ɣːvər/	whatever the reason
ginealach (*m*)	/gʲinəɫ̪əx/	generation
gu h-àraid (*adv*)	/gə haːrɛdʲ/	especially
litreachas (*m*)	/ʎiht̪rəxəs/	literature
measail air	/misal ɛrʲ/	fond of
Port Rìgh	/pɔʀst̪ ʀiː/	Portree
Ratharsair	/ʀa-əʀsɛrʲ/	Isle of Raasay
seadh dìreach	/ʃɣɣ dʲiːrʲəx/	yes, indeed
sin as coireach	/ʃin əs kɣrʲəx/	that (which) is the reason
taghadh (*vn*)	/t̪ɣ-əɣ/	electing, choosing
teagasg (*m*)	/tʲegəsk/	teaching
thoir air (*vb*)	/hɔrʲ ɛrʲ/	cause
tìr-mòr (*m*)	/tʲirʲ moːr/	mainland
ùr-nodha (*adj*)	/uːr n̪o-ə/	brand new

12

CÒMHRADH (CONVERSATION)

Bàrd ainmeil a' bruidhinn air prògram rèidio

Ceasnaiche	Fàilte oirbh do phrògram na seachdain seo. Tha am bàrd ainmeil Niall MacLeòid a-staigh còmhla rium an-diugh. Feasgar math dhuibh, a Nèill. Ciamar a tha sibh?
Niall	Tha gu dòigheil. Tha mi fìor thoilichte a bhith an seo nur cuideachd feasgar an-diugh.
Ceasnaiche	A-nis, innsibh beagan dhuinn mu ur deidhinn fhèin an toiseach. Càite an do rugadh sibh?
Niall	Rugadh is thogadh mi ann an Ratharsair. Àite brèagha. Tha mi a-nis a' fuireach air tìr-mòr ged-thà. Bha m' athair ri iasgach. Bha e air a chumail a' dol. Bhiodh e aig muir fad an t-siubhail. Dh'fheumadh e sin a chionn bha teaghlach mòr aige. Bha ceathrar bhràithrean agam agus triùir pheathraichean.
Ceasnaiche	Càite an d' fhuair sibh ur foghlam?
Niall	Fhuair an toiseach ann an Ratharsair agus an dèidh sin ann am Port Rìgh. Nuair a dh'fhàg mi an sgoil, chaidh mi dhan an oilthigh an Dùn Èideann. Chuir mi seachad ceithir bliadhna an sin. Is e Gàidhlig agus Beurla a rinn mi ann. Chòrd an dà chuspair sin rium glan – le chèile. Bhuilicheadh ceum MA orm ann an naoi-deug trì fichead is a dhà.
Ceasnaiche	Dè a rinn sibh an dèidh dhuibh a bhith anns an oilthigh?
Niall	Chuir mi a-staigh airson dreuchd teagaisg ann an àrd-sgoil is chaidh mo thaghadh airson na h-obrach. Bha mi a' teagasg an dà chuid Gàidhlig is Beurla is beagan Fraingis cuideachd.
Ceasnaiche	Dè a thug oirbh tòiseachadh air sgrìobhadh agus cuin a thòisich sibh air sgrìobhadh?
Niall	B' àbhaist dhomh a bhith a' sgrìobhadh tric nuair a bha mi òg. Tha cuimhne agam gun do sgrìobh mi pìos bàrdachd nuair a bha mi sia bliadhna a dh'aois. Tha e agam fhathast.
Ceasnaiche	An ann anns a' Ghàidhlig as motha a bha sibh a' sgrìobhadh?
Niall	Is ann, is ann anns a' Ghàidhlig a bha mi a' sgrìobhadh mar bu trice. Cha b' urrainn dhomh an aon rud a dhèanamh anns a' Bheurla ge bè air bith gu dè an t-adhbhar, tha fhios agaibh. Nuair a bha mi òg, bhinn a' cluinntinn tòrr òrain bho na seann daoine a thigeadh a-steach a chèilidh oirnn. Bhinn gan ionnsachadh. Tha mi cinnteach gun robh sin na chuideachadh mòr dhomh mar bhàrd. Ghabhte òrain is dh'innste sgeulachdan a h-uile h-oidhche anns an taigh againne, gu h-àraid anns a' gheamhradh. Bha fìor dheagh bhàrdachd anns na h-òrain sin is anns na sgeulachdan cuideachd. Bha mi eagalach measail air na h-òrain. Is dòcha gur h-e sin as coireach gur h-e Gàidhlig a thagh mi seach Beurla nuair a thòisich mi air sgrìobhadh an toiseach.
Ceasnaiche	Dè ur beachd air na thathar a' sgrìobhadh anns a' Ghàidhlig an-diugh?

Niall	Deagh bheachd air a' chuid as motha dheth, feumaidh mi a ràdh. Feumar a ràdh ged-thà gum bheil cuid dhen an litreachas ùr-nodha nas fheàrr na chèile. Thathar a' foillseachadh mòran leabhraichean Gàidhlig a h-uile bliadhna seach mar a b' àbhaist. Is e comharradh math a tha sin. Tha feadhainn dhen a' ghinealach òg air leth math.
Ceasnaiche	Seadh dìreach. Tha mi duilich ach chan eil an còrr ùine againn. Tha an ùine air ruith agus feumaidh sinn a fhàgail mar sin an-dràsta chun na seachdain seo a' tighinn. Sin agaibh e. Tapadh leibh, a Nèill, airson tighinn a-staigh a bhruidhinn ruinn. Tha sinn fada nur comain. Beannachd leibh.
Niall	Mar sin leibh.

TRANSLATION

A famous poet speaking on a radio programme

Interviewer	Welcome to this week's programme. The famous poet Neil Macleod is here with me today. Good evening, Neil. How are you?
Neil	Fine. I am very happy to be here in your company this evening.
Interviewer	Now, tell us a bit about yourself first. Where were you born?
Neil	I was born and brought up in Raasay. A beautiful place. I now live on the mainland, however. My father was at the fishing. He was kept going [i.e. busy]. He used to be at sea all the time. He had to be because he had a big family. I had four brothers and three sisters.
Interviewer	Where were you educated?
Neil	In Raasay at first and after that in Portree. When I left school, I went to the university in Edinburgh. I spent four years there. It was Gaelic and English that I did there. I enjoyed those two subjects a lot – both of them. I was granted an MA degree in the year nineteen sixty two.
Interviewer	What did you do after being in the university?
Neil	I applied for a teaching post in a secondary school and I was chosen for the work. I was teaching both Gaelic and English and a bit of French too.
Interviewer	What caused you to begin writing and when did you start to write?
Neil	I used to write often when I was young. I remember that I wrote a piece of poetry when I was six years of age. I still have it.
Interviewer	Was it in Gaelic that you wrote mostly?
Neil	Yes, it was in Gaelic that I most often wrote. I couldn't do the same thing in English for some reason or other (whatever be the reason), you know. When I was young, I used to hear lots of songs from the old people that would come in to visit us. I used to learn them. I am certain that that was a great help to me as a poet. Songs were sung and stories were told every night in our house, especially in the winter. There was really good poetry in those songs and in the stories too. I was terribly fond of the songs. I suppose that is the reason that it was Gaelic rather than English that I chose when I started writing at first.
Interviewer	What is your opinion of what is being written in Gaelic nowadays?

12

Neil	A good opinion of most of it, I must say. It must be said, however, that some of the modern literature is better than the rest. Many Gaelic books are published every year compared to the way it used to be. That's a good sign. Some of the young generation are exceptionally good.
Interviewer	Yes indeed, I am sorry but we have no more time. The time has run out and we must leave it like that until next week. That's it. Thank you, Neil, for coming in to speak to us. We are very indebted to you. Goodbye.
Neil	Goodbye.

12

Appendix 1

Vowel changes with slenderisation

The following vowels are affected by slenderisation as follows:

VOWEL	VOWEL + i	EXAMPLES	EXAMPLES WITH SLENDERISATION
ea	ei i	each, caileag fear, cailleach	eich, caileig fir, caillich
ia	èi	fiadh, Niall	fèidh, Nèill
eò	iùi	ceòl	ciùil
eu	èi eòi	geug beul	gèig beòil
io	i	fionn	finn
ìo	i	sìol	sìl
o ò	ui ùi	cnoc bòrd	cnuic bùird

The following vowels may or may not change form with slenderisation. There are no hard and fast rules to tell us if a particular word will change form or not; the vowel changes must be learnt for each noun in question:

VOWEL	VOWEL + i	EXAMPLES	EXAMPLES WITH SLENDERISATION
a	ai	cat	cait
	oi	cas	cois
	ui	falt	fuilt
	i	mac	mic
ò	òi	sròn	sròin
	ùi	bòrd	bùird

Appendix 2

Prepositions and prepositional pronouns

aig 'at'	air 'on'	do 'to, for'	gu 'to'
agam	orm	dhomh	thugam
agad	ort	dhut	thugad
aige	air	dha	thuige
aice	oirre	dhi	thuice
againn	oirnn	dhuinn	thugainn
agaibh	oirbh	dhuibh	thugaibh
aca	orra	dhaibh	thuca
bho 'from'	**fo 'under'**	**le 'with'**	**ri 'with, to'**
bhuam	fodham	leam	rium
bhuat	fodhad	leat	riut
bhuaidhe	fodha	leis	ris
bhuaipe	foidhpe	leatha	rithe
bhuainn	fodhainn	leinn	ruinn/rinn
bhuaibh	fodhaibh	leibh	ruibh/ribh
bhuapa	fodhpa	leotha	riutha
de 'of'	**ro 'before'**	**tro 'through'**	**ann an 'in'**
dhìom	romham	tromham	annam/unnam
dhìot	romhad	tromhad	annad/unnad
dheth	roimhe	troimhe	ann
dhith	roimpe	troimpe	innte
dhinn	romhainn	tromhainn	annainn/unnainn
dhibh	romhaibh	tromhaibh	annaibh/unnaibh
dhiubh	rompa	trompa	annta/unnta
mu 'about'	**à 'out of'**		
umam	asam		
umad	asad		
uime	às		
uimpe	aiste		
umainn	asainn		
umaibh	asaibh		
umpa	asta		

Appendix 3

Forms of the article

The article may be grouped into four main varieties: **an, an*, na, nam**. These are as follows:

ARTICLE	FORMS	ENVIRONMENT	FUNCTION
an	**am**	before labials **b p f m**	nom. sing. masculine
	an t-	before vowels	
	an	otherwise	
an*	**a'***	before lenitable consonants except **d t s f**	nom. sing. feminine prepositional sing.
	an t-	before **s sl sn sr**	genitive sing. masculine
	an*	before **f**	
	an	before **d t** and otherwise	
na	**na h-**	before vowels	genitive sing. feminine
	na	otherwise	nominative plural
nan	**nam**	before labials **b p f m**	genitive plural
	nan	otherwise	

Recall that * indicates that a form lenites a following word.

Appendix 4

Nasalisation (eclipsis)

Forms of the article ending in **-n/-m** can affect the pronunciation of the following consonants: **c t p g d b** to varying degrees in Gaelic dialects. There are two main varieties:

GAELIC ORTHOGRAPHY	TYPE A	TYPE B
an càr	a(n) gàr	ang hàr
	[ə(ŋ) gʰaːr]	[əŋ haːr]
an taigh	a(n) daigh	an haigh
	[ə(ṉ) dʰɣj]	[əṉ hɣj]
am pinnt	a(m) binnt	am hinnt
	[ə(m) bʰiːɲdʲ]	[əm hiː dʲ]
an gobha	a(n) gobha	a ngobha
	[ə(ŋ) go-ə]	[ə ŋo-ə]
an duine	a(n) duine	a nuine
	[ə(ṉ) duɲə]	[ə [ṉ]uɲə]
am bainne	a(m) bainne	a mainne
	[ə(m) baɲə]	[ə maɲə]

Both types are localised pronunciations, 'A' belonging, broadly speaking, to most dialects and 'B' to a number of dialects of the north west, e.g. Lewis, parts of Skye and Raasay.

Appendix 5

Paradigm of the regular verb '**mol**' ('praise')

PRESENT

tha mi a' moladh	I am praising, I praise
tha thu a' moladh	you are praising, you praise
tha e/i a' moladh	he/she is praising, he/she praises
tha sinn a' moladh	we are praising, we praise
tha sibh a' moladh	you are praising, you praise
tha iad a' moladh	they are praising, they praise
tha Anna ga moladh	Anne is praising it/her, Ann is being praised

PAST

INDEPENDENT		DEPENDENT	
mhol mi	I praised	**cha do mhol mi**	I did not praise
mhol thu	you praised	**cha do mhol thu**	you did not praise
mhol e/i	he/she praised	**cha do mhol e/i**	he/she did not praise
mhol sinn	we praised	**cha do mhol sinn**	we did not praise
mhol sibh	you praised	**cha do mhol sibh**	you did not praise
mhol iad	they praised	**cha do mhol iad**	they did not praise
mholadh Iain	John was praised	**cha do mholadh Iain**	John was not praised

FUTURE

INDEPENDENT (i)	RELATIVE - INDEPENDENT (ii)	
molaidh mi	**mholas mi**	I will praise
molaidh tu	**mholas tu**	you will praise
molaidh e/i	**mholas e/i**	he/she will praise
molaidh sinn	**mholas sinn**	we will praise
molaidh sibh	**mholas sibh**	you will praise
molaidh iad	**mholas iad**	they will praise
molar Mòrag	**mholar Mòrag**	Morag will be praised

Apdx

DEPENDENT

nach mol mi?	will I not praise?
nach mol thu?	will you not praise?
nach mol e/i?	will he/she not praise?
nach mol sinn?	will we not praise?
nach mol sibh?	will you not praise?
nach mol iad?	will they not praise?
nach molar Calum?	will Calum not be praised?

CONDITIONAL/PAST HABITUAL

Independent

mholainn	I would praise, I used to praise
mholadh tu	you would praise, you used to praise
mholadh e/i	he/she would praise, he/she used to praise
mholamaid/mholadh sinn	we would praise, we used to praise
mholadh sibh	you would praise, you used to praise
mholadh iad	they would praise, they used to praise
mholte Anna	Ann would be praised, Ann used to be praised

Dependent

The dependent forms are the same as the independent forms without the lenition.

IMPERATIVE

mol	praise
moladh e/i	let him/her praise
molamaid	let us praise
molaibh	praise (*pl*)
moladh iad	let them praise
molar iad	let them be praised

To negate the imperative, the above forms are preceded by **na.**

Apdx

Appendix 6

Grave and acute accents

As pointed out in the introductory section on pronunciation, modern Scottish Gaelic orthographic conventions do not distinguish between the two long **è** sounds, nor between the two long **ò** sounds which are current in the modern language. This distinction used to be represented by the use of grave and acute accents. The following lists include the majority of words used in this book which would have been spelled with acute accents, **é** and **ó**, pronounced as /e:/ (i.e. like 'ay' in 'say') and /o:/ (i.e. like 'o' in 'owe') respectively. All other words in this book containing grave accented **è** and **ò** are to be pronounced as /ɛ:/ (i.e. like 'ai' in 'fair', e.g. **stèisean**)) and /ɔ:/ (i.e. like 'au' in 'caught', e.g. **òl**) respectively. As a rule of thumb, **è** in modern Scottish Gaelic is normally pronounced as /e:/ (i.e. like 'ay' in 'say'), and **ò** as /ɔ:/ (i.e. like 'au' in 'caught'); for the pronunciaiton of **èa**, which is different, see introduction to pronunciation.

è representing older acute **é** /e:/

a' bhòn-dè, an-dè, cèile, cèilidh, Cèitean, dè, dèidh, Èideann, èirich, Èirinn, èisg, èist(eachd), fèidh, fhèin (pèin), gèig, gèire, glè, Grèig, grèine, lèine, lèir, rè, sgèine, sèithear, sgèith, Sgèithe, slèibhtean, stèidhich(te), stèite, t(h)èid, tè (tèigin), Trèig.

ò representing older acute **ó** /o:/

bò, cò, còig, còigeamh, còignear, fòghnaidh, fòn, fònadh, mòr, Mòrag, mòran, Pòlainn.

Appendix 7

The dental rule

The dental rule is a rule which explains the environments in which lenition can be blocked. If we delete the vowel sounds in the word 'dental', we are left with the main dental sounds of Scottish Gaelic, namely **d n t l** (**s** can also be categorised as dental). When a leniting word ends in one of the dental sounds and the following word (which would normally be lenitable) begins with one of the dental sounds (**d t**), the lenition is blocked. This can be described as follows:

Leniting word*	+	Lenitable Words
-d		d-
-n	+	t-
-t		(s-)
-l		

Examples:

	LENITION OPERATES		LENITION BLOCKED	
Article **an***	**a' chlach**	the stone	**an deoch**	the drink
	a' bheinn	the mountain	**an tè**	the woman, the one
Noun phrases	**sgian bheag**	a small knife	**sgian-dubh**	skean dhu (a black knife)
	clann Chaluim	Calum's children	**Clann Dòmhnaill**	Clan MacDonald
Adjective **seann***	**seann chàr**	an old car	**seann duine**	an old man
	seann ghloine	an old glass	**seann taigh**	an old house
Adjective **aon**	**aon chàr**	one car	**aon duine**	one person
	aon bhròg	one shoe	**aon tè**	one woman
Adjective **gun**	**gun bhròg**	without a shoe	**gun teagamh**	without a doubt

There is an increasing tendency to jettison the dental rule in noun phrases, e.g. **cairt-shiubhail** 'passport', **Càrn Sheumais** 'James' Cairn', **sìn-s(h)eanair** 'great grandfather'; note the 'new' contrast between **sgian-dubh** 'a skean dhu' (i.e. a particular type of black knife) and **sgian dhubh** 'a (generic) black knife'.

Reading Practice

1   Iolaire Loch Trèig

Uair dha robh an saoghal, bha iolaire anns na beanntan a-muigh taobh Loch Trèig. Bha i a' fuireach ann an coire an sin ris an can iad An Coire Meadhain. A' bhliadhna seo thàinig geamhradh fuar agus mòran sneachd, le cur is cathadh. Oidhche dhe na h-oidhcheannan bha an iolaire a' faireachdainn an fhuachd. 'Cha do dh'fhairich mi a leithid de dh'fhuachd riamh', thuirt i rithe fhèin. 'Saoil', thuirt i, 'an robh oidhche na b' fhuaire na seo riamh ann?'

Bha dreathann donn a' fuireach faisg oirre is chaidh i far an robh an dreathann. 'An do dh'fhairich thu oidhche na b' fhuaire na seo riamh?' thuirt i ris. 'Cha do dh'fhairich', ars an dreathann donn, 'ach dh'fhaodadh e a bhith gun robh a leithid ann. Chan eil fhios agamsa. Ach tha gobhar dhubh ann am Bun Ruaidh is tha i fada nas sine na mise. Bidh fhios aicese.'

Chaidh an iolaire chun na goibhre is chuir i an dearbh cheist oirrese. 'Cha do dh'fhairich', thuirt a' ghobhar, 'ach tha damh fèidh', ars ise, 'ann an Coille Innse a tha fada nas sine na mise agus bidh fhios aigesan.' Ràinig an iolaire Coille Innse is lorg i an damh fèidh ann an coire fasgach. Is e an aon fhreagairt a fhuair i an sin. 'Thàinig mi', ars esan, 'an seo à Inbhir Làire is mi nam dhamh òg is cha do dh'fhairich mi oidhche na b' fhuaire. Ach tha breac ann an Lochan na Làirig a tha fada nas sine na mise. Bidh fhios aigesan.'

Chaidh an iolaire chun a' bhric. 'An do dh'fhairich thu oidhche riamh na b' fhuaire na seo?' thuirt i.

'O dh'fhairich', thuirt am breac, 'fada fada na b' fhuaire. Bha mise anns an loch seo an oidhche a bha ann is bha an oidhche cho fuar is gun do chaill mi mo fhradharc leis an fhuachd. Bha an oidhche sin fada na b' fhuaire na an oidhche a-nochd.'

Bha an iolaire toilichte sin a chluinntinn is thill i dhachaigh.

The Eagle of Loch Trèig

Once upon a time there was an Eagle in the mountains out by Loch Trèig. She lived in a corry there that they call (the) Middle Corry. One year there came a cold winter and a lot of snow, with fall and drift (blizzard). One particular night the Eagle was feeling the cold. 'I've never known such cold', she said to herself. 'I wonder if there was ever a colder night than this.' There was a Wren living near the Eagle and the Eagle went to the Wren. 'Have you ever known a colder night than this?' she asked. 'No. I haven't', said the Wren, 'but such there might have been. I do not know. But there's a Black Goat in Bun Roy and she's far older than me. She'll know.'

The Eagle went to the Goat and put the very same question to her. 'No, I haven't', said the Goat, 'but there's a Stag in the Wood of Inch who is far older than me and he'll know.' The Eagle reached the Wood of Inch and found the Stag in a sheltered corry. She got the same answer there. 'I came here from Inverlair', said he, 'when I was a young stag and I have not known a colder night. But there is a Salmon in Lochan na Lairig who is far older than me. He'll know.'

The Eagle went to the Salmon. 'Have you ever known a colder night than this?' she asked. 'Oh yes', said the Salmon, 'a far, far colder night. I was in this loch that night and the night was so cold that I lost my sight with the cold. That night was far colder than this night tonight.' The Eagle was glad to hear that and returned home.

2 Alasdair Mac Mhaighstir Alasdair (c 1695–1770) agus Donnchadh Bàn Mac an t-Saoir (c 1724–1812): dithis(t) bhàrd ainmeil

Rinn Donnchadh Bàn òran dhan an tè a phòs e, Màiri Bhàn Òg: 'A Mhàiri Bhàn Òg is tu an òigh a tha air m' aire'. Bhathas a' ràdh gun robh seòrsa de dh'fharmad aig Mac Mhaighstir Alasdair ri Donnchadh Bàn. Is e duine foghlaimte a bha ann an Alasdair. Cha robh sgoil aig Donnchadh ann. Ach bha Donnchadh cho measail aig an t-sluagh fada is farsaing air feadh na Gàidhealtachd, mar dhuine agus mar bhàrd, agus bha fios aig Alasdair gur h-ann mar sin a bha.

An dèidh do Dhonnchadh Bàn agus Màiri Bhàn Òg pòsadh, thuirt Mac Mhaighstir Alasdair latha ri Donnchadh: 'Tha mi a-nis air Màiri fhaicinn agus chan eil i idir cho brèagha is a thuirt thusa a bha i anns an òran'. 'O ged-thà chan fhaca tusa i le mo shùilean-sa', arsa Donnchadh Bàn.

Alexander MacDonald (c 1695–1770) and Duncan Bàn MacIntyre (c 1724–1812): two famous bards

Duncan Bàn (fair-haired) made a song to the girl he married, Màiri Bhàn Òg (Young fair-haired Mary): 'Màiri Bhàn Òg, you are the maiden in my thoughts'. It was said that Alasdair mac Mhaighstir Alasdair was kind of jealous of Duncan Bàn. Alasdair was an educated man. Duncan had no schooling. But Duncan was so popular with people in general, far and wide throughout the Gaidhealtachd as a poet and as a man, and Alasdair knew that that was so.

After Duncan Bàn and Màiri Bhàn Òg married, mac Mhaighstir Alasdair said to Duncan one day: 'I've now seen Màiri and she isn't at all as beautiful as you said she was in the song.' 'Ah, but you didn't see her with my eyes', said Duncan Bàn.

3 Donnchadh Bàn agus 'Moladh Beinn Dòbhrain'

Bhathar ag innse gun robh Donnchadh Bàn Mac an t-Saoir, am bàrd, ag òl còmhla ri cuideachd an latha a bha seo ann an taigh-seinnse Chill Fhinn. Cò a thachair a bhith an làthair ach Dòmhnall mac Raghnaill na Sgèithe, Dòmhnallach à Gleann Comhann. Is e bàrd a bha annsan e fhèin.

Bha an dithis(t) bhàrd a' còmhdach mu mhaise nam beanntan, gach fear aca a' moladh na dùthcha aige fhèin. Is ann a thuirt duine a bha anns an èisteachd: 'Is e bàird a tha annaibh le chèile. Carson nach dèan sibh òran am fear mu na beanntan is na slèibhtean sin agus thig sinn cruinn an seo a-rithist an ceann mìos. Am fear a tha a' chuideachd seo a' meas a rinn an t-òran as fheàrr, faodaidh e a bhith ag òl an-asgaidh fad na h-oidhche.'

Sin mar a bha. Bha òran aig Dòmhnall mac Raghnaill mu bheanntan Ghlinne Comhann. Ach is e an t-òran a bha aig Donnchadh Bàn 'Moladh Beinn Dobhrain'.

Duncan Bàn and 'The Praise of Ben Doran'

They used to tell that Duncan Bàn MacIntyre the poet was drinking along with a group of companions one day in the tavern of Killin. Who happened to be present but Donald son of Ranald of the Shield, a MacDonald from Glencoe. He was a poet himself. The two poets were arguing about the beauty of the mountains, each of them praising his own district. Then a man who was there listening said: 'You are poets both of you. Why doesn't each of you make a song about those moors and mountains and we'll meet here again in a month's time. The one whom the company here reckons made the better song, he can drink free all night.'

That's how it was. Donald son of Ranald had a song about the mountains of Glencoe. But the song that Duncan had was 'The Praise of Ben Doran'.

4 Foghlam anns a' Ghàidhlig

Tha cùrsa an Fhoghlaim Ghàidhealaich annasach anns an dà sheagh: tha e a' dùsgadh ùidh agus tha e na adhbhar iongantais. Nuair a sheallar air na chaidh a sgrìobhadh ann an Gàidhlig, shaoileadh duine gun deach òigridh na Gàidhealtachd a oideachadh nan cànan fhèin ann an sgoiltean na Stàite bho shean. Ach cha b' ann mar sin a bha. Bha sgoiltean paraiste thall is a-bhos air feadh na Gàidhealtachd fad ghinealach ach cha robhar a' teagasg Gàidhlig annta ann. Is e sgoiltean de ghnè eile a chùm taic ri leughadh is sgrìobhadh agus tha ceangaltas ri a lorg a thaobh litearrachd bho linn Chaluim Chille an Eilean Idhe, anns an t-siathamh ceud, a dh'ionnsaigh an latha an-diugh.

Anns na linntean Meadhanach bha sgoiltean nam filidh (is dòcha caochladh sheòrsaichean dhiubh an àiteachan fa-leth) a' toirt foghlam ann an Gàidhlig do na sgrìobhadairean agus do theaghlaichean nan uaislean. Mhair a bheag no a mhòr dhe a shusbaint gu ruige an t-ochdamh ceud deug. Ach na bu tràithe na sin a-rithist bhathas air modh-litreachaidh na Gàidhlig a leasachadh agus a chur an sàs ann a bhith a' sgrìobhadh cainnt chumanta an t-sluaigh. Rinneadh tomhas dhen obair sin fo sgèith Seanadh Earra-Ghàidheal anns an Eaglais Stèite.

Ann an 1709 chaidh Comann a stèidheachadh ann an Dùn Èideann, le barrantas rìoghail, airson sgoiltean a chur air bhonn gus leughadh is sgrìobhadh a ionnsachadh do mhuinntir na Gàidhlig an Alba agus gu sònraichte airson am Bìoball agus leabhraichean cràbhach a chur an eòlas nan Gàidheal. B' sin an SSPCK (Scottish Society for the Propagation of Christian Knowledge). Aig toiseach tòiseachaidh b' e rùn a' Chomainn foghlam Beurla a thoirt don t-sluagh Ghàidhealach: bha Gàidhlig is Laideann le chèile, uime sin, air an toirmeasg anns na sgoiltean. Ach cha deach leotha. Is e buil a bha ann gun tàinig an Comann seo gu bhith na chùl-taic don chànan, a' misneachadh agus a' cuideachadh an dà chuid teagasg agus clò-bhualadh leabhraichean Gàidhlig.

Bha comainn eile a chuireadh air bhonn gus taic a thoirt do sgoiltean Gàidhlig. Cha robh ach aon cheann-uidhe anns an amharc aca: fiosrachadh sgriobtaireil a chraobh- sgaoileadh. Nuair a thàinig an Dealachadh (1843) agus a dh'fhàg mòran dhen t-sluagh an Eaglais Stèite, chuir an Eaglais Shaor a cuid sgoiltean fhèin air chois. A thuilleadh orra sin, bha caochladh chòmhlan eile ann, car dhen aon seòrsa, a chuir ris an obair chèanta. Ma tha laigead ri a chur às leth òrdachadh an fhoghlaim sin air fad, is e gun robh e ro cheangailte ri riaghladh eaglaiseach. Ach a dh'aindeoin sin thug na sgoiltean litearrachd do ghinealaichean dhe na Gàidheil.

Nuair a thugadh a-mach Achd an Fhoghlaim leis an Stàit, ann an 1872, cha robh àite no cothrom air a thoirt dhan Ghàidhlig. A chionn is gum feumadh a h-uile leanabh a-nis dol dhan sgoil, agus leis gur h-e Beurla an aon chainnt ionnsachaidh a bha innte, thug an t-Achd buille mhairbhteach dhan chànan. Ann an 1918 thàinig achd a thug inbhe air choreigin dhan Ghàidhlig: chuireadh mar fhiachaibh air ùghdarras an fhoghlaim anns gach sgìreachd Ghàidhealaich ullachadh freagarrach a dhèanamh às leth an teagaisg. Ann an 1946 chaidh Gàidhlig a chur air a' chlàr-oideachaidh ann am beagan sgoiltean anns na bailtean mòra,

Glaschu gu h-àraid, airson a' chiad uair. Ann an 1949 stèidhich Siorrachd Inbhir Nis post fear-eagraidh Gàidhlig ann an sgeama dà-chànanach. Bhon uair sin thàinig leasachaidhean eile ann an Roinn na Gàidhealtachd agus ann an Roinn nan Eilean. Tha toradh na h-obrach sin fhathast ri a mheas. Chaidh a' chiad sgoil Ghàidhlig neo-eisimeileach, Sgoil Ghàidhlig Ghlaschu (anns am faighear foghlam aig ìre sgoil-àraich, bun-sgoil agus àrd-sgoil), a stèidheachadh ann an Glaschu anns a' bhliadhna 2006.

Education in Gaelic

The course of Gaelic education is remarkable in two senses: it arouses interest and astonishment. When one considers how much has been written in Gaelic, one would think that the youth of the Gaidhealtachd had been instructed in their own language in the schools of the state from olden times. But that was not the case. There were parish schools here and there throughout the Gaidhealtachd for generations but Gaelic was simply not taught in them. It was schools of another kind that maintained reading and writing and a continuity of literacy can be traced from the time of Columba in Iona, in the sixth century, to the present day.

In the Middle Ages the poets' schools (diverse kinds perhaps in different places) gave instruction in Gaelic to writers and the families of the aristocracy. The substance of that, to a lesser or greater degree, survived until the eighteenth century. But earlier than that again the orthography of Gaelic had been developed and used in writing to represent the common speech of the people. A certain amount of that work was done under the aegis of the Synod of Argyll in the Established Church.

In 1709 a Society was set up in Edinburgh, under royal charter, to establish schools in order to teach reading and writing to the Gaelic speakers in Scotland and particularly to give Gaels a knowledge of the Bible and books of piety. This was the SSPCK (Scottish Society for the Propagation of Christian Knowledge). At the outset the aim of the Society was to provide education in English to the Gaelic population. Gaelic and Latin together were therefore forbidden in the schools. But they did not succeed in that policy. The result was that this Society came to be a support for the language, encouraging and helping both teaching and publishing Gaelic books.

Other societies were set up to support Gaelic schools. These had the sole aim of disseminating knowledge of the Scriptures. When the Disruption came (1843) and many of the people left the Established Church, the Free Church set up its own schools. In addition to these, there were a variety of other bodies, more or less of the same kind, who supplemented the same work. If there is any weakness to be found in this educational set-up, it is the fact that it was too closely tied to ecclesiastical control. But despite that, the schools made generations of Gaels literate.

When the Education Act of 1872 was passed, no place or opportunity was given to Gaelic. Since every child had now to go to school, and since English was the only language of instruction, the Act gave Gaelic a fatal blow. In 1918, a new act came which gave some status to Gaelic: the educational authority in every Gaelic-speaking district was obliged to make adequate provision for the teaching of Gaelic. In 1946 Gaelic was placed on the curriculum of a few city schools, especially in Glasgow, for the first time. In 1949 Inverness-shire established the post of Gaelic organiser in a scheme for bilingualism. Since then other developments have come in the Highland Region and in the Western Isles. The effects of this work have still to be assessed. The first independent Gaelic school, The Gaelic School in Glasgow (where nursery, primary and secondary education is provided), was established in Glasgow in the year 2006.

Key to Exercises

LESSON 1

Exercise 1.1: 1 Tha Màiri toilichte. 2 Tha Iain làidir. 3 Tha mi blàth. 4 Tha iad fuar. 5 Tha sinn an seo. 6 Tha leabhar aig Anna. 7 Tha càr aig Seumas. 8 Tha deoch agam. 9 Tha taigh againn. 10 Tha balach aice.
Exercise 1.2: 1 Chan eil Anna sgìth. 2 Chan eil Seumas an sin. 3 Chan eil cù aig Màiri. 4 Chan eil airgead againn. 5 A bheil Iain fuar? 6 A bheil deoch aig Dòmhnall? 7 A bheil airgead aca? 8 Chan eil agam ach sgillinn. 9 Nach eil Dòmhnall toilichte? 10 Nach eil càr aige?

LESSON 2

Exercise 2.1: 1 Is mise Anna. 2 Is esan Calum. 3 Is ise Peigi. 4 Cha tusa Seumas. 5 Chan iadsan an clas Gàidhlig. 6 Chan ise Màiri. 7 Nach tusa Dòmhnall? Cha mhi. 8 An tusa Iain? Is mi. 9 Is iadsan Peigi agus Màiri. 10 Is sibhse/tusa an tidsear.
Exercise 2.2: 1 an leabhar. 2 an ceòl. 3 a' chraobh. 4 a' phìob. 5 a' bhean. 6 an fheannag. 7 an t-sràid. 8 an sporan. 9 am pàipear. 10 an tè.
Exercise 2.3: 1 mo phiuthar. 2 do mhàthair/ur màthair. 3 a h-athair. 4 am mac. 5 a chas. 6 ar cù/an cù againn. 7 an airgead/an t-airgead aca. 8 do bhò/a' bhò agad. 9 a h-obair/an obair aice. 10 a sùil.
Exercise 2.4: 1 bòrd beag. 2 bò mhòr. 3 balach math. 4 oidhche dhorcha. 5 bròg shalach. 6 bàta dearg. 7 seann bhàta. 8 deagh chaileag (= caileag mhath). 9 droch shìde. 10 seann chàr gorm.
Translation: 1 a small table. 2 a big cow. 3 a good boy. 4 a dark night. 5 a dirty shoe. 6 a red boat. 7 an old boat. 8 a good girl. 9 bad weather. 10 an old blue car.

LESSON 3

Exercise 3.1: 1 Dè a tha thu/sibh a' smaoineachadh? 2 Tha Anna a' fuireach (ann) an Dùn Èideann. 3 A bheil thu/sibh a' tuigsinn Fraingis? 4 Tha Iain a' sgrìobhadh bàrdachd. 5 Tha Màiri a' dèanamh rannsachadh. 6 A bheil thu/sibh a' tighinn a-mach? 7 Tha iad ag iarraidh cupa cofaidh. 8 Tha Seumas ag obair (ann) an Glaschu. 9 A bheil thu/sibh a' faireachdainn ceart gu leòr? 10 Chan eil mi a' tuigsinn.
Exercise 3.2: 1 Is mise Iain./Is e mise Iain. 2 Is ise Anna./Is e ise Anna. 3 An (e) esan an tidsear? Is e. 4 Chan e Seumas an tidsear agam/mo thidsear. 5 Is e Màiri an nurs. 6 Is e Dòmhnall a h-athair. 7 Nach e Uilleam do mhac? Chan e. 8 Is e Catrìona a' phiuthar mhòr. 9 Is tusa/Is e thusa Seòras beag. 10 Is e Màiri am ministear ùr aca/am ministear ùr.
Exercise 3.3: 1 a' chaileag seo. 2 a' bhùth sin. 3 am baile ud. 4 am boireannach sin an sin. 5 (Is e) Seo mo phiuthar. 6 (Is e) Sin an sgian. 7 Tha an t-aran an siud. 8 (Is e) Sin a' bheinn ud a-rithist. 9 Tha seo fuar. 10 Tha sin glè mhath.
Exercise 3.4: (a) a naoi. (b) a còig. (c) a sia. (d) a h-ochd-deug. (e) a seachd. (f) a naoi-deug. (g) a h-aon. (h) a còig-deug.

LESSON 4

Exercise 4.1: **An robh** mi aig an taigh Diluain? **An cuala** mi fuaim shuas an staidhre? **An deach** mi suas? **Am faca** mi meàirleach? **An do rinn** e bùrach? **An do rinn** e bùrach? **An tuirt** mi: 'Cò thusa?' **An tàinig** am Poileas agus **an do rug** iad air a' mheàirleach? **An d' fhuair** am meàirleach buille? **An tug** e an t-airgead air ais? **An do ràinig** iad an stèisean? **An robh** e duilich?

Nach robh mi aig an taigh Diluain? **Nach cuala** mi fuaim shuas an staidhre? **Nach deach** mi suas? **Nach fhaca** mi meàirleach? **Nach do rinn** e bùrach? **Nach tuirt** mi: 'Cò thusa?' **Nach tàinig** am Poileas agus **nach do rug** iad air a' mheàirleach? **Nach d' fhuair** am meàirleach buille? **Nach tug** e an t-airgead air ais? **Nach do ràinig** iad an stèisean? **Nach robh** e duilich?

Exercise 4.2: 1 Bha mi toilichte. 2 Chunnaic mi Anna an-dè. 3 Chaidh Iain a-mach. 4 Thàinig iad a-steach/a-staigh. 5 Chuir sinn seachad bliadhna an sin. 6 Cha do rinn thu d' obair/an obair agad. 7 An d' fhuair thu an t-airgead? 8 Nach do ràinig thu/sibh Dùn Èideann fhathast? 9 Cha tuirt i sìon. 10 Chuala mi Màiri a-raoir.

Exercise 4.3: 1 Òl do thì/an tì agad./Òlaibh ur tì/an tì agaibh. 2 Ith do dhìnnear/an dìnnear agad./Ithibh ur dìnnear/an dìnnear agaibh. ('Gabh' may also be used in place of 'ith'.) 3 Seas/seasaibh (suas). 4 Suidh/suidhibh (sìos). 5 Bi/bithibh sàmhach. 6 Thig/thigibh a-steach/a-staigh. 7 Thoir/thoiribh sin do Sheumas. 8 Na dèan/dèanaibh sìon. 9 Faigh/faighibh e an-diugh./Faigh/faighibh an-diugh e. 10 Dùin an doras mas e do thoil e./Dùinibh an doras mas e ur toil e.

Exercise 4.4: 1 a Dhonnchaidh. 2 a Mhairead. 3 a Mhìcheil. 4 a Mhurchaidh. 5 a Shìne.

LESSON 5

Exercise 5.1: 1 Tha Iain na chadal. 2 A bheil thu nad dhùisg?/A bheil sibh nur dùisg? 3 Tha Màiri na laighe/na sìneadh. 4 Bha e na sheasamh an sin. 5 Tha sinn nar suidhe.

Exercise 5.2: 1 Is e ministear a tha ann an Iain. 2 Is e seinneadair a tha ann an Anna. 3 Is e tidsear a tha ann an Seonag. 4 Is e croitear a tha ann an Uilleam. 5 Is e oileanach a tha ann an Dòmhnall. 6 Is e oileanach a tha annam cuideachd. 7 Is e dotair a tha innte. 8 Is e borbair a tha annaibh. 9 An e tidsear a tha annaibh/annad? 10 An e ministear a tha ann?

Exercise 5.3: (a) Is /Is e sinne a chuala Anna a' seinn aig a' chèilidh a-raoir. (b) Is e Anna a chuala sinn a' seinn aig a' chèilidh a-raoir. (c) Is ann a' seinn a chuala sinn Anna aig a' chèilidh a-raoir. (d) Is ann aig a' chèilidh a chuala sinn Anna a' seinn a-raoir. (e) Is ann a-raoir a chuala sinn Anna a' seinn aig a' chèilidh. (f) Is ann a chuala sinn Anna a' seinn aig a' chèilidh a-raoir.

Exercise 5.4: 1 I like (the) Gaelic. 2 She prefers John. 3 Would you prefer beer? 4 Would you like a cup of tea? 5 They don't prefer brown bread. 6 Doesn't Ann like dancing/to dance? 7 I don't like meat. 8 I would prefer beer to whisky. 9 Do you like Run Rig? 10 Would you not prefer pibroch?

Exercise 5.5: 1 ann an taigh. 2 air bòrd. 3 le duine. 4 tro bhaile. 5 ro Sheumas. 6 bho àm gu àm. 7 a dh'Inbhir Nis. 8 à Dùn Èideann/bho Dhùn Èideann. 9 aig geata. 10 fo chàr.

LESSON 6

Exercise 6.1: 1 aig an doras. 2 anns an t-seòmar. 3 leis a' bhalach. 4 dhan a' chaileig. 5 ron a' chèilidh. 6 leis an airgead. 7 anns a' chàr. 8 anns a' Bheurla. 9 fo chrao(i)bh. 10 tron a' bhaile.

Exercise 6.2: 1 Dhùin Seumas an uinneag. 2 Choisich Anna dhachaigh. 3 Cheannaich Màiri am pàipear. 4 Dh'òl Catrìona a tì/an tì aice. 5 Sheinn/Ghabh Iain òran. 6 Leugh Calum am pàipear. 7 Dh'innis e dhomh. 8 Dh'ionnsaich mi (a') G(h)àidhlig. 9 Dh'ith i aran. 10 Ruith Uilleam agus dhùin e an doras. **Exercise 6.3:** 1 Cò a dhùin an doras? 2 Cuin a chaidh iad a-mach? 3 Càite an do chuir thu/sibh an iuchair? 4 Cha do dh'innis mi dha. 5 An do chòrd an cèilidh riut/ruibh? 6 Leugh mi an leabhar sin nuair a bha mi òg. 7 Fàg e far an d' fhuair thu e. 8 (Is e) Sin an duine a sheinn aig a' chèilidh. 9 Chan fhaca mi Seumas ma bha e ann. 10 Thàinig e ged a bha e sgìth.

LESSON 7

Exercise 7.1: 1 mac an t-sagairt. 2 dath an t-sneachd(a). 3 mullach a' chnuic. 4 doras na sgoile. 5 piuthar mo bhràthar. 6 iuchair an taighe. 7 càr mo pheathar. 8 biadh a' chait. 9 athair Sheumais. 10 leabhar Catrìona. **Exercise 7.2:** 1 Tha sinn a' fàgail an taighe an-diugh. 2 A bheil iad ag ithe a' bhidhe? 3 Cò a tha a' gabhail an òrain? 4 Chan eil iad ag èisteachd ris a' cheòl. 5 Bha sinn ag òl na tì. 6 An robh thu ag innse na naidheachd do dh'Anna? 7 Tha i a' tuigsinn na Gàidhlig. 8 Tha iad a' ceannach a leabhair. 9 Tha mi a' fosgladh an dorais. 10 Tha i a' dùnadh na h-uinneig(e). **Exercise 7.3:** 1 air mo chùlaibh. 2 air do bheulaibh/air ur beulaibh. 3 os a chionn. 4 ri a taobh. 5 às ar n-aonais. 6 coltach riutha. 7 còmhla rium. 8 timcheall oirnn. 9 seachad air. 10 chun an dorais.

LESSON 8

Exercise 8.1: 1 Òlaidh Anna a tì/an tì aice. 2 Ionnsaichidh mi (a') G(h)àidhlig. 3 Cuin a ghabhas tu/sheinneas tu an t-òran?/Cuin a ghabhas sibh/sheinneas sibh an t-òran? 4 Cha cheannaich i aran geal uair sam bith. 5 Am falbh iad gu moch anns a' mhadainn? 6 Bruidhnidh mi ris ma thilleas e. 7 Càite am fàg sinn an t-airgead? 8 Cò a chuidicheas mi? 9 Leughaidh mi am pàipear nuair a dhùisgeas mi. 10 Ciamar a dhùineas tu/sibh an doras? **Exercise 8.2:** 1 na caileagan agus na balaich. 2 anns na bailtean. 3 fo na bùird. 4 bho na Gàidheil. 5 air na cnuic. 6 tidsearan nan sgoiltean. 7 leabhraichean nam balach. 8 cànan nan Gàidheal. 9 airgead nam boireannach. 10 an dèidh nan oidhcheannan. **Exercise 8.3:** (a) trì uinneagan. (b) deich sgoiltean. (c) seachd brògan. (d) dà chlas. (e) ochd craobhan. (f) dà chàr dheug. (g) còig pìoban deug. (h) ochd òrain d(h)eug. (i) dà chois. (j) dà uinneig/uinneag dheug. **Exercise 8.4:** 1 A bheil thu gam chluinntinn? 2 A bheil sibh ga fhaicinn? 3 Tha Iain gan coinneachadh. 4 An robh na balaich gur bualadh? 5 Cò a tha gar n-iarraidh? 6 Bha Anna gad fhaighneachd. 7 Tha mi ga fhreagairt an-dràsta. 8 A bheil thu gar fàgail an seo? 9 A bheil thu ga ceannach? 10 Bha iad ga sheinn/ghabhail.

LESSON 9

Exercise 9.1: 1 Chan abair (cha chan) mi sìon ris. 2 Dè a bheir thu do bhean an taighe? 3 An cluinn thu na h-eòin a' seinn?/A bheil thu a' cluinntinn nan eun a' seinn? 4 An dèan thu an obair air mo shon/dhomh? 5 Am faigh iad na lathaichean saora aca/an lathaichean saora a-màireach? 6 Chì sinn iad nuair a ruigeas iad Glaschu. 7 An tèid do bhràthair dhan a' chèilidh? 8 Cha tig iad dhachaigh dìreach an dèidh na sgoile. 9 Gheibh e an trèan nuair a thig e. 10 An dèan thu/sibh do dhìcheall/ur dìcheall an uair seo a Iain?

Exercise 9.2: 1 An aithne dhut/dhuibh am balach a thilg a' chlach? 2 (Is e) Sin am boireannach a sheinn/ghabh an t-òran brèagha ud a-raoir. 3 Càite a bheil an leabhar nach do leugh thu? 4 (Is e) Seo an seòmar anns an do dh'fhàg mi an iuchair./(Is e) Seo an seòmar a dh'fhàg mi an iuchair ann. 5 An e sin am boireannach dhan an do dh'innis thu an naidheachd?/An e sin am boireannach a dh'innis thu an naidheachd dhi? 6 Is toil leam an sgioba leis an do chluich mi./Is toil leam an sgioba a chluich mi leis. 7 An toil leat/leibh an ceòl ris an robh Dòmhnall ag èisteachd?/An toil leat/leibh an ceòl a bha Dòmhnall ag èisteachd ris? 8 An rathad mun an robh sinn a' bruidhinn?/An rathad a bha sinn a' bruidhinn mu a dheidhinn? 9 An e sin an duine ris an do thachair thu?/An e sin an duine a thachair thu ris? 10 An aithne dhut am fear-lagha a fhuair a mhac an ceum aige an-uiridh?

Exercise 9.3: 1 leis a' chat bheag. 2 air a' bhòrd gheal. 3 dhan a' chaileig mhòir/dhan a' chaileag mhòr. 4 anns an t-solas gheal. 5 dath na deise ùire/dath na deise ùir. 6 faclan an òrain bhrèagha. 7 ceòl na pìoba-mòire/ceòl na pìob-mhòir. 8 cosgais a' chamara dhaoir. 9 leis a' chàraid lagha(i)ch. 10 air an rathad cheàrr.

Exercise 9.4: *Vigesimal:* (a) dà fhichead leabhar is a còig. (b) trì fichead each is a sia-deug. (c) ceithir fichead sèithear is a seachd. (d) naoi bliadhna deug air fhichead a dh'aois. (e) trì fichead bliadhna is a dhà a dh'aois. (f) trì fichead bliadhna is a deich a dh'aois. *Decimal:* (a) ceathrad is a còig leabhar/ceathrad leabhar is a còig. (b) seachdad is a sia each/seachdad each is a sia. (c) ochdad is a seachd sèithear/ochdad sèithear is a seachd. (d) trithead is a naoi bliadhna a dh'aois/trithead bliadhna is a naoi a dh'aois. (e) seasgad is a dhà bliadhna a dh'aois/seasgad bliadhna is a dhà a dh'aois. (f) seachdad bliadhna a dh'aois.

LESSON 10

Exercise 10.1: 1 Cha chuirinn suas ri sin. 2 Cuin a dhùisgeadh tu/sibh anns a' mhadainn? 3 Carson a chreideadh Iain sin? 4 Nigheadh iad iad fhèin anns an abhainn. 5 Lorg/fhuair sinn àite far an gabhamaid/gabhadh sinn anail. 6 Chan itheadh/cha ghabhadh iad grèim. 7 Cha ghabhainn ach druthag bheag. 8 Am postadh tu/sibh an litir seo dhomh/air mo shon? 9 Thuigeadh iad cuid mhath dheth gu dearbh. 10 Dh'fhosglainn an doras dhut/dhuibh/sibh(air do shon/air ur son) nam biodh fios agam gun robh thu/sibh ann.

Exercise 10.2: 1 Theirinn/chanainn gum bheil Iain nas sine na Màiri. 2 Nam biodh an t-sìde na b' fheàrr, shuidheamaid/shuidheadh sinn a-muigh. 3 Dh'innis mi dhut/dhuibh gum buinigeadh tu/sibh an duais a bu mhotha. 4 Bha Uilleam a' fuireach anns an Òban nuair a bha e na b' òige. 5 Is e Seumas (an duine) as sine anns an teaghlach aige. 6 Tha e nas fhasa nuair a tha an sgian nas gèire. 7 Tha Peigi nas treasa na Ailean ged a tha i nas lugha na e. 8 Sin a' chraobh as àirde a chunnaic mi riamh. 9 Tha a' Ghàidhlig cho doirbh ris a' Bheurla. 10 Chan eil an tidsear cho beairteach ris an fhear-lagha.

Exercise 10.3: 1 Thuirt Iain gun robh e a-muigh a-raoir. John said that he was out last night. 2 Chuala mi gun tàinig Seumas. I heard that James came. 3 An rud a chunnaic mi. The thing that I saw. 4 An naidheachd a chuala tu. The news that you heard. 5 Thuirt Anna gur h-e ministear a tha ann. Ann said that he is a minister. 6 Tha mi a' smaoineachadh gur h-e co-là-breith Sheumais a tha ann an-diugh. I think that it is James' birthday today. 7 Leugh mi gur h-ann an-diugh a thachair e. I read that it was today that it happened. 8 Tha iad a' ràdh/ag ràdh gur h-ann air a' Ghàidhealtachd a bha iad a' fuireach. They say that it was in the Highlands that they lived.

Exercise 10.4: 1 caileagan òga. young girls. 2 an fheadhainn gheala. the white ones. 3 cait dhubha. black cats. 4 clasaichean mòra. big classes. 5 balaich mhodhail. well-behaved boys. 6 daoine làidir. strong men/people. 7 bùird ghlana. clean tables. 8 pàistean matha. good children. 9 leabhraichean inntinneach. interesting books. 10 boireannaich bheairteach. rich women.

LESSON 11

Exercise 11.1: 1 Is toil leam ithe. 2 Feumaidh mi falbh. 3 Bu toil leis cuideachadh. 4 Tha i ag iarraidh bruidhinn. 5 Bha e a' dol a thighinn. 6 Thàinig i a choimhead. 7 Tha dùil aca ri fuireach anns an Òban. 8 Bu chòir dhut a dhol gu Baile Àtha Cliath./Tha còir agad a dhol gu Baile Àtha Cliath. 9 Nach eil thu a' dol a dh'èisteachd? 10 Is urrainn do Pheigi snàmh.

Exercise 11.2: 1 Feumaidh mi m' obair/an obair agam a dhèanamh. 2 Is urrainn dhi Gàidhlig a bhruidhinn. 3 Bu chòir dhut/Tha còir agad càr ùr a cheannach./Bu chòir dhuibh/Tha còir agaibh càr ùr a cheannach. 4 Tha Iain ag iarraidh leabhar a sgrìobhadh. 5 Is fheàrr dhut/Is fheàrr dhuibh an doras a dhùnadh nad dhèidh/nur dèidh. 6 Cha b' urrainn dhuinn an dotair a phàigheadh. 7 Tha sinn a' dol a dh'fhaighinn bainne. 8 Thàinig Anna a thogail a mic. 9 Tha cuimhne aig Dòmhnall air an leabhar sin a leughadh. 10 B' urrainn do Pheigi Gàidhlig a bhruidhinn.

Exercise 11.3: 1 Is toil leis a ithe. 2 Bha dùil aig Anna a sheinn/ghabhail aig a' chèilidh. 3 Bha an t-eagal air Iain a tarraing. 4 Feumaidh na balaich òga an glanadh/Tha aig na balaich òga ri an glanadh. 5 Chaidh Calum ga coimhead. 6 Is fheàrr le Màiri a teagasg. 7 Bu chòir dhut/Tha còir agad ar creidsinn. 8 Tha Anna a' dol gan dùsgadh. 9 Bu toil leinn do chuideachadh/ur cuideachadh. 10 Tha cuimhne aig Seumas air sin a ràdh/Tha cuimhne aig Seumas air a bhith ag ràdh sin.

Exercise 11.4: 1 Tha Raibeart dìreach air falbh. 2 Tha Seonag air tighinn/a thighinn. 3 Tha Iain air an litir a sgrìobhadh. 4 Tha e air cuideam a chur air. 5 Tha iad air dol/a dhol a-mach. 6 Bidh Màiri air tòiseachadh anns an oilthigh an t-seachdain seo tighinn/an ath-sheachdain. 7 Tha Anna air an seann taigh a reic mu dheireadh. 8 Bhiodh Seumas air Gàidhlig a ionnsachadh. 9 Tha Iain air cus a ithe/ghabhail mar-thà. 10 An dèidh do Niall am fiosrachadh gu lèir a chruinneachadh...

LESSON 12

Exercise 12.1: 1 Bhinn glè thoilichte nan tigeadh iad. 2 Dh'òladh e tì ceart gu leòr. 3 Chitheadh iad an càirdean/na càirdean aca aig an sgoil. 4 Rachamaid/Rachadh sinn dhan an taigh-t(h)asgaidh a h-uile mìos. 5 Chan fhaigheadh tu suidheachan air a' phlèan a-nis. 6 An abradh tu/an canadh tu gun rachadh Iain dhan an dràma/dealbh-chluich? 7 Am faigheadh tu am bus aig a' chùil sin? 8 Bheireadh tu air an aiseag mu dheireadh aig naoi uairean. 9 Cha chluinneadh tu a leithid sin ann an àite sam bith eile. 10 Cha toireadh màthair Dhòmhnaill cead dha a dhol a-mach.

Exercise 12.2: 1 Seinnear an t-òran. 2 Dh'fhosgladh an uinneag. 3 Leagadh an seann taigh. 4 Caillear airgead a h-uile bliadhna. 5 Leanadh Iain dhachaigh an-dè. 6 Nighte e a h-uile latha. 7 Chan fhacas is cha chualas an t-eun bhon an t-seachdain seo a chaidh. 8 Theirear/canar gun robh e a' fuireach ann an Dùn Èideann nuair a bha e na b' òige/nas òige. 9 Mharbhadh e feadh na h-oidhche. 10 Rugadh is thogadh mi an Èirinn.

Mini-dictionary

This mini-dictionary contains some extra vocabulary not appearing in the lessons.

Gaelic—English

a *(ppn)* her
à *(prp)* from, out of
a particle used before numerals when counting
a *(rel pron)* that, which
a* *(ppn)* his
abair *(vb)* say
abhainn *(f)* river, **aibhne** (G), **aibhnichean** *(pl)*
àbhaist *(f)* customary state
a' bhòn-dè *(adv)* the day before yesterday
a' bhòn-raoir *(adv)* the night before last
a' bhòn-uiridh *(adv)* last year
a-bhos *(adv)* over here (location at speaker)
ach *(cjn)* but
acras *(m)* hunger
actair *(m)* actor, **actairean** *(pl)*
ad *(f)* hat, **adaichean** *(pl)*
a dh'aithghearr *(adv)* soon
adhar *(m)* sky
adhbhar *(m)* reason, **adhbhair** *(pl)*
agus *(cjn)* and
a h-uile every
aig *(prp)* at
Ailean *(m)* Allan
aimsir *(f)* weather, **aimsirean** *(pl)*
ainm *(m)* name, **ainmean, ainmeannan** *(pl)*
ainmeil *(adj)* famous
air *(prp)* on
airgead *(m)* money
airson *(cmp prp)* for (the sake of) (followed by G)
aiseag *(m)* ferry, **aiseagan** *(pl)*
àite *(m)* place, **àiteachan, àitichean** *(pl)*
aithne *(f)* knowledge

aithneachadh *(vn)* recognising, knowing
aithnich *(vb)* recognise, know
àlainn *(adj)* beautiful
Alba *(f)* Scotland
àm *(m)* time, **amannan** *(pl)*
a-mach *(adv)* out, outwards (motion)
a-màireach *(adv)* tomorrow
am-bliadhna *(adv)* this year
a-muigh *(adv)* out (location)
an etc. *(art)* the
an/m *(interr prt pos)*
a-nall *(adv)* over here (motion towards speaker)
an ath-bhliadhna *(adv)* next year
an ath-oidhch(e) *(adv)* next night
an ath-sheachdain *(adv)* next week
an-còmhnaidh *(adv)* always
an-dè *(adv)* yesterday
an-diugh *(adv)* today
an-dràsta *(adv)* now
an-earar *(adv)* the day after tomorrow
a-nis *(adv)* now
anmoch *(adv)* late
ann *(adv)* there
ann an *(prp)* in
Anna *(f)* Ann
a-nochd *(adv)* tonight
a-nuas *(adv)* down, downwards; up, upwards (towards the speaker)
an-uiridh *(adv)* last year
a-null *(adv)* over there (motion away from speaker)
a-null thairis *(adv)* abroad (motion to)
a-raoir *(adv)* last night
an seo *(adv)* here
an sin *(adv)* there
an siud *(adv)* there, yonder
an toiseach *(adv)* first
aodach *(m)* cloth, clothes, **aodaichean** *(pl)*
aodann *(m)* face, **aodainnean** *(pl)*

aois *(f)* age, **aoisean** *(pl)*
aon *(num)* one
aon* *(adj)* one, same
aonan *(m)* one
ar *(ppn)* our
aran *(m)* bread, **arain** *(pl)*
àrd *(adj)* high, tall
àrd-sgoil *(f)* secondary school,
  àrd-sgoiltean *(pl)*
a-rithist *(adv)* again
ars(a) *(def vb)* says, said
a-staigh *(adv)* in, inside (location)
a-steach *(adv)* in, inwards (motion)
as t-earrach *(adv)* in Spring
as t-fhoghar *(adv)* in Autumn
as t-oidhche *(adv)* at night
as t-samhradh *(adv)* in Summer
ath* *(adj)* next
athair *(m, irreg)* father, **athraichean** *(pl)*
atharrachadh *(vn)* changing
atharraich *(vb)* change

baga *(m)* bag, **bagaichean** *(pl)*
baile *(m)* town(ship), **bailtean** *(pl)*
bainne *(m)* milk, **bainneachan** *(pl)*
balach *(m)* boy, **balaich** *(pl)*
balgam *(m)* mouthful, **balgaman** *(pl)*
ball-coise *(m)* football
balla *(m)* wall, **ballachan,**
  ballaichean *(pl)*
bàn *(adj)* fair (of hair)
banca *(m)* bank, **bancaichean** *(pl)*
bàrd *(m)* poet, **bàird** *(pl)*
bàrdachd *(f)* poetry
bàrr *(m)* top
bas *(f)* palm, **boisean** *(pl)*
basaidh *(m)* basin, **basaidhean** *(pl)*
basgaid *(f)* basket, **basgaidean** *(pl)*
bàta *(m)* boat, **bàtaichean** *(pl)*
beachd *(m)* opinion, **beachdan** *(pl)*
beag *(adj)* small
beagan *(m)* a little, a small amount/
  number
beairteach *(adj)* rich
Bealltainn *(f)* May (Day)
bean *(f, irreg)* wife, **mnathan** *(pl)*
beannachd *(m)* blessing,

beannachdan *(pl)*
beannachd leibh goodbye *(pl or formal)*
beinn *(f, irreg)* mountain, **beanntan** *(pl)*
beir (air) *(vb)* take hold, catch, bear
beò *(adj)* alive
beul *(m)* mouth
Beurla *(f)* English
(a) bhith *(inf)* being, to be
bho* *(prp)* from; *(cjn)* since
bho chionn *(cjn)* since
bi *(vb)* be
biadh *(m)* food, **bidhe** (G),
  bidheannan *(pl)*
blas *(m)* taste
blasta *(adj)* tasty
blàth *(adj)* warm
blàths *(m)* warmth
(a') B(h)liadhna Ùr *(f)* New Year
bò *(f)* cow, **bà** *(pl)* (rare: **crodh** *(m, coll)*,
  more common as *pl*)
bochd *(adj)* poor
bodach *(m)* old man, **bodaich** *(pl)*
boin *(vb)* belong to, relate to
boireannach *(m)* woman, **boireannaich**
  (pl)
borbair *(m)* barber, **borbairean** *(pl)*
bòrd *(m)* table, **bùird** *(pl)*
bracaist *(m)* breakfast, **bracaistean** *(pl)*
bradan *(m)* salmon, **bradain** *(pl)*
bràthair *(m, irreg)* brother, **bràithrean**
  (pl)
breac *(m)* trout, **bric** *(pl)*
breac *(adj)* speckled
breith *(vn)* taking hold, catching, bearing
brèagha *(adj)* lovely, fine
bris(t) *(vb)* break
bris(t)eadh *(vn)* breaking
bròg *(f)* shoe, **brògan** *(pl)*
brònach *(adj)* sad
brot *(m)* soup
bruidhinn (ri) *(vb)* speak (to)
bu, b' past & conditional of **is**
b' aithne do knows
bu chaomh le would like
bu toil le would like
b' urrainn do could
buaidh *(f)* influence

buail *(vb)* strike
bualadh *(vn)* striking
buidhe *(adj)* yellow
builich *(vb)* grant, bestow, confer
buinig *(vb)* win
buinigeadh *(vn)* winning
bun-sgoil *(f)* primary school,
  bun-sgoiltean *(pl)*
buntàta *(m, coll)* potatoes
bùrach *(m)* mess
bus *(m)* bus, **busaichean** *(pl)*
bùth *(f)* shop, **bùthan, bùithtean** *(pl)*

cabhag *(f)* hurry
cabhsair *(m)* pavement, **cabhsairean** *(pl)*
cadal *(m)* sleep
(a') C(h)àisg *(f)* Easter
caileag *(f)* girl, **caileagan** *(pl)*
caill *(vb)* lose
cailleach *(f)* old woman, **cailleachan** *(pl)*
cairteal *(m)* quarter, **cairtealan** *(pl)*
cairt-shiubhail *(f)* passport
caisteal *(m)* castle, **caistealan** *(pl)*
càite *(interr pron)* where?
call *(m)* loss, pity
Calum *(m)* Calum
camanachd *(f)* shinty
can (ri) *(vb)* say to
cànan *(m)*/**cànain** *(f)* language,
  cànanan/cànainean *(pl)*
cantainn/cantail *(vn)* saying
caoin *(vb)* cry
caoineadh *(vn)* crying
caora *(f)* sheep, **caoraich** *(pl)*
càr *(m)* car, **càraichean** *(pl)*
càradh *(vn)* fixing
caraid *(m)*, friend, relative, **càirdean** *(pl)*
  relatives, **caraidean** friends
càrn *(m)* cairn, **càirn, cùirn** *(pl)*
cas *(f)* foot, leg, **casan** *(pl)*
cat *(m)* cat, **cait** *(pl)*
cathair *(f)* chair; city **cathraichean** *(pl)*
Catrìona *(f)* Catherine
cead *(m)* permission
ceann *(m)* head, **cinn** *(pl)*
ceann-suidhe *(m)* president, **cinn-s(h)uidhe** *(pl)*

ceannach *(vn)* buying
ceannaich *(vb)* buy
ceàrr *(adj)* wrong
ceart gu leòr *(adv)* all right, OK
ceasnaiche *(m)* interviewer,
  ceasnaichean *(pl)*
ceathrar *(m)* four people
cèiliche *(m)* visitor, **cèilichean** *(pl)*
cèilidh *(m, f)* ceilidh, dance, social visit,
  cèilidhean *(pl)*
ceist *(f)* question, **ceistean** *(pl)*
Cèitean *(m)* May, **Cèiteanan** *(pl)* *(pl*
  rarely used)
ceithir *(num)* four
ceòl *(m)* music
ceòl-mòr *(m)* pibroch
ceum *(m)* step, degree, **ceumannan** *(pl)*
cha(n) *(neg prt)* not
cho as *(adv)*
chun *(prp)* to (followed by G)
ciamar (a) how?
clach *(f)* stone, **clachan** *(pl)*
cladach *(m)* shore, **cladaichean** *(pl)*
clann *(f, coll)* children
clas *(m)* class, **clasaichean** *(pl)*
clì *(adj)* left
cluas *(f)* ear, **cluasan** *(pl)*
cluich *(vb, vn)* play(ing)
cluinn *(vb)* hear
cluinntinn *(vn)* hearing
cnoc *(m)* hill, **cnuic** *(pl)*
cò (a) who? *(interr pron)*
cùil *(f)* corner, **cùiltean** *(pl)*
co-dhiubh *(adv)* anyway, however
co-dhiù *(cjn)* whether
cofaidh *(m)* coffee
coibhneil *(adj)* kind
còig *(num)* five
còignear *(m)* five people
coille *(f)* wood, **coilltean** *(pl)*
coinneachadh *(vn)* meeting
coinneamh *(m)* meeting,
  coinneamhan *(pl)*
coinnich *(vb)* meet
còir *(f)* right
coire *(m)* kettle
coireach *(adj)* faulty, guilty

coiseachd *(vn)* walking
coisich *(vb)* walk
colaiste *(f)* college, **colaistean** *(pl)*
co-là-breith *(m)* birthday
cò mheud how many?
coltach ri *(cmp prp)* like
coltas *(m)* appearance, **coltais** *(pl)*
comharradh *(m)* sign, **comharraidhean** *(pl)*
comhfhurtail *(adj)* comfortable
còmhla ri *(cmp prp)* along with
còmhlan ciùil *(m)* band (of music)
companach *(m)* companion, **companaich** *(pl)*
còrd ri *(vb)* enjoy (accord with)
còrdadh ri *(vn)* enjoying, (according with)
cosgais *(f)* cost, **cosgaisean** *(pl)*
còta *(m)* coat, **còtaichean** *(pl)*
cothrom *(m)* chance, **cothroman** *(pl)*
craobh *(f)* tree, **craobhan** *(pl)*
creach *(f)* plunder, ruin, ruination, **creachan** *(pl)*
mo chreach *(interj)* alas
creid *(vb)* believe
creidsinn *(vn)* believing
croitear *(m)* crofter, **croitearan** *(pl)*
cruaidh *(adj)* hard
cruinneachadh *(un)* gathering
cruinnich *(vb)* gather
cù *(m, irreg)* dog, **coin** *(pl)*
cuideachadh *(vn)* helping
cuideachd *(adv)* also
cuideigin *(m)* somebody, someone
cuidich *(vb)* help
cuimhne *(f)* memory
cuin (a) when?
cuingichte *(adv)* restricted, limited to
cuir *(vb)* put, send
cùirt *(f)* court, **cùirtean** *(pl)*
cùm *(vb)* keep
cumail *(vn)* keeping
cupa *(m)* cup, **cupannan** *(pl)*
cur *(vn)* putting, sending
cùrsa *(m)* course, **cùrsaichean** *(pl)*
cus *(adv)* too much, too many (very many)

cuspair *(m)* subject, **cuspairean** *(pl)*

dà* *(num)* two, **a dhà** (when counting)
dachaigh *(f)* home, **dachaighean** *(pl)*
dad nothing (in *neg* and *interr* sentences)
Dàmhair *(m)* October, **Dàmhairean** *(pl)*
damhan-allaidh *(m)* spider, **damhain-allaidh** *(pl)*
dannsa *(m)* dance, **dannsaichean** *(pl)*
dannsa *(vn)* dancing
dath *(m)* colour, **dathan** *(pl)*
de *(prp)* of
dè (a) *(interr pron)* what?
deagh* *(adj)* good (precedes noun)
dealbh *(f, m)* picture, **dealbhannan, deilbh** *(pl)*
dealbh-chluich *(f)* drama, **dealbh-chluichean** *(pl)*
dèan *(vb)* do, make
dèanamh *(vn)* doing, making
dearbh* *(adj)* very
dearg *(adj)* (bright) red
deas *(adj)* right(-hand), south
deich *(num)* ten
deichnear *(m)* ten people
deigh *(f)* ice
deireadh *(m)* end
deise *(f)* suit, **deiseachan** *(pl)*
dhachaigh *(adv)* home(wards)
deiseil *(adj)* ready
deoch *(f)* drink, **dighe/dibhe** (G, *irreg*), **deochannan** *(pl)*
dian *(adj)* intense, hard
Diardaoin Thursday
Diciadain Wednesday
Didòmhnaich Sunday *v* **Latha na Sàbaid**
Dihaoine Friday
dìleas *(adj)* loyal
Diluain Monday
Dimàirt Tuesday
dìnnear/dinnear *(f)* dinner, **dìnnearan/dinnearan** *(pl)*
dìreach *(adj)* just, straight
Disathairne Saturday
dithis(t) *(f)* two people

do* *(ppn)* your
do* *(prp)* to, for
do-dhèante *(adj)* impossible
doirbh *(adj)* difficult
dòirt *(vb)* pour
dol *(vn)* going
Dòmhnall *(m)* Donald
dona *(adj)* bad
donn *(adj)* brown
doras *(m)* door, doorway, **dorais, dorsan** *(pl)*
dorcha *(adj)* dark
dòrtadh *(vn)* pouring
dragh *(m)* worry, **draghannan** *(pl)*
dotair *(m)* doctor, **dotairean** *(pl)*
dràibh *(vb)* drive
dràibheadh *(vn)* driving
dram(a) *(m)* dram (drink), **dramaichean, dramannan** *(pl)*
dràma *(m)* drama
dreuchd *(f)* post, job, office, **dreuchdan** *(pl)*
droch* *(adj)* bad (precedes noun)
duais *(f)* prize, reward, **duaisean** *(pl)*
dualchainnt *(f)* dialect, **dualchainntean** *(pl)*
dubh *(adj)* black
Dùbhlachd *(f)* December, **Dùbhlachdan** *(pl)*
duilich *(adj)* sorry; hard, difficult
duilleag *(f)* leaf, **duilleagan** *(pl)*
dùin *(vb)* close
duine *(m)* man, person, **daoine** *(pl)*
dùisg *(vb)* waken
Dùn Èideann *(m)* Edinburgh
dùnadh *(vn)* closing
dùsgadh *(vn)* wakening
dùthaich *(f)* country, district, land, **dùthchannan** *(pl)*

each *(m)* horse, **eich** *(pl)*
eachdraidh *(f)* history, **eachdraidhean** *(pl)*
eagal *(m)* fear
eaglais *(f)* church, **eaglaisean** *(pl)*
Earrach *(m)* Spring, **Earraich** *(pl)*

-eigin some *v* **rudeigin, cuideigin, uaireigin**
èigh *(vb)* shout
èigheach(d) *(vn)* shouting
eile *(adj)* other, else
eilean *(m)* island, **eileanan** *(pl)*
Èirinn *(f)* Ireland
èist *(vb)* listen
èisteachd *(vn)* listening
esan *(pron)* he

fa leth particular, singly, separately
fada *(adj)* long
fàg *(vb)* leave
fàgail *(vn)* leaving
faic *(vb)* see
faicinn *(vn)* seeing
faigh *(vb)* get
faighinn *(vn)* getting
faighneachd *(vn)* asking
faighnich (de) *(vb)* ask (information of)
faireachdainn *(vn)* feeling
fairich *(vb)* feel
faisg (air) *(prp)* near, close (to)
falamh *(adj)* empty
falbh *(vb, vn)*) go(ing) away
falt *(m)* hair
faod *(def vb)* may
Faoilleach/Faoilteach *(m)* January, **Faoillich/Faoiltich** *(pl)*
far *(prp)* off (followed by G)
far an *(cjn)* where, the place that
fàs *(vb, vn)* grow(ing)
feadh *(prp)* during, throughout
feadhainn *(f)* some (people or things)
feannag *(f)* crow, **feannagan** *(pl)*
fear *(m)* man, **fir** *(pl)*
fear *(pron)* one, **feadhainn** *(f, coll* used for *pl)*
fear-lagha *(m)* lawyer, **fir-lagha** *(pl)*
feasgar *(m)* evening, **feasgair** *(pl)*
feòil *(f)* meat
feuch (ri) *(vb)* see; make sure, try
feuchainn (ri) *(vn)* making sure, trying
feum *(def vb)* must
feur *(m)* grass

fhathast *(adv)* yet
fhèin self
fiadh *(m)* deer, **fèidh** *(pl)*
fichead *(m)* twenty, **ficheadan** *(pl)*
fidheall *(f)* fiddle, **fidhlean** *(pl)*
fidhlear *(m)* fiddler, **fidhlearan** *(pl)*
fiodh *(m)* wood
fion *(m)* wine
fios *(m)* knowledge
fiosrachadh *(m)* information
fìrinn *(f)* truth
fliuch *(adj)* wet
fo* *(prp)* under
foghain *(vb)* suffice
Foghar *(m)* Autumn, **Foghair** *(pl)*
foghlaimte *(adj)* learned, educated
foghlam *(m)* education
foillseachadh *(vn)* publishing, revealing
foillsich *(vb)* publish, reveal
fòn *(m)* phone
fòn *(vb)* phone
fònadh *(vn)* phoning
fosgail *(vb)* open
fosgladh *(vn)* opening
Fraingis *(f)* French
fraoch *(m)* heather
freagairt *(f)* reply, answer,
  freagairtean *(pl)*
freagarrach *(adj)* suitable
fuadaichean *(pl)* Clearances
fuaim *(m)* sound, **fuaimean** *(pl)*
fuar *(adj)* cold
fuil *(f)* blood
fuireach *(vn)* living (in), staying
fuireach ri *(vn)* waiting for
fuirich *(vb)* live (in), stay
fuirich ri *(vb)* wait for
furasta *(adj)* easy

gabh *(vb)* take; eat
gabh *(vb)* **mo lethsgeul** excuse me
gabh *(vb)* **òran** sing a song
gabhail *(vn)* taking; eating
gach every
Gàidheal *(m)* Gael, **Gàidheil** *(pl)*
Gàidhealtachd *(f)* Highlands
Gàidhlig *(f)* Gaelic

galar *(m)* disease
Gall *(m)* Lowlander, **Goill** *(pl)*
Galltachd *(f)* Lowlands
gaol *(m)* love
garaids *(f)* garage, **garaidsean** *(pl)*
geal *(adj)* white, bright
geama *(m)* game, **geamaichean** *(pl)*
geamair *(m)* gamekeeper, **geamairean**
  (pl)
Geamhradh *(m)* Winter,
  Geamhraidhean *(pl)*
(a') G(h)earmailt *(f)* Germany
Gearmailtis *(f)* German
geàrr *(adj)* short
geàrr *(vb)* cut
gearradh *(vn)* cutting
Gearran *(m)* February, **Gearrain** *(pl)*
geata *(m)* gate, **geataichean** *(pl)*
ged (a) *(cjn)* although
ged-thà however
geug *(f)* branch, twig, **geugan** *(pl)*
geur *(adj)* sharp
Giblean *(m)* April, **Gibleanan** *(pl)*
gille *(m)* boy, **gillean** *(pl)*
ginealach *(m)* generation,
  ginealaich(ean) *(pl)*
glan *(adj)* clean; fine, nice
glas *(adj)* grey, grey-green
glas *(vb)* lock
Glaschu *(f)* Glasgow
glasraich *(f)* vegetables
glè* very
gleusta *(adj)* canny, prudent
glic *(adj)* clever, wise
gloine *(f)* glass, **gloineachan** *(pl)*
gobha *(m)* smith, **goibhnean** *(pl)*
goid *(vb)* rob, steal
goirid *(adj)* short
goirt *(adj)* sore
gòrach *(adj)* silly, foolish
gorm *(adj)* blue
greas *(vb)* hurry up
greas ort (you) hurry up!
grian *(f)* sun, **grèine** (G)
grunn *(m)* a good deal, a lot
gu *(prp)* to, to the point of
gu bràch *(adv)* ever

gu bràch tuilleadh evermore
gu dearbh *(adv)* indeed
gu dòigheil *(adv)* fine
gu dona *(adv)* badly
gu lèir *(adv)* completely
gu leòr *(adv)* plenty
gu luath *(adv)* quickly
gu math *(adv)* well
gu mì-fhortanach *(adv)* unfortunately
gu snog *(adv)* nicely
gu sònraichte *(adv)* especially
gun(*) *(prp)* without
gun *(cjn)* that
gu ruige *(prp)* to
gus *(prp)* until
guth *(m)* voice, **guthan** *(pl)*

i *(pron)* she
iad *(pron)* they
Iain *(m)* John
iarr *(vb)* ask, request, want
iarraidh *(vn)* asking, requesting, wanting
iasg *(m)* fish, **èisg** *(pl)*
iasgach *(m)* fishing
idir *(adv)* at all
ìm *(m)* butter
innis (do) *(vb)* tell (to)
innse *(vn)* telling
inntinneach *(adj)* interesting
ionnsachadh *(vn)* learning
ionnsaich *(vb)* learn
is *(def vb)* is
is aithne do know (of person)
is beag air dislikes
is caomh le likes
is coingeis le it doesn't matter to
is dòcha probably, perhaps
is toil le likes
is urrainn do can
ise *(pron)* she
ìseal *(adj)* low
ith *(vb)* eat
ithe *(vn)* eating
iuchair *(f)* key, **iuchraichean** *(pl)*
Iuchar *(m)* July, **Iuchair** *(pl)*

lag *(adj)* weak

lagachadh *(vn)* weakening
lagaich *(vb)* weaken
lagh *(m)* law, **laghannan** *(pl)*
laghach *(adj)* kind
làidir *(adj)* strong
laigh *(vb)* lie down
laighe *(vn)* lying down
làmh *(f)* hand, **làmhan** *(pl)*
làr *(m)* floor, **làir** *(pl)*
latha *(m)* day, **lathaichean** *(pl)*
Latha na Sàbaid Sunday *v*
    Didòmhnaich
lathaichean saora *(pl)* holidays
le *(prp)* with
leabaidh *(f, irreg)* bed, **leapannan** *(pl)*
leabhar *(m)* book, **leabhraichean** *(pl)*
leabharlann *(m)* library,
    leabharlannan *(pl)*
leag *(vb)* knock down, fell
leagail *(vn)* knocking down, felling
lean *(vb)* follow
leantainn/leantail *(vn)* following
leig *(vb)* let, allow
leigeil *(vn)* letting, allowing
lèine *(f)* shirt, **lèintean** *(pl)*
lethphinnt *(m)* half-pint,
    lethphinntean *(pl)*
lethsgeul *(m)* excuse, **lethsgeulan** *(pl)*
lethuair *(f)* half-hour, **lethuairean** *(pl)*
leudachadh *(vn)* expanding
leudaich *(vb)* expand
leugh *(vb)* read
leughadh *(vn)* reading
liath *(adj)* (light) blue, grey
lìon *(vb)* fill
lionn *(m)* beer, **lionntan** *(pl)*
litir *(f)* letter, **litrichean** *(pl)*
litreachas *(m)* literature
loch *(m)* lake, **lochan** *(pl)*
luath *(adj)* fast, swift
Lùnastal *(m)* August, **Lùnastail** *(pl)*
ma *(cjn)* if
mac *(m)* son, **mic** *(pl)*
madainn *(f)* morning, **madainnean,**
    maidnean *(pl)*
maighstear-sgoile *(m)* schoolmaster
mair *(vb)* last, endure

Màiri *(f)* Mary
manaidsear *(m)* manager, **manaidsearan** *(pl)*
mar *(prp)* as, like
mar sin leibh goodbye to you *(pl or formal)*
Màrtainn *(m)* Martin
mar-thà *(adv)* already
Màrt *(m)* March, **Màirt** *(pl)*
mas e do thoil e please, *lit* if it is your wish
math *(adj)* good
ma-thà then! so!
màthair *(f)* mother, **màthraichean** *(pl)*
meadhan *(m)* middle, **meadhanan** *(pl)*
meadhanach *(adj)* middling
meàirleach *(m)* robber, **meàirlich** *(pl)*
meal *(vb)* enjoy
meal do naidheachd congratulations
mear *(adj)* merry
measail air fond of
mì-fhortanach *(adj)* unfortunate
mi *(pron)* I
mìle *(m)* thousand, **mìltean** *(pl)*
milis *(adj)* sweet
mìn *(adj)* smooth
ministear *(m)* minister, **ministearan** *(pl)*
mionaid *(f)* minute, **mionaidean** *(pl)*
mìos *(m, f)* month, **mìosan** *(pl)*
mo* *(ppn)* my
modh cainnte *(m)* mode of speaking
modh *(m)* good manners, politeness
modhail *(adj)* well-behaved, polite
mol *(vb)* praise
moladh *(vn)* praising
moladh *(m)* recommendation
mòr *(adj)* big
Mòrag *(f)* Morag
mòran *(m)* much, many
mu *(prp)* about
mu dheidhinn *(prp)* about, concerning (followed by G)
mu dheireadh *(adv)* (at) last
muillean *(m)* million, **muilleanan** *(pl)*
muir *(f)* sea, **marannan** *(pl)*
mura *(cjn)* if not

mus *(cjn)* before
na *(pron)* what, that which
nach *(interr prt neg* etc.*)*
naidheachd *(f)* news, **naidheachdan** *(pl)*
naoi *(num)* nine
naonar *(m)* nine people
neoni *(m)* nothing, zero
nigh *(vb)* wash
nighe *(vn)* washing
nighean *(f)* daughter, girl **nigheanan** *(pl)*
no *(cjn)* or
nochd *(vb)* appear
nochdadh *(vn)* appearing
nuair (a) *(cjn)* when, the time that
nurs *(f)* nurse, **nursaichean** *(pl)*

obair *(f)*, work, **obraichean** *(pl)*
obair *(vn)* working
(an t-) Òban *(m)* Oban
ochd *(num)* eight
ochdnar *(m)* eight people
òg *(adj)* young
Ògmhios *(m)* June, **Ògmhiosan** *(pl)*
oidhche *(f)* night, **oidhcheannan** *(pl)*
Oidhche Challainn *(f)* Hogmanay, New Year's Eve
Oidhche Shamhna *(f)* Halloween
oifigear *(m)* officer, official, **oifigearan** *(pl)*
oifis *(f)* office, **oifisean** *(pl)*
oileanach *(m)* student, **oileanaich** *(pl)*
oilthigh *(m)* university, **oilthighean** *(pl)*
òl *(vb, vn)* drink(ing)
orains *(m)* orange-juice
orainsear *(m)* orange, **orainsearan** *(pl)*
òran *(m)* song, **òrain** *(pl)*
ospadal *(m)* hospital, **ospadail** *(pl)*

pailteas *(adv)* enough, plenty
pàipear *(m)* paper, **pàipearan** *(pl)*
pàipear-naidheachd *(m)* newspaper, **pàipearan-naidheachd** *(pl)*
pàirc *(f)* park, **pàircean** *(pl)*

Paras *(m)* Paris
pàrlamaid *(f)* parliament,
   pàrlamaidean *(pl)*
pàrtaidh *(m)* party, **pàrtaidhean** *(pl)*
pathadh *(m)* thirst
peann *(m)* pen, **pinn** *(pl)*
peant *(m)* paint, **peantaichean** *(pl)*
Peigi *(f)* Peggy
peitean *(m)* jumper, **peiteanan** *(pl)*
pinc *(adj)* pink
plèan *(m)* plane, **plèanaichean** *(pl)*
pinnt *(m)* pint, **pinntean** *(pl)*
pìob *(f)* pipe, **pìoban** *(pl)*
pìobaire *(m)* piper, **pìobairean** *(pl)*
pìos *(m)* piece
piuthar *(f, irreg)* sister, **peathraichean**
   (pl)
pòg *(f)* kiss, **pògan** *(pl)*
poileas *(m)* police, **poileis** *(pl)*
port-adhair *(m)* airport, **puirt-adhair**
   (pl)
pòs *(vb)* marry
pòsadh *(vn)* marrying
post *(m)* postman, **postaichean, puist**
   (pl)
prìosanach *(m)* prisoner, **prìosanaich**
   (pl)
prògram *(m)* programme, **prògraman**
   (pl)

rach *(vb)* go
ràdh *(vn)* saying
Raghnall *(m)* Ronald
rannsachadh *(vn)* (re)searching
rannsaich *(vb)* (re)search
rathad *(m)* road, **rathaidean/**
   rothaidean *(pl)*
rè *(prp)* during (followed by G)
reòite *(adj)* frozen
reul *(m)* star, **reultan** *(pl)*
ri *(prp)* to, for etc.
riamh *(adv)* ever
rionnag *(f)* star
ro/roimh *(prp)* before
ro* too
ruadh *(adj)* (darker) red, red (of hair)
rudeigin *(m)* something

ruig *(vb)* reach, arrive at
ruigsinn/ruighinn *(vn)* reaching,
   arriving at
rùisg *(vb)* peel
ruith *(vb, vn)* run(ning)
rùsgadh *(vn)* peeling

sagart *(m)* priest, **sagairt** *(pl)*
salach *(adj)* dirty
salann *(m)* salt
sam bith any, at all
sàmhach *(adj)* quiet
Samhain *(f)* November, **Samhainean**
   (pl)
Samhradh *(m)* Summer,
   Samhraidhean *(pl)*
saoil *(vb)* wonder
saor *(adj)* free
Sasa(i)nn *(f)* England
seachad *(adv)* past
seachd *(num)* seven
seachdain *(f)* week, **seachdainean** *(pl)*
seachdnar *(m)* seven people
seall *(vb)* look, show
sean *(adj)* old
seann* *(adj)* old (precedes noun)
seas *(vb)* stand
seasamh *(vn)* standing
seinn *(vb, vn)* sing(ing)
seinneadair *(m)* singer,
   seinneadairean *(pl)*
seòrsa *(m)* type, **seòrsaichean** *(pl)*
seòlta *(adj)* cunning, clever
seòmar *(m)* room, **seòmraichean** *(pl)*
Seumas *(m)* James
sgadan *(m)* herring, **sgadain** *(pl)*
sgeilp *(f)* shelf, **sgeilpichean** *(pl)*
sgeul *(m)* sign, news, story,
   sgeòil *(pl)*
sgeulachd *(f)* story, **sgeulachdan** *(pl)*
sgian *(f, irreg)* knife, **sgeinean** *(pl)*
sgillinn *(f)* penny, **sgillinnean** *(pl)*
sgiobalta *(adj)* tidy, neat, deft
sgìth *(adj)* tired
sgìths *(m)* tiredness
sgoil *(f)* school, **sgoiltean** *(pl)*
sgrìob *(f)* trip, **sgrìoban** *(pl)*

sgrìobh *(vb)* write
sgrìobhadh *(vn)* writing
sguir *(vb)* ceasing, stopping
sgur *(vn)* cease, stop
sia *(num)* six
sianar *(m)* six people
sibh *(pron)* you *(pl)*, you *(sing, formal)*
sìde *(m, f)* weather
sìn *(vb)* stretch (out)
sìneadh *(vn)* stretching (out)
sinn *(pron)* we
sìol *(m)* seed, **síl** *(pl)*
sìon *(m)* a particle, a small bit
sìon *(m)* anything
  (in *interr* and *neg* sentences and in
  phrase **a h-uile sìon** everything)
shìos *(adv)* down (location)
shuas *(adv)* up (location)
sionnach *(m)* fox, **sionnaich** *(pl)*
sìos *(adv)* down, downwards
  (motion away from speaker)
siubhad *(def vb)* go on, continue
siùcar *(m)* sugar
siuga *(m)* jug, **siugaichean** *(pl)*
slàinte *(f)* health, **slàintean** *(pl)*
smaoineachadh, smaointinn *(vn)*
  thinking
smaoinich *(vb)* think
smoc *(vb)* smoke (of tobacco)
smocadh *(vn)* smoking (of tobacco)
snàmh *(vb, vn)* swim
sneachd(a) *(m)* snow, **sneachdannan**
  (pl)
snog *(adj)* nice
solas *(m)* light, **solais** *(pl)*
sònraichte *(adj)* especial
speal *(f)* scythe, **spealan** *(pl)*
sporan *(m)* purse, **sporain,**
  sporannan *(pl)*
spreadh *(vb)* burst
spreadhadh *(vn)* bursting
sràid *(f)* street, **sràidean** *(pl)*
sreap *(vb, vn)* climb(ing)
sròn *(f)* nose, **srònan** *(pl)*
staidhre *(f)* stair, **staidhrichean** *(pl)*
stèidhichte/stèite *(adj)* established
stèisean *(m)* station, **stèiseanan** *(pl)*

stiall ort *(vb)* on you go, continue
suas *(adv)* up, upwards (motion away
  from speaker)
suidh *(vb)* sit down
suidhe *(vn)* sitting down
suidheachan *(m)* seat,
  suidheachain, suidheachanan *(pl)*
sùil *(f)* eye, **sùilean** *(pl)*
Sultain *(f)* September, **Sultainean** *(pl)*
suiteas *(m, coll)* or **suiteis** *(pl)* sweets
suitidh *(m)* sweet

tachair *(vb)* happen
tachair ri *(vb)* meet (with)
tachairt *(vn)* happening
tachairt ri *(vn)* meeting (with)
tadhail air *(vb)* visit (on)
tadhal air *(vn)* visiting (on)
tagh *(vb)* choose, elect, select
taghadh *(m)* election, electing
taghadh-pàrlamaid *(m)*
  parliamentary election
taigh *(m)* house, **taighean** *(pl)*
taigh-beag *(m)* toilet,
  taighean-beaga *(pl)*
taigh-bidhe *(m)* restauruant, **taighean-**
  bidhe *(pl)*
taigh-òsta *(m)* hotel, pub,
  taighean-òsta *(pl)*
taigh-tasgaidh *(m)* museum,
  taighean-tasgaidh *(pl)*
taingeil thankful
taobh *(m)* side, **taobhan** *(pl)*
tapadh leat thank you *(informal)*
tapadh leibh *(pl or formal)*
tarraing *(vb, vn)* pull(ing)
tarsainn (air) *(prp)* across
tè *(f, pron)* woman; one, **feadhainn**
  (f, coll used for pl of 'one')
teagaisg *(vb)* teach
teagamh *(m)* doubt, **teagamhan** *(pl)*
teagasg *(vn)* teaching
teaghlach *(m)* family,
  teaghlaichean *(pl)*
teanga *(f)* tongue, **teangannan** *(pl)*
teann *(adj)* tight
Teàrlach *(m)* Charles

teich *(vb)* escape, flee
teicheadh *(vn)* escaping, fleeing
teine *(m)* fire, **teintean** *(pl)*
telebhisean *(m)* television
teth *(adj)* hot
tha *(vb)* is
thall *(adv)* over there (location not at speaker)
thall thairis *(adv)* abroad (location)
theab *(def vb)* almost
thig *(vb)* come
thoir (do) *(vb)* give, bring (to)
thoir gaol do *(vb)* love
t(h)u *(pron)* you
tì *(f)* tea
tidsear *(m)* teacher, **tidsearan** *(pl)*
tighinn *(vn)* coming
tilg *(vb)* throw
tilgeil *(vn)* throwing
till *(vb)* return
tilleadh *(vn)* returning
timcheall air *(cmp prp)* around
tinn *(adj)* sick
tiocaid *(f)* ticket, **tiocaidean** *(pl)*
tìr-mòr *(m)* mainland
t(h)iugainn, thugainn *(def vb)* come along, let's go
tiugh *(adj)* thick
tog *(vb)* lift, build
togail *(vn)* lifting, building
toilichte *(adj)* happy
toirt (do) *(vn)* giving, bringing (to)
toll *(m)* hole, **tuill** *(pl)*
toll-iuchrach *(m)* keyhole, **tuill-iuchrach** *(pl)*
tòrr *(m)* a lot, **torran** *(pl)*

trèan *(f)* train, **trèanaichean** *(pl)*
trì *(num)* three
tric *(adv)* often
triùir *(m)* three people
tro/troimh *(prp)* through
trobhad *(def vb)* come along
trom *(adj)* heavy
truinnsear *(m)* plate, **truinnsearan** *(pl)*
tuig *(vb)* understand
tuigsinn *(vn)* understanding
tuil *(f)* flood, **tuiltean** *(pl)*
tuilleadh *(m)* more
tuit *(vb)* fall
tuiteam *(vn)* falling
turas *(m)* trip, journey, **turais, tursan** *(pl)*

uabhasach *(adj, adv)* terrible; terribly; very much (intensifier)
uaine *(adj)* green
uair one o'clock
uaireigin *(adv)* sometime
uan *(m)* lamb, **uain** *(pl)*
uasal *(adj)* high, noble
ugh *(m)* egg, **uighean** *(pl)*
uile *(adj)* all
Uilleam *(m)* William
uinneag *(f)* window, **uinneagan** *(pl)*
uinnean *(m)* onion, **uinneanan** *(pl)*
uisge *(m)* water, **uisgeachan** *(pl)*
uisge-beatha *(m)* whisky
ur *(ppn)* your (pl and sing, formal)
ùr *(adj)* new
ùrlar *(m)* floor, **ùrlair** *(pl)*

Index

The numbers refer to pages, *not* sections.

Index

Index